New York University Studies in Near Eastern Civilization Number XIII

General Editor
Bayly Winder

ALSO IN THIS SERIES

Number I: F. E. Peters, *Aristotle and the Arabs*

Number II: Jacob M. Landau, *Jews in Nineteenth-Century Egypt*

Number III: Lois Anita Giffen, *Theory of Profane Love Among the Arabs: The Development of the Genre*

Number IV: Lewis V. Thomas, *A Study of Naima*, Norman Itkowitz, editor

Number V: Carl Max Kortepeter, *Ottoman Imperialism During the Reformation: Europe and The Caucasus*

Number VI: Linda Fish Compton, *Andalusian Lyrical Poetry and Old Spanish Love Songs: The Muwashshah and Its Kharja*

Number VII: Peter J. Chelkowski, *Ta'ziyeh: Ritual and Drama in Iran*

Number VIII: Arthur N. Young, *Saudi Arabia: The Making of a Financial Giant*

Number IX: Donald Quataert, *Social Disintegration and Popular Resistance in the Ottoman Empire, 1881–1908: Reactions to European Economic Penetration*

Number X: Tawfiq Al-Hakim, *The Return of Consciousness*, Bayly Winder, translator

Number XI: F. E. Peters, *Jerusalem and Mecca: The Typology of the Holy City in the Near East*

Number XII: Bruce Masters, *The Origins of Western Economic Dominance in the Middle East: Mercantilism and the Islamic Economy in Aleppo, 1600–1750*

New York University Studies
in Near Eastern Civilization

The participation of the New York University Press in the University's commitment to Near Eastern Studies provides Americans and others with new opportunities for understanding the Near East. Concerned with those various peoples of the Near East who, throughout the centuries, have dramatically shaped many of mankind's most fundamental concepts and who have always had high importance in practical affairs, this series, New York University Studies in Near Eastern Civilization, seeks to publish important works in this vital area. The purview will be broad, open to varied approaches and historical periods, including the range of social scientific approaches. It will, however, be particularly receptive to work in two areas that reflect the University and that may have received insufficient attention elsewhere. These are literature and art. Furthermore, taking a stand that may be more utilitarian than that of some other publications, the series will welcome translations of important Near Eastern literature. In this way, an audience, unacquainted with the languages of the Near East, will be able to deepen its knowledge of the cultural achievements of Near Eastern peoples.

Bayly Winder
General Editor

MYSTICAL ISLAM

An Introduction to Sufism

JULIAN BALDICK

NEW YORK UNIVERSITY PRESS
New York and London

First published in the U.S.A. in 1989 by
NEW YORK UNIVERSITY PRESS
Washington Square
New York, NY 10003

Library of Congress Cataloging-in-Publication Data

Baldick, Julian
    Mystical Islam: an introduction to Sufism / Julian Baldick.
        p.   cm. — (New York University studies in Near Eastern
    civilization: no. 13)
    Includes bibliographical references.
    ISBN 0–8147–1138–3: — ISBN 0–8147–1139–1 (pbk.)
    1. Sufism — History.   I. Title.   II Series.
BP188.5.B35   1989
297'.4'09—oc20
                                                            89–12751
                                                                 CIP

To Feroza

CONTENTS

Acknowledgements		viii
Introduction		1
1	Sufism's beginnings	13
2	From construction to systematization (*c.* 922–*c.* 1240)	50
3	Elders and empires (*c.* 1240–*c.* 1700)	86
4	Into the modern world	132
	Conclusions	169
	Notes	179
	Bibliography	185
	Index I: Brotherhoods, sub-brotherhoods, branches and offshoots	195
	Index II: Names of persons mentioned	200
	Index III: Technical terms	203

ACKNOWLEDGEMENTS

I must acknowledge a very deep indebtedness to my teachers in Sufi studies, R. C. Zaehner, Henry Corbin, Sayyid Sadiq Gawharin and Simon Digby. Thanks are also due to Albert Hourani, who first suggested that I should write this book, for his wise counsels, and to Sebastian Brock and Alexis Sanderson for advice concerning eastern Christianity and Indian religions. It goes without saying that the opinions expressed here are entirely my own. I must also express my thanks to the staff of I.B.Tauris and in particular to Anne Enayat; to King's College, London, for granting me sabbatical leave, and to Peter Clarke for taking over my duties in my absence; to Colin Wakefield, for bibliographical assistance; and above all, to my wife, for her great patience and help.

INTRODUCTION

Presenting Islam's main mystical tradition, Sufism, is a task which is perhaps easiest to carry out when addressing those who have read nothing about Islam or mysticism. In this area presuppositions die harder than elsewhere. The stock image of Islam as the stern, forbidding religion of the desert still prevails, as does the notion of mysticism as a universal search for union with God or some other ultimate source of existence. Here it may be as well to say a few words about Islam itself before going on to discuss the problem of defining mysticism.

Islam is not just a religion: it is also a civilization. In the areas of its greatest concentration in Asia and Africa it has produced a shared cultural heritage, which is often far more important than regional or ethnic elements. It has given rise to societies having distinct political institutions and military and legal traditions peculiar to the Muslim world. For our purposes, however, it is necessary to consider Islam mainly as a religion. The Arabic word *islam* itself is usually translated as 'submission' (that is, to God). The term has also been taken to mean 'entering into a covenant of peace with God'. Sometimes the religion is seen as an old one, essentially the pure faith of the biblical patriarchs and prophets, which the Jews and Christians have corrupted: this is the view of the Muslims themselves. Sometimes it is seen as a new religion, founded in Arabia by the Prophet Muhammad in the seventh century CE. Conventionally, Islam is described as being built around five pillars: the attestation of belief that there is no god except God and that Muhammad is his Messenger; the prescribed acts of worship; the alms tax; the fast in the month of Ramadan; and the pilgrimage to Mecca. But this conventional description, as will be seen, is unsatisfactory. To be sure, these are the basic legal requirements of Islam, but the religion itself has always been dominated by other patterns, to an extent which has not usually been realized.

The declared intentions of the earliest Muslims showed that they wished to restore an earlier articulation of faith, that would accept Jesus as the Messiah, but preserve the old laws of the Jews. Jesus would be seen as a man and a prophet, not as God or the Son of God. There would be no priests, but there would be specially favoured 'friends of God'. In a way Islam is Christianity: technically, from a Christian standpoint, it is a Christian sect, since it recognizes Jesus as the Christ; from a Muslim standpoint, it is the religion of the Messiah, which the Christians have deformed. In another perspective, of course, Islam is not Christianity: it developed very gradually as a new arrangement of regulations and doctrines, carefully defined practices and elaborate theories. It has no church or clergy, and rejects the standard Christian doctrines of incarnation and the Trinity.

Since Islam denies the possibility that God might dwell within a man (whether Jesus or anyone else), as the spirit dwells within the body, serious difficulties arise with regard to the already vexed problem of defining mysticism. Usually, definitions of mysticism present it as consisting of ideas and practices which lead to 'union with God', or being united with some other ultimate source of existence. But the mystics of Islam not only reject the notion that a man can find God dwelling within himself, but also nearly always condemn the concept of 'unitive fusion' (*ittihad*), according to which God and man become one. The word 'union' has often been used to translate various Arabic terms used by Muslim mystics to describe their experiences, but these terms would be more accurately rendered as 'togetherness', 'joining', 'arriving', 'conjunction' and 'the realization of God's Uniqueness'. In any case, definitions of mysticism encounter the obstacles posed by Indian religions, with complexities and sophistication of thought that defy comprehension.

It seems better to avoid attempting a dictionary-style definition, and concentrate instead on isolating specific elements which the label 'mysticism' covers. Secrecy is certainly one, indicated by the word's root meaning, from which we also have the idea of mystery. The sense of a higher, privileged knowledge is another element, connected to the idea of intimate communion or experience, which, perhaps by its very nature (as opposed to a requirement for secrecy), cannot be disclosed. Other elements which must be included are the means indicated to obtain this experience, and the thinking that surrounds both the means and the final goal. What has now been listed will probably be enough for our purposes. It should be borne in mind that mysticism in Islam is not limited to the Sufi tradition, the subject here.

The English word *Sufism* is used to designate a set of practices, an ideal, and one of the Islamic religious sciences. It is employed to translate the term *tasawwuf*, which means literally 'wearing wool' (wool, *suf*, being the dress of eastern Christian and Muslim world renouncers), but also, and far more commonly, means 'belonging to the faith and doctrine of the people called the Sufis', or 'trying to become a Sufi'. As for the name *Sufi* itself, its derivation from the word for wool does not exclude the possibility of a punning reference to the Greek *sophos*, 'wise'.

The subject of the origin of the term Sufi will be discussed below, in the first chapter. Here I shall give a preliminary reply to the classic question 'What is Sufism?', which the Sufis have always been fond of asking, and of answering with poetic or allusive evocations of their experiences (which one could hardly call definitions). Sufism is a mystical tradition which, when compared to Christian and European institutions, could be put somewhere between monasticism and Freemasonry. It has many of the characteristics of monasticism, but does not usually preach celibacy. It does enjoin mortification of the flesh, and exalts the ideal of poverty, but it includes ordinary members of society in its ranks, with no distinction of clerical versus lay. It emphasizes the love of God, and teaches that God and the Sufis have a special relationship which goes back to a primordial Covenant: the Sufis are God's friends, perpetually engaged in remembrance (*dhikr*) of him. Sufism also constitutes a Path (*tariqa*), which begins with repentance and leads through a number of 'stations' (*maqamat*), representing virtues such as absolute trust in God, to a higher series of ecstatic 'states' (*ahwal*). These culminate in the 'passing away' (*fana'*) of the mystic (or perhaps just of his lower soul, or of his human attributes) and the subsequent 'survival' (*baqa'*) of his transformed personality (or perhaps just of his higher soul, or alternatively of his essence now adorned by the attributes of God).

Sufism has other aspects, such as deliberate self-abasement in disreputable conduct and apparently libertine behaviour, sometimes manifested in the contemplation of human beauty as a means to the contemplation of God himself. It has themes which would often be called Gnostic, that is to say relating to a higher form of knowledge, reserved for an elite, such as the ascent of the soul through the heavens and the liberation of a divine spark of light in man from amid the darkness of matter.

Sufism should be distinguished from other traditions in the Muslim world which have also represented strongly mystical trends. One of these is the Islamic continuation of Greek philosophy. This was to come very close to Sufism, especially when it developed what is called the 'wisdom of Oriental Illumination' (*hikmat al-ishraq*), a colourful blend of neo-Platonism and Gnostic light imagery. But there are important differences. The Hellenized philosophers of Islam, like the Sufis, have been elitist, but, unlike the Sufis, they have made no attempt to instruct or win over a wider audience. They have remained a tiny minority, scornful of the masses. What has interested them has been not the pure love of God, but an ordered vision of the universe, which is both presented and dominated by a mysterious Angel. They have been concerned not so much with 'passing away' as with the problem of existence itself. This they have tried to solve by conceiving of themselves as travelling in an upward movement of self-integration into the complex astronomical structures of space, to escape from their miserable exile among their unsatisfactory fellow humans. Their work has provided inspiration for certain twentieth-century German and French writers, notably the poet Rainer Maria Rilke, who explained that the figure of the Angel which dominates his *Duino Elegies* − a superhuman being who enables one to flee from men into a transformed world of real existence − is not Christian but Islamic.[1] But the Sufis have rejected the philosophers' concentration on the Angel in favour of the pure love of God himself.

It is also important to recognize the differences between Sufism and Shiism, the main minority sect of Islam, which is characterized by its extreme devotion to Muhammad's family, and has also developed pronounced mystical tendencies. Perhaps it is misleading to speak of 'Shiism'. The corresponding Arabic word, *tashayyu'*, means rather 'belonging to the Party', and it might be better to talk of the Party (*shi'a*) itself. The majority of the Shiites, called the Twelvers because they venerate twelve early Leaders in Muhammad's family, and expect the last to return as a messiah, used to be seen as united around a single doctrine, however much this changed over the centuries. But Peter Antes has pointed out that the opposite was the case, and more recent research has confirmed the view that the Shiites have most often been deeply divided, with an esoterically inclined wing on the one hand encountering stiff opposition from lawyers and theologians on the other.[2]

Perhaps it is inevitable that a party of this kind, with its emphasis on leadership and messianic expectation of social justice, should be split into two warring but complementary factions. Shiites are often mystics, and indeed in later Islamic history can also be Sufis, but Sufism itself is not the ideology of a party, however much some Sufis have pursued revolutionary goals. Moreover, just as the philosophers have distinguished themselves from the Sufis by their emphasis on union with a powerful Angel, so too the Shiite mystics have tended to cut themselves off from the Sufi quest for God by looking for a supreme experience of self-identification with their Leaders.

A historical approach to Sufism

The perspective which has been chosen is that of the history of religions, in the European, not the American sense. In the United States the expression 'history of religions' is used to mean 'religious studies' or 'studies pertaining to religion' of whatever kind. Ironically, this sometimes means rejecting history in order to effect an alleged reproduction of the psychological states attributed to the believers studied. In Europe, 'the history of religions' means a sub-discipline of history, history as applied to religions. This does not mean that the historian of religions is always (or indeed often) trying to write history in the ways common among professional historians. Frequently, the meagre evidence available in a given period or area, or the small amount of research already done, will not allow him to do that. In any case what concerns him most is the analysis of patterns or configurations as they pass from one religion to another, or from one period of religious history to the next. Thus the history of religions examines the modes of change in these patterns, rather than the events which are supposed to have happened.

Now such an approach might seem harmless enough, but it inevitably encounters much opposition. Generally this has come from scholars of an older generation, who are confident that religions have been instituted by founders, more or less as the legends, with some exaggeration, relate. Opposition also comes from those who say that a religion must be understood in its own terms, and in the perspectives of its own adherents. But Islam presents itself as a purified version of earlier beliefs, and the Muslims themselves have always had resolutely historical overviews of their faith as the heir to previous revelations. To argue that Islam consists largely of patterns repeated from its religious antecedents is not particularly unislamic, while to cast doubt on the veracity of the legends surrounding Muhammad is merely to continue the Muslims' own long and sustained attack upon what they have always perceived as the fabrication, on a massive scale, of 'Traditions' concerning him.

The search for patterns in the history of religions has often been confused with the structuralism fashionable in France in the 1960s. Structuralism has sometimes meant the imposition of an artificial grid of structures upon the subject studied, in order to produce clarity in the mind of the investigator or in his writings. Sometimes it has assumed that reality itself, including the human mind, is structured universally and definitively. The history of religions has looked instead to find concrete instances of the repetition of patterns, expressed explicitly in literary texts or material remains, with such clarity of definition as to make acceptance of historical continuity beyond dispute. The relationship of a pair of Indo-European twins with a goddess in both India and Scandinavia reappears in the seduction of two Muslim angels by Venus, after going through the 'Bounteous Immortals' or archangels of ancient Iran: the articulation of the concepts of health, immortality and fertility is so exactly reproduced in the later myth as to forestall any accusation of arbitrariness in the investigator's procedure and the suggestion that these concepts belong to a universal structure in human psychology as opposed to a common inheritance.

This is not to say that structuralism has come and gone without leaving anything of value for the study of Sufism. On the contrary, the analysis of myths as pursued by Claude Lévi-Strauss will certainly continue to be helpful in examining the legends of the Sufi 'friends of God': the stories have formal literary properties which are found all over the world. Similarly, the post-structuralism of the late 1960s onwards has performed an invaluable task in breaking down the illusions of order and unity which have plagued modern western thought. In Islam one will no longer see a spiritual reproduction of cosmic harmony, but rather the conflict of opposing forces in disorder and contradiction. But in the 1980s, at least on the continent of Europe, the importance of returning to traditional scholarship and avoiding excessive theorizing has been recognized. Most encouragingly, continental European social scientists have moved away from their previous enthusiasm for generalizations, and begun to co-operate with specialists in the literary and historical study of Islamic mysticism. A new generation of anthropologists has acquired the expertise to study the contemporary history of Sufis with a command of the relevant documentation which may surprise British and American observers.

The approach here will therefore be historical, without attempting the premature task of a history of Sufism itself. Accordingly it will be necessary, in considering the rise of Islam as studied by historians, to bear in mind the background of peoples belonging to two ancient linguistic groupings: on the one hand the Indo-European grouping, which spreads from India to Ireland; and on the other the Semitic grouping, which contains the Hebrew, Syriac and Arabic languages. Within the Indo-European grouping is the Indo-Iranian category, with its archaic caste system, and the Iranian monarchical and military traditions which were to have a profound effect on Islamic civilization and society. Also within the Indo-European group are the Greeks, who were to give the Muslims philosophy and sciences such as alchemy and astronomy. The Greeks were also to bring a mystical strand to Islam, notably through eastern Christianity. The Semitic grouping was to transmit to Islam the idea of God's continuing action in history, in between Creation and the Last Judgement. It was also to bring the concept of prophethood, as something which had begun with Adam and had been renewed up to its last manifestation in Muhammad. After this, the Sufi mystics were to see themselves as the heirs to the prophets, by virtue of being God's special friends.

Avoiding Christian terms

In approaching Islam and Sufism, certain words commonly borrowed from Christianity will be avoided: 'orthodoxy', 'heresy', 'clergy', 'fundamentalism' and 'saint'.

Many writers have presented the Muslim mystics as a force opposed to 'the orthodox'. It is difficult to see who 'the orthodox' would be. Collectors of sayings attributed to the Prophet? There are Sufis among them. Theologians, upholding the use of reason against the devout transmitters of Muhammad's words? There are Sufis among these as well. Besides, Islam is not really so much a religion of doctrine as one of law and experience. There is no central authority to say what an 'orthodox' dogma would be, while the power to condemn someone as an unbeliever belongs to any qualified jurist. Since there is no orthodoxy there can be no heresy. Similarly, there is no clergy in Islam: the Muslim lawyers are in effect rabbis, not cut off from other believers by any form of ordination. Almost all Muslims have seen themselves as expected to follow the basic example of Muhammad as recorded by his associates or relatives: to speak, like contemporary journalists, of 'Muslim fundamentalism' is to employ an empty tautology, a catch-all label which permits no real clarity of definition. As for the word 'saint', it has been applied to Muslims by modern British writers with such liberality that one trembles to think what would happen if they were to reimport it into the United Kingdom: a halo would have to replace every mitre and every tonsure, every coronet and every mortar-board. There is no process of canonization in Islam, nor any authority capable of conducting it. A vast number of words have been mistranslated as 'saint', terms which mean 'elder', 'guide', 'noble', etc. The expression most often rendered as 'saint', *wali Allah*, means 'friend of God'. The idea of the friend, the protégé or 'client' of God, who is also the protector and patron of lesser Muslims, is so essential a feature of Islam that one loses all sense of perspective if one confuses it with the Christian concept of sainthood, with its connotations of heroic piety and officially endorsed innocence.

The most misleading of all expressions, 'the sacred and the profane', has often been employed to mistranslate references in Sufi literature to 'the real and the metaphorical' (since for the Muslim mystic what is beautiful in this world is a metaphor for the real Beauty of God). Linguists have demonstrated that in Indo-European languages two different ideas have been conflated in words such as 'sacred' and 'holy': that of sacrosanctity, of being cut off from everything else, and that of life-giving and health-increasing force. Modern writers in the sociology of religion insist that *the sacred* is sharply divided from *the profane*. But to say that the sacrosanct is clearly cut off from what is not sacrosanct is just another tautology, and if one were to say that God's 'blessing', his life-increasing force, is separated from the rest of nature, one would be contradicted by all the Islamic evidence. As for the word *profane*, applied to virtually everything by modern writers, to find its original religious meaning one must go back to the Latin *profanus*, which, as Émile Benveniste has shown, meant not an abstract opposite of 'the sacred', but rather 'that which is put outside the consecrated space, and thus becomes fit for common use'.[3] The Muslim equivalent is *halal*, 'that which has been made lawful to men by God', as opposed to what he has forbidden, not as opposed to his Sacrosanctity or his 'blessing'.

An outline

The original intention was to produce something like the late Marijan Molé's *Les Mystiques musulmans* (1965), which is an excellent summary of the research done up to that time. But it was immediately apparent that Molé's concentration on the beginnings of Sufism would not be appropriate today, and that other periods of Sufi history deserved increased coverage. Accordingly, more or less equal space has been given to all of the fourteen centuries of Islam. I have also tried to achieve some geographical balance, looking at Sufism both in the central and in the more outlying parts of the Muslim world. Thus in the third and fourth chapters, which consider the history of Sufism from about 1240 to the present, attention is given to the Indian subcontinent, Africa and Indonesia, in order to reflect Islam's own expansion. Usually I have incorporated the results of recent scholarship, mentioning the name of the specialist whose work has been used, summarizing selected aspects of his findings and sometimes adding comments at the end. Occasionally I have introduced elements from my own research (on Sufi legends, the 'youngmanliness' (*futuwwa*) tradition, Persian poetry, fourteenth-century India and sixteenth-century Central Asia).

The first chapter was written in the wake of the recent revolution in the study of Islam's origins, a revolution which resembles the one in biblical studies in the nineteenth century, and which has been brought about by academics in Britain. However, I have taken a path indicated by German specialists in looking for Islam's antecedents in 'Jewish Christianity' – a perilous term, here used to mean the recognition of Jesus as the Messiah along with the observance of Jewish law. As for the origins of Sufism itself, it has been necessary to attack a position often taken for granted, namely that it grew out of the Koran. The success of this view is due largely to its adoption by the famous French Islamist Louis Massignon (1883–1962). Massignon's opinions in other fields (such as the history of the Muslim craft guilds, urban topography and medieval banking) have been badly discredited, and it is therefore not surprising that his contribution to the study of Islamic mysticism should now be criticized. This is not, however, to fail to appreciate his personal greatness and learning. As for the argument put forward against Massignon here, namely that Sufism grew out of eastern Christianity, it is one that is easily misunderstood. It is often misinterpreted as a suggestion that the Muslims, after acquiring the new religion of Islam from Muhammad, later came into contact with Christians and borrowed mysticism from them. On the contrary, the argument is that Islam took much longer to develop than has usually been supposed, and that in the slow process of development Christian materials were used to build the mystical side of the religion, the side which was to become Sufism.

The second half of the first chapter, devoted to the Sufis of the ninth and early tenth centuries, reopens an old controversy about an Indian influence upon one Muslim mystic. Now the reader may wonder why I have gone into so much detail to support the claim that this influence took place, when the evidence speaks so clearly for itself. There are two reasons: the massive hostility with which the claim has been greeted (doubtless owing to the ideological positions of its opponents); and the need to know precisely what that influence was. In fact this influence was not, as often suspected, the introduction of the all-important doctrine of 'passing away', but rather it involved the transmission of ideas which the Sufis themselves did not want.

The second chapter considers a number of tenth- and eleventh-century treatises on Sufism. Some of these are dry and pedestrian, and it may be wondered why so much space has been given to them. The answer is again twofold. On the one hand it is important to look at the inconsistencies and contradictions which they contain, in order to find the patterns of thought in the background, which the authors have failed to reconcile. On the other hand it is also important to try to see how in the eleventh century Islam turned its back on the cultural and scientific renaissance which had recently occurred, and consequently how the Muslim world was later to be in a less advantageous position than the Christian West – with results which are still with us today.

Some readers will be surprised to find the famous Muhammad Ghazali (d. 1111), often hailed as the greatest Muslim after the Prophet, dismissed here as an inconsistent popularizer and relegated to a station beneath his Sufi brother. But this view has long been anticipated by criticisms of Ghazali made in medieval Spain and modern Iran, and is based on the best recent study of his politics.

This chapter and the following one summarize analyses which I have made elsewhere of long Persian Sufi poems, generally admired as the finest classics of eastern Islamic literature. It is argued that they have structures which have long been ignored. The suggestion has been made that I was claiming to have succeeded in finding these where other specialists had searched in vain. In fact I was only trying to point out the obvious, where others had not looked.

The third chapter avoids discussing some of the most talented of Sufi writers, who belonged to the school of Sufism's greatest systematizer, Ibn 'Arabi (d. 1240). This is because their work is not really suitable for inclusion in a survey of the present kind: it consists of commentaries on the books of a very difficult and abstruse thinker. Instead, it has seemed better to concentrate on India, where the records of conversations between masters and disciples give us the immediacy of everyday life. The richness of this Indian Sufi literature has hardly been noticed in the West.

In the second half of the chapter more attention has been given to social and economic factors, when examining Sufism in the Ottoman Empire. It must be admitted that here the evidence is so fragmentary that one wonders how it can be used. Little is known, as is usual in Islamic history, about the size of populations, the division of the harvest and the volume of trade. However, as in India, one obtains brief glimpses of the way in which the Sufis lived, what they bought and ate, and the sources of their income.

The fourth chapter has again demanded a variety of angles of approach. So little work has been done on eighteenth-century Islam that it appeared best to select three representative figures and look at what they had to say. The nineteenth century demanded a focus upon its burgeoning bureaucracy, while what has been written about Sufism and 'reformism' seemed to require sceptical investigation. The twentieth century has naturally presented particularly great problems. It has been necessary to discuss the work of highly influential British and American social scientists, about whom certain reservations have already been voiced elsewhere. Comparison with the publications of their European colleagues has resulted in a verdict heavily in favour of the latter. Perhaps this is not surprising. The English-language books examined here reflect work done from the 1950s to the 1970s, and attitudes which now require substantial revision, if not outright rejection. The continental European studies, on the other hand, represent the recent shift back to traditional scholarship, noted above.

Finally, after the historical survey, I have tried to place Sufism in the wider context of Islamic civilization as a whole, in particular by considering the relations between Sufism and music, the visual arts, law and politics. Here it has been necessary to ask how the place of Sufism in Islam might be compared with that of Christian monasticism in European society; and also, looking to the future, whether Islam could ever dispense with Sufism.

There is one last possible objection which I should address. Why have I appeared to rely so heavily on western research, and made so little use of contemporary scholarship in Muslim countries? My indebtedness to eastern specialists is far greater than is apparent on the surface. Iranian scholars have shown me great kindness and patience. Their contribution to the present study has come through the help given by invaluable oral advice, editions of texts and indispensable reference works. Scholars in Arab countries also excel in the subtler aspects of linguistic and literary problems, which are unsuitable for treatment here. Turkey has produced experts in social and economic history equal to the finest in the West, and their achievements are amply reflected in Suraiya Faroqhi's work. On the Indian subcontinent Muslim historians have done essential groundwork in separating genuine from forged materials, and, if their political preoccupations are such as to inspire reserve, then British colonialism is not without blame.

1 SUFISM'S BEGINNINGS

BACKGROUND AND ORIGINS

In order to study the origins of Islamic mysticism one must first of all examine the historical background to the rise of Islam in the seventh century CE. This is a most exciting subject today, since considerable changes have recently taken place in the attitudes of western scholars. There has been much controversy, largely related to the respective roles played in the emergence of the new religion by Arabia on the one hand and the rest of the Middle East on the other. An older generation of academics still continues to concentrate on archaeological and anthropological evidence in Arabia itself, regarding it as likely to shed light on the influence of tribal life on the beliefs and practices of the earliest Muslims. Younger specialists are more inclined to look for a continuity of patterns from the ancient civilizations in the countries which the Arabs invaded, in circumstances which are seen as particularly significant.

The Middle East, in the early seventh century, was dominated by two great empires: the later Roman (or early Byzantine) Empire, which had for long governed Egypt, Syria, Palestine and what is now Turkey; and the Persian (or Iranian) Empire, which consisted mainly of Iran and Iraq. Both these states had been seriously weakened by a number of factors, notably war, bad government and the persecution of religious minorities. Conditions were as favourable as could be imagined for the onslaught which came from the Arabian peninsula. As for this peninsula itself, very little is known about it before Islam. The literary sources are of a later period and appear to reflect Muslim efforts to create an idealized picture of the religion's beginnings. This picture minimizes the probability that the Arabs were already heavily influenced by the peoples whom they were about to conquer. Moreover, it is likely that the Muslims projected back into the Arabian past developments which really took place within the conquered territories.

According to Islamic historical tradition, as preserved in works of the eighth and ninth centuries, the founder of Islam, the Prophet Muhammad, was born around 570 at Mecca, in central western Arabia. About 610 he began to receive revelations, which, he came to believe, were brought to him by the Archangel Gabriel. These called on him to start a rigorously monotheistic practice of worship. The revelations were later collected as the Koran ('Recitation' or 'Reading'). After encountering much opposition, in 622 Muhammad moved to Medina, some 200 miles to the north. There he founded a new state, and, by his own example and a vast number of oral instructions, instituted the religion of Islam. He died at Medina in 632.

After Muhammad's death most of the Middle East was conquered by his successors, the caliphs (*khulafa'*, 'deputies'). Under the leadership of one of these, 'Umar (reigned 634–44), the Arabs quickly overran Palestine, Egypt, Syria, Iraq and Iran. Then internal dissension arose, before one family, the Umayyads, were able to establish control over most Muslims in the conquered territories and centralize government in Damascus. This family extended the new empire in both the west and the east, so that by the early eighth century it embraced most of Spain and part of what is now Pakistan.

The Islamic historical tradition, in its presentation of the religion's beginnings, has to be seen as reflecting subsequent political and doctrinal bias. The main biography of the Prophet, composed in the mid-eighth century and edited in the ninth, is so far removed from Muhammad's lifetime as to make the historian wonder if it can be used at all. For our present purpose, the search for the origins of Islamic mysticism, its value must remain doubtful. Inevitably, modern writers produce versions of it in which the miracles are omitted and Muhammad emerges as a mystic and visionary. More serious scholarship indicates that the biography is the result of long regional rivalries; of the projection into one man's life of developments which must have taken place much later; and of the transposition into an Arabian setting of processes which belong to the Fertile Crescent in the north. As for the traditional picture of events between Muhammad's death and the fall of the Umayyads in 750, here too there has been much disagreement about whether it should be accepted or replaced, and whether it is possible for the historian to make any positive contribution in this field. Scholars have taken conflicting positions on the question of using the records of the communities conquered by the Muslims. Differing views have also been expressed about the geographical location of Muhammad's activities. No attempt is made here to resolve these differences, however, since our concern is not with events, but with the continuity of configurations of religious ideas.

The influence of earlier religious traditions

The peoples of the territories conquered by the Arabs, as they converted to the new religion, must have continued to express certain motifs and modes of thought which contributed to the developing Islamic creed, and in particular to its spiritual dimensions. In examining the religious background to the rise of Islam there are elements and configurations which seem to have been preserved within Sufism; it will sometimes be necessary to look ahead to Sufi themes when analysing the pre-Sufi evidence. A number of themes have already been mentioned as characteristic of Sufism, and these have their antecedents in the various religions of the pre-Islamic Middle East.

Greatest attention needs to be given to eastern Christianity. In recent years more weight has been accorded to the view that Islamic mysticism, and in particular Sufism, grew out of Christian spirituality. In particular, the very word *sufi* has usually been seen as reflecting a Christian influence, being derived from the Arabic word for wool (*suf*), which was the characteristic clothing material of eastern Christian monks, and was taken over by the early mystics of Islam. Other styles of dress adopted by the Sufis are also anticipated in pre-Islamic Christianity: the patchwork frock made from rags, and the use of the colour of mourning, black for the Christians, dark blue for the Muslims.

When we look for Christian antecedents of aspects of Sufism it is the doctrines and practices of the monastic life which are most striking. On the doctrinal side one expects Christianity to anticipate Sufism in such areas as the contemplation of God, the adaptation of Greek philosophy to a devotional framework, and the delineation of the mystic's progress through a hierarchy of stages. On the practical side one is led to focus on the mortification of the flesh, the espousal of poverty and the repetition of special prayers.

Arthur Vööbus, the greatest historian of Christian asceticism in Syria, Iraq and Iran, notes the particular emphasis, in the Christian literature of these countries (which was composed in Syriac, and consequently has a distinctive and unified character of its own), on a Covenant between God and men: this we shall find stressed in classical Sufism. Of special interest, in the eastern Christian communities, are the 'Sons of the Covenant', who are not members of the clergy, or monks, but live among fellow believers while pursuing mortification of the flesh and devotional exercises. Here we see 'solitaries' within society, in an anticipation of the Sufi mystics; the latter perceive themselves as bound in a Covenant with God, and belong to a religion which has neither priests nor (in theory at least) monks, but only Muslims. Thus Sufis are often in the midst of other men while rejecting the world.

One dominant motif in early Christian spirituality is comparatively rare in Sufism: the characteristically Christian veneration of celibacy. Vööbus notes the use of the root *q-d-sh* in Syriac, both to denote sexual continence and, in effect, to designate sanctity itself. This helps us to understand the absence of a concept of sainthood in Sufism: as eastern Christians pass from Syriac to Arabic they will use the term *qiddis*, 'saint', but the Muslims, along with their refusal to accept the ideal of celibacy, will not. There are no 'cut-off points' in Islam, at which a man is consecrated and set apart as a priest, or canonized and seen as a *sanctus*, a saint. The Muslims do, in a very different perspective, perpetuate the early Christian idea of friendship with God (an idea made familiar in recent years by Peter Brown). Here friendship means not what it does today, but rather a finely balanced understanding of mutual obligations: the 'friend of God' (*wali Allah*) is both his client, in the Roman sense of a dependant, and also the patron, in the Roman sense of a protector, of lesser men, possessing and channelling freedom of access to the highest source of power. Early Islam inherited from the Roman Empire a temporal institution of clienthood, by which a non-Arab convert to the Muslim faith acquired dependent legal status, and became a sort of second-class, associate member of the community.[1] Here one sees a striking counterpart to the spiritual concept.

Islam also mirrors the regional varieties of eastern Christian devotionalism. Egypt, although the legendary birthplace of Christian monasticism, engaged in moderate abstinence but did not proceed to higher speculation. Syria, punishing the flesh more severely, with its 'browsers' who ate nothing but plants and its wearers of heavy iron chains (another element continued among Muslim extremists on the fringes of Sufism), produced visionary experiences and ecstasy. Iraq was the most sophisticated of all, in its academic adaptations of the Greek philosophical tradition.

One particular Christian expression continues to play a major role in Sufism: that of 'remembrance of God', in Greek *mneme Theou*, which is found first among the Stoic philosophers and is also connected with the use, in the Hebrew Bible, of the term *zakar*, 'remembering'. This is a form of prayer, but not in the sense of asking for something. It is connected with the celebrated 'Jesus prayer', the continually repeated invocation of the name of Jesus, a distinctive feature of eastern Christianity. In Islam the term is the same, *dhikr Allah*, 'remembrance of God', in the repetition of a short formula.

The specialists have demonstrated beyond doubt that another Sufi practice comes from early Syrian Christianity: that of deliberately incurring 'blame' (Syriac *shituta*; Arabic *malama*) through apparently reprehensible conduct: pretending to engage in illicit sexual relations, behaving like a madman, sitting on a dunghill, and so on. This has remained an important facet of Sufi poetry and teaching up to our own day: the mystic puts himself in a position where he is indifferent to the opinions held by others about him, or indeed prefers to be despised.

This doctrine of blame, already old, is repeated in the works of Isaac of Nineveh, the most important Christian mystical writer of seventh-century Iraq. Isaac is a representative of the Nestorian Church, which, through its emphasis on the humanity of Jesus, came close to Islam's rejection of his divinity, and enjoyed good relations with the early Muslims. He also teaches the doctrine of trust or confidence in God to provide one's sustenance: this too continues as a major topic in Sufism. Isaac is the most useful thinker in our search for a pattern, configuration or structure which is reproduced in Islam. Up to now we have encountered only isolated themes, but Isaac provides a fair amount of systematization, which corresponds with Sufi theory and clearly establishes the Christian character of Islamic mysticism. His teachings are repeatedly set out according to a threefold model, which consists of (1) the body; (2) the lower soul (known in Sufism as the *nafs*, the 'self'); (3) the higher soul or spirit (known in Sufism as the *ruh*). This triad is a dominant feature in Isaac's portrayal of the Path. In Islam the concept of the Path (*tariqa*) is often identified with Sufism itself. Isaac uses the term in the Sufi manner to indicate the mystic's upward progress. His version of the Path consists of three phases: (1) repentance; (2) purification; (3) perfection. The description of the Sufi Path always begins with repentance. Isaac gives an enumeration of the *virtues* and the *degrees* upon which the mystic ascends. In the first phase there are works of righteousness, performed with the body: fasting, alms-giving and vigils. In the second phase are neighbourly love, humility and other virtues of the lower soul. These two phases involve labour on the part of the mystic. Now, in the third phase instead of labour, at the level of the higher soul or spirit, are the gifts bestowed by God: delight, exultation and love.[2] In the same way, the classical descriptions of the Sufi Path distinguish, among the various stages of ascent, between those at the bottom, which are obtained through the mystic's own efforts, and those at the top, which are given by God alone. To be sure, neither Isaac and his Christian contemporaries nor the early Sufis possess fully developed systems. Different writers not only have different patterns, but are also often self-contradictory. However, the ordered correspondence between Isaac's explicit arrangement of his triads and the mainstream of classical Sufi theory demonstrates a repeated configuration.

In the past scholars expressed great hopes that light could be cast upon the origins of Sufism through further research into one peculiar Christian sect or grouping, known as the Messalians or 'Prayerites' because of their apparently continuous praying. Unfortunately, very little is known about them, and we are dependent upon biased and hostile references from outsiders. Immense caution is needed when evaluating these, especially when they include accusations of libertinism. Isaac of Nineveh asserts that the Messalians claim to be perfect, and consequently above normal restrictions. Such accusations are made by fairly early Sufi writers against extremists on the fringes of Sufism, and it is only later that mainline Sufi thinkers support the idea that perfection puts the mystic above the law. Even then, they will not advocate committing actual violations of Islamic legality. Given the correspondence between Isaac of Nineveh and mainstream Sufism, it is unlikely that the latter would owe much to some 'Messalian' libertines. Moreover, it is not clear that references to the Messalians by seventh-century authors represent more than a literary tradition of attacking a sect already dead. They were probably extinct (if indeed they ever existed as a separate grouping) by the end of the eighth century, when Sufism was yet to emerge. As for works in which authors put forward their own ideas, and which were previously labelled as 'Messalian' by scholars (the famous *Book of Degrees* and the *Homilies of Pseudo-Macarius*), recent research has shown this label to be inappropriate. The word 'Messalian' may just have been a pejorative epithet.

A much more promising perspective, not only for studying the roots of Sufism, but for finding the origins of Islam itself, is provided by 'Jewish Christianity'. This term is also riddled with difficulties. Here it will be used in the sense of observing the Jewish law while recognizing Jesus as the Christ. Such a combination brings with it a number of practices and beliefs, resulting from its own internal logic, and also false accusations from outsiders that more practices and beliefs existed.

Scholars have argued that a wide range of early 'Jewish-Christian' opinions and observances were misleadingly attributed to one particular sect, the Ebionites, whose name means 'the poor'.

This designation is highly relevant to the subject of mysticism in early Islam. 'A poor man' is the literal and original meaning of the words which have passed into English as 'fakir' and 'dervish' (Arabic *faqir*; Persian *darwish*). These words acquired the connotations of 'a man of the spiritual life' or 'a mystic'. We shall often use the term 'dervish' below. Like 'fakir', it has a wider meaning than the word 'Sufi': not all dervishes are Sufis. Moreover, the term 'dervish' indicates more the dimension of practice, while 'Sufi' designates more that of theory: the dervish is a Sufi in action, and the Sufi is a dervish in the abstract.

Reliable evidence shows that the Jewish Christians of the first few centuries CE (if not the Ebionites themselves) adopted a number of positions later taken over by Islam: retaining Jewish law in religious matters, and thus insisting on circumcision and rejecting Saint Paul; believing that Jesus was the Messiah, but just as a man, *not* as the Son of God; seeing Adam as a prophet; insisting on ablutions before worship and after sexual intercourse; and, in their later development, rejecting sexual continence and insisting on marriage. Some of them lived in the north of the Arab world, in Syria, before the Muslim conquest. It seems probable that they had a great influence at an early stage of Islam's development. Even if this is not the case, it would appear that from fairly early on the Muslims adopted their main pattern of belief and practice.

On the other hand Judaism itself does not seem to have made much of a direct contribution to Islamic mysticism, but rather to have provided the legal boundaries within which the expression of spirituality had to be confined. The Sufis are often accused of erring by using expressions which belong to Christianity, while Muslim lawyers are sometimes criticized for being too much like Jewish rabbis. While Sufis frequently think that Christians hold important secret opinions, the praiseworthy aspects of Judaism are found by Muslims to lie in the straightforward observance of ritual purity. Thus one Sufi observes that Syriac (as the language of eastern Christians) represents what is highest and most hidden, whereas Hebrew (as the language of Judaism) represents what is lowest and most obvious, and Arabic (as the language of Islam) unites the two extremes.[3] There does not appear to be any significant presence of specifically Jewish asceticism or mysticism in the background to the rise of Sufism. The time of Philo Judaeus (fl. 40 CE), the great exponent of symbolic interpretation of the scriptures, had long since passed. Only the 'Merkabah' or 'Throne of God' type of mysticism flourished before Islam. Here the description of the soul's journey to God's Throne, with its crossing of seven planetary spheres, resembles the visionary accounts in the Greek philosophical tradition as continued in the Muslim world rather than what is found in Sufism. Moreover, the sources show us not so much Judaism as Gnosticism (which will be discussed shortly) in Judaic dress. As the late Gershom Scholem, the greatest specialist in the study of Jewish mysticism, observed, there was no authentically Judaic mystical tradition in the lands of Islam before the Kabbalah arose in southern France around 1200. This is underlined by the fact that up to the thirteenth century Jews in Muslim countries just imitated Sufi writings.[4]

Christianity's contribution to the rise of Sufism is further apparent in the obvious influence from the neo-Platonist school of Greek philosophy. Plato himself had already provided a firm basis for early Christian spirituality: the doctrines of the contemplation of eternal Ideas and intimate knowledge of them; the soul's ascent from the false reality of the senses; and the love of true Beauty. The neo-Platonist school of Plotinus (d. 270 CE) and his followers had developed these doctrines into a great system, dominated by the triad of the One, Reason and the Soul. This system exercised an immense influence upon Christian mystical thought, with which it was indeed often identical. There were neo-Platonist philosophers in the background to the rise of Islam who were not Christians, but the process of transmitting Greek philosophy to the Muslims was essentially conducted by the Christians as translators and teachers, throughout the ninth century and well into the tenth. Thus to ask whether the origins of Sufi thought are neo-Platonist as opposed to Christian, or vice versa, would be to pose a false problem.

One striking and distinctive Sufi practice has antecedents in Plato: that of 'gazing at beardless boys' (*nazar ila 'l-murd*), justified by the explanation that one is contemplating Absolute Beauty in human form. This practice has provoked many condemnations, and has also provided much inspiration for classical lyric poetry in the Muslim world. There has been speculation about the possibility of a directly inherited tradition, passing from late antiquity into Islam. Certainly, there is a *literary* tradition of expressing love for beardless boys, which goes from later Greek literature into classical Arabic prose. But the Sufi practice of 'gazing' itself could either have been inspired by Plato's writings or have come from Central Asian sources (as we shall see) and then been justified by reference to him.

The neo-Platonist triad of the One, Reason and the Soul dominates the great Sufi didactic poems composed in Persian in the late twelfth century and the thirteenth. There is no doubt that as Sufism developed it took many teachings from this source, but scholars have tended to see little coming from it into the earliest beginnings of Sufism. They may be wrong, misled by the Sufis' own portrayal of their earliest representatives as heroic ascetics, followed only later by intellectuals, in parallel to the Path's beginnings in self-mortification before subsequent contemplation.

Another strand of the Greek philosophical tradition has been much neglected in the study of Sufism's origins: that of the Cynics. These uncouth vagrants, who rejected society's institutions to take a 'short cut' to the philosophers' goal of enlightenment, behaved very much as did the more extreme of the eastern Christian mystics who deliberately incurred 'blame'. It is likely that this practice passed from the Cynics into Christianity before going into Sufism and libertine groups on its fringes. There is no evidence that Cynics continued to exist in the sixth and seventh centuries CE: it is usually considered that they were absorbed into Christian monasticism. Here they survived as 'wanderers' (*gyrovagi*) who, as such, were disreputable. Their successors in the Muslim world were generally classed as dervishes rather than as Sufis, and cut themselves off from Sufism by openly breaking Islamic law.

The Cynics may well owe their origin (as is perhaps reflected in the alleged oriental roots of their most famous early Greek representative, Diogenes) to the ancient religious tradition of Central and North Asia, shamanism, which is characterized by magic, rain-making, healing and the flight of the shaman through the heavens. One problem is that the word 'shamanism' is used to mean this type of religion found all over the world. There is some evidence to suggest a direct influence from Central Asian shamanism upon Sufism as it first emerged. The use of the Sufi dance (itself resembling shamanistic practice) to produce rain is one example. The veneration of beauty (notably human beauty) is attested among the Turks of Central Asia before their conversion to Islam (but it has been argued that this belongs to the Gnostic religion of Manichaeanism, discussed below). Legends of Sufis as 'flyers' are particularly common in the north-east of the Muslim world, near the frontier with unconverted Turks. The deliberate provoking of 'blame' is also characteristic of this area in early Sufism. Modern western writers tend to be deeply suspicious of suggestions of shamanistic influences, and argue that these phenomena are universal. Indeed they are, but they are typical of tribal and nomadic religion, and we may see, in the constant influx of nomadic Turkic tribes from the north-east, a continuing source of renewal.

The flight of the shaman (whether as an influence imported from Central Asia, or as representing an indigenous religious tradition of a type found everywhere) is perhaps the ancestor of the ascent of the soul in Gnosticism, a mystical movement which arose in the mediterranean and in the Middle East from the second century CE onwards, and is distinguished by an emphasis on a higher knowledge (*gnosis*) reserved for an elite. This movement's teachings are based on the idea that in man there is a spark of divine light which has been imprisoned in earthly matter. It has recently been shown that the Gnostics appear in the Koran under the name of the Sabians, and also that Gnostic activity is connected with Jewish Christians in the north of the Arab world before Islam.[5] One cannot dismiss the likelihood that Gnostic elements were present in Islam from the very beginning.

It was as rulers of Iraq, however, that the Muslims were to find Gnosticism at its strongest. We must be careful here, as earlier scholars used the term Gnosticism to cover too wide a range of ideas, both in the background to the rise of Islam, and then in Islam itself. Recent research has shown what might have been expected: the original elite was by its very nature severely restricted, and consequently so was its Islamic progeny. This progeny is found in Islam's principal minority sect: that of the Shiites. Even there, the Gnostics live on not in the main Shiite sub-sect, constituted by the 'Twelvers', who recognize twelve Leaders after Muhammad and are strongest in Iran, but in the smaller sub-sects, whose members are called 'extremist Shiites' by western academics, such as the Isma'ilis, led by the Aga Khan, and the Druze of the Lebanon. Similarly, when Gnostic influences are detected in Sufism, where they are identified by the use of a distinctive imagery of light and darkness, they are found in the works of exceptionally sophisticated thinkers, whose teachings were evidently reserved for a small number of people. Such influences do not appear to have had a much wider impact. What holds good for Gnosticism holds good for the main Gnostic religion, Manichaeanism, which is named after the prophet who inaugurated it, Mani (d. *c.* 274). The fact that Mani was brought up in a Jewish-Christian sect, however, is of great importance for the comparative study of Manichaean and Islamic origins. Various features of Manichaeanism, notably its rejection of the flesh, were taken over by Christianity before Islam: direct influence on Sufism would have been limited.

Manichaeanism used to be called 'an Iranian religion'. Nowadays it would be better to call it 'one of the religions of Iran'. There does not seem to be a major Iranian religious contribution to Islam or Sufism. In the past there has, inevitably, been an attempt to see Islamic mysticism as an Aryan or Indo-European racial reaction of the conquered Iranians to their Arab, Semitic rulers. But the main Iranian religion before Islam was notably lacking in spirituality. This religion, called Mazdaism by some modern writers because of its worship of a chief god called Ahura Mazda, and Zoroastrianism by others after the name of its supposed founder (Zarathushtra or Zoroaster), was in a very weak condition at the time of Islam's appearance. Class ridden, hostile to asceticism, resorting to the persecution of Christian and Manichaean mystics, it had become an empty shell of taboos and rituals, the original meanings of which had long been lost. The only element within it of interest for our purposes seems to be borrowed from shamanism: the flight of the soul in a simulation of death, with the help of a hallucinogenic drug. On the other hand, it will be argued below (when we come to the fourteenth century) that the Islamic institution of 'youngmanliness' (*futuwwa*), which is often compared to European chivalry, and was combined with Sufism, is of Iranian origin. But this is a military rather than a specifically religious tradition.

The question of Indian influences on early Sufism has been much debated. There would appear to have been important borrowings, over the centuries, in the field of meditational techniques, but not at a particularly early date. Methods of breath control were evidently taken by the Sufis from India and then transmitted to eastern Christianity, where there is no firm evidence for their existence before the late thirteenth century. It is essential to distinguish between, on the one hand, influences in the form of techniques, such as worshipping upside down suspended in a well, or the use of the rosary, transmitted from Buddhism through Islam to Christianity; and, on the other hand, doctrinal influences. The latter seem notably absent.

We shall see one instance of doctrinal influence from traditional Indian religion, 'Hinduism', upon a ninth-century Muslim mystic, but we shall also see that this was immediately isolated and contained, being perceived as manifestly alien to the Sufis' objectives. In the thirteenth and fourteenth centuries one encounters elaborate theories of colours in one Sufi brotherhood, with the establishing of a system of correspondences between these colours and spiritual organs within the mystic, in a manner very similar to what is found in Hindu Tantrism. We shall come across these spiritual organs in the work of an eighteenth-century Indian Sufi: there they are located in the body according to Tantric teachings. But such borrowings are not central to Sufi doctrine or relevant to the study of its origins. As for the influence of Buddhism, it would appear to have come via Manichaeanism, and then through the impact of Manichaeanism on Christian monasticism and extremist Shiism. Thus the legend of the Buddha himself, accompanied by repeated complaints about the persecution of ascetics, seems to have been transmitted by Manichaeans to the Isma'ili Shiites before turning into the story of a penitent Sufi prince. Such contributions are both minor and indirect.

The influence of the Koran

The Koran presents enormous difficulties for the modern student. These difficulties stem largely from the bewildering arrangement of its contents. Biblical stories, allusions to contemporary events and attacks on opponents are mixed together in a way which appears to make the task of disentanglement impossible. The old method of distributing the fragments of the Koranic text into parts of Muhammad's biography has now been discredited, as the application of the methods of biblical criticism has begun. Moreover, the traditional view that the Koran was put together in its present form during the reign of 'Uthman (644–56) has been much criticized: it would seem that this was done much later, perhaps in the early eighth century, after a period of doctrinal changes. Here, in looking at the Koran as a source of inspiration for the development of Sufism, we shall follow the order of likely influences (Christian, Jewish-Christian and Gnostic) as enumerated above.

The Koran contains a striking expression of sympathy for Christians, and notably Christian monasticism:

> You will find that the people most hostile to the believers are the Jews and the polytheists; and you will find the closest in love to the believers to be those who say, 'We are Christians.' That is because some of them are priests and monks, and they are not proud. And when they hear what has been sent down to the Messenger you see their eyes overflow with tears, because of the truth which they recognize. (5: 82–3)

There are also attacks on Christians, notably for taking their monks as lords beside God (9: 31). The monks are condemned for enriching themselves (9: 34). In one important passage the Koran says, referring to Jesus: 'And we made in the hearts of those who followed him kindness and mercy and monasticism (*rahbaniyya*) – they started it (we did not prescribe it for them) in seeking God's acceptance, but they did not observe it as it should be observed' (57: 27). Here one can see an anticipation of the course later taken by Sufism: monasticism will be seen by Sufis as a specifically Christian institution, practised by Christians in a way which is not quite right, and which somehow obscures a true, underlying and ideal essence.

The Koran also speaks of an original Covenant between God and man (a theme much emphasized, it has been noted, in eastern Christianity): 'And when your Lord took from the sons of Adam, from their loins, their seed, and made them bear witness against themselves – "Am I not your Lord?" – they said, "Yes, we bear witness"' (7: 172). This passage is central to all Sufi doctrine. Moreover, the Koran speaks of a privileged class of people, the 'friends of God' (*awliya' Allah*, 10: 62). It also speaks of love between God and these privileged people, notably in a passage much quoted by the Sufis: 'a people whom he loves and who love him, humble towards the believers, disdainful towards the unbelievers, striving in the way of God, not fearing the reproach of anyone' (5: 54). The Koran also repeatedly and frequently emphasizes the Christian theme of 'remembrance of God' (*dhikr Allah*, 5: 91, 13: 28, etc.) There is a somewhat ambiguous carnal soul (*nafs*), which urges evil (12: 53), but can be rendered tranquil (89: 27) and be found acceptable by God (89: 28). There is also a Spirit (*ruh*), which is God's, and part of which he breathed into Adam (15: 29) and Mary (66: 12). This Spirit, we are told, will give rise to questioning: the answer is that it belongs to the 'affair' (or 'command', *amr*) of God (17: 85). In Sufism there is a great mystery about the relationship between this Spirit of God and the spirit or higher soul within man. The Koran also speaks of man's heart (*qalb*, 2: 97, 2: 204, etc.) Thus Sufism will depict a battle between the lower or carnal soul and the spirit, with the heart in the middle.

The subject of a possible Jewish-Christian mystical element in the Koran is closely bound up with the problem of Gnostic influences, and the specifically Jewish-Christian teaching of a 'True Prophet' who is manifested first in the person of Adam and later in that of Jesus. The statement that Muhammad is the 'Seal of the Prophets' (33: 40) gives us a Manichaean term from a Jewish-Christian context. The Koran's declaration that Jesus was not killed on the Cross, but only appeared to be (4: 157), had long been thought by earlier scholars to reflect a Gnostic source. The dramatic discovery in Egypt of Gnostic texts which contain this doctrine has brought ample confirmation.[6] But when the

Koran says that God is the light of the heavens and the earth (24: 35) we have a familiar Christian image (given a remarkable poetic development) and need not look to Gnosticism's habitual concern with the light and the dark.

In general, however, it must be said that the elements just discussed, which seem most favourable to Sufism's development, are not representative of the Koran as a whole: the text is noteworthy for its rigour and severity, and the mystics of Islam have had to work hard to produce inner meanings which reflect personal communion with God. But it would be entirely wrong to see the Koran as coterminous with the earliest phase of Islam itself. The text is there for a liturgical purpose, as its very name shows – 'Reciting', 'Reading (from Scripture)' – and so a large part of it presents familiar biblical stories in Arabic.

The harshness of its attacks on adversaries is what one would expect from an atmosphere of sectarian strife, and is consistent with the hypothesis of a Jewish-Christian element in the religion's formation. That does not exclude the possibility of extensive mystical beliefs in the beginnings of Islam. For some scholars have recently come to realize that the Koran did not play so great a part in the rise of Islamic doctrines and institutions as had previously been thought. In Islamic law, for example, it could not, by its very nature, make a particularly extensive contribution. It is important for the Muslim more for what it is, namely the uncreated speech of God, than for what it actually says. Moreover, recent research has shown that in early Islam God's speech was by no means restricted to the Koran; he was seen as speaking in the first person via Muhammad in sayings collected outside the Koranic text. Furthermore, even when utterances attributed to Muhammad were not seen as reflecting God's speech, in the eighth century they were accorded an authority which in practice equalled that of the Koran, however surprising this may seem today.

The influence of the Traditions

Originally, the Tradition or 'report' (*hadith*, literally 'news') was just a statement that an early and authoritative Muslim had said or done something, or condoned someone else's action by his silence. As time went on only statements about Muhammad were held to be valid in mainstream Islam (while the Shiites accepted statements about their Leaders), and had to be provided with increasingly full pedigrees, in the form of lists of transmitters from one generation to the next. The Muslims themselves have always admitted that forgery and invention, in both the statements and the pedigrees, took place on a massive scale, but have nonetheless maintained that a substantial bedrock of sound Traditions was preserved in the ninth-century canonical collections. Some western scholars have been much more sceptical, and have tried to date the Traditions to periods of Islam's development and argue that they mirror doctrinal and political changes.

Now the importance of the Traditions to the study of Sufism's origins is fundamental. Earlier scholarship decided that Traditions of a mystical nature, notably those in which God speaks in the first person, were all ninth-century forgeries, invented by the Sufis for their own purposes. This standpoint was consistent with such scholars' overall view of the beginnings of Islam, one typical of attempts to write religious history in the nineteenth and twentieth centuries: the founder was an austere prophet of God's absolute transcendence, whose pure faith was later corrupted by alien visionaries. Islam was therefore seen as an originally harsh and cold intrusion, which was later given mildness and warmth by Sufism, a product of foreign borrowings and man's need for solace.

In recent years, however, it has been shown that the Traditions used by Sufis, and notably those of the 'sacrosanct Tradition' (*hadith qudsi*) type, which present God's own speech, are not likely to be any later in origin than the others in the ninth-century collections. Our chances of determining that a given Tradition was really originated by Muhammad are non-existent, unless new evidence is discovered. But the Sufi Traditions seem to be as early as the rest, and probably belong to what now appears as the main source: the large-scale production of Traditions in Iraq from the beginning of the eighth century. Most probably, as the new religion of Islam was gradually built up from its Jewish-Christian base – whether this base was there at the very start, or was subsequently borrowed, or was spontaneously recreated – it produced on the one hand legal Traditions out of Jewish materials in the Babylonian Jewish community in Iraq; and on the other mystical Traditions out of Christian materials in the Nestorian Church in Iraq.

Thus some of the 'sacrosanct Traditions' are recognizably reflections of Christian source materials: God speaks of men who love one another *in him*, as in New Testament usage. He says, 'I was sick and you did not visit me', etc. (cf. Matthew 25: 41–5); also, 'I have prepared for my pious servants what no eye has seen, and no ear has heard, and has not occurred to the heart of any man.' This saying is found in almost identical wording in the Coptic Gospel of Thomas. One particular 'sacrosanct Tradition' is a cornerstone of all later Sufi doctrine:

My servant does not stop drawing close to me by extra acts of devotion until I love him. Then when I love him I am his hearing by which he hears, his sight by which he sees, his hand by which he grasps and his foot by which he walks.

Other Traditions, in which it is not God who is presented as speaking through the intermediary of the Prophet, but Muhammad alone, give the spiritual life in Islam both its direction and its boundary: 'Poverty is my glory', and 'There is no monasticism in Islam'. Moreover, it is Traditions which make up the earliest standard biography of Muhammad, composed in the mid-eighth century and edited in the early ninth. Here we find a brief sketch of the story of Muhammad's ascension to heaven and appearance before God: a familiar Middle Eastern motif with shamanistic antecedents. Islam has always linked this story with a passage in the Koran (17: 1), where an unnamed person goes on a mysterious journey by night. It has been convincingly pointed out, however, that there is no reason to identify this person with Muhammad or the night journey with his ascension. But the mystics of Islam have given the combination a rich and colourful expansion, finding in it a prototype for their own experiences. In another legend, set in Muhammad's boyhood, in which mysterious visitors open his breast and extract his heart, we again find a well-known element of shamanistic religion, where it is an indispensable initiatory procedure. Sometimes the story of Muhammad having his breast opened is put just before his ascension.

Legends of early mystics

Other stories connect Muhammad with figures much venerated in Sufism: notably Salman the Persian, a convert from Christianity, alleged in an early Christian source to have had a hand in the composition of the Koran; and a man called Uways in South Arabia, who is said to have communicated with Muhammad by telepathy, and thereby to have inaugurated a curious tradition in Sufism in which disciples are presented as being instructed by the spirits of physically absent or dead masters. Legend also tells of associates of Muhammad called the people of the *suffa*, a long bench in Medina which was supposed to have been their sole home, as they devoted themselves to piety and poverty. This led to the postulation of a fanciful derivation, which is linguistically impossible, of the word *sufi* from *suffa*.

Legends of eighth-century figures venerated in Sufism do not present them as Sufis, but as 'world renouncers' (*zuhhad*) or 'devotees' (*nussak*). They are shown as sternly pious ascetics who achieve massive feats of self-mortification. Needless to say, many of the stories about them are repetitions of anecdotes about Christian monks. What is needed, however, is to find patterns, rather than isolated tales, to establish the continuation of ideas into Islam.

Such a pattern is provided by the legends of two women called Rabi'a. One of these, Rabi'a of Basra in Iraq, is the most famous woman of Islamic mysticism. She is thought to have died in 801. We are told that before repenting and taking to the desert she was a slave girl. One version of her legend says that she 'fell into minstrelsy'. It would seem that here we have a reminiscence of the celebrated converted prostitutes of early eastern Christianity. For at that time the singing slave girls of Iraq provided sexual and cultural services in the manner of classical Athenian courtesans and the Japanese geisha. This tallies with anecdotes of this Rabi'a's witty replies and her recital of verses about love. We need not take seriously, however, the claim, often repeated by modern scholars, that she introduced the theme of love into Islamic mysticism. This is based on verses attributed to her by a source 200 years later; the source also ascribes these verses to four other figures. Popular belief confuses her tomb with that of Saint Pelagia of Jerusalem, a penitent entertainer and courtesan whose cult on the Mount of Olives is attested from the sixth century.

In contrast to her we find another Rabi'a, alleged by sources from the late tenth century onwards to have lived in Syria in the early ninth. She is supposed to have been married to a leading Sufi, but not to have had intercourse with him. Here we have a continuation, rare in Islam, of a practice common in early Christianity, where it is often put beneath the patronage of Mary the mother of Jesus. Thus behind the contrasting Rabi'as we can see pairs of contrasting Marys. Behind Rabi'a of Basra we can see Mary Magdalen, who is identified with the anonymous penitent in Luke (7: 37–50) by a Nestorian writer of ninth-century Iraq, and Mary of Egypt, who is supposed to have repented of a life of promiscuity after the intervention of Mary the mother of Jesus, and is also believed to be buried at the shrine of Pelagia. Behind Rabi'a of Syria and her Sufi husband we can see the shadows of Mary the mother of Jesus and Saint Joseph, and also Mary and Theophilus of Antioch, representatives of the Syrian tradition of 'blame'. Mary and Theophilus of Antioch dress up as a prostitute and a juggler, but are really a pious and sexually abstinent married couple. Thus the two Rabi'as reflect the pre-Islamic cultural colourings of Iraq, with its wit and sophistication, and Syria, with its more simple but rigorous asceticism. The pair of the penitent courtesan and the sexually abstinent wife form a pattern which continues in Sufi biographies.

Eighth-century texts

Great care should be taken when approaching the vexed question of eighth-century texts. The leading specialists disagree vehemently about the dating of works ascribed to this century. Even when they agree that a given text was composed before 800, they advance vastly different theories about the part of the century to which it should be attributed. Again, there is the problem of such a text being edited by Muslim writers after 800. Some arguments advanced in favour of the authenticity of a work are patently naive, such as the suggestion that a text should be accepted as authentic until proved otherwise. Given the obvious temptation for Muslims to ascribe teachings to a famous early figure, such an argument can carry no weight at all.

It seems unwise to build historical reconstructions upon, for example, the mystical commentary on the Koran attributed by Muslims to the sixth Leader (*Imam*) of the Shiites, Ja'far (d. 765). We possess this commentary only in editions made in the early tenth century. The rigorously sceptical work of John Wansbrough has suggested that the task of elaborating the interpretation of the Koran fell into successive (if overlapping) stages, as with Hebrew scripture: there would have been a concern first with moralistic story-telling, then with law, then with the transmission of the text itself, and only finally with rhetorical analysis and the symbolic interpretation characteristic of Sufism.

The origin of the term sufi

From this we come to the problems of the first appearances of the term *sufi* and its meaning. Here I am indebted to the recent work of Göran Ogén, without being in agreement with him. Much has been made of an isolated statement that the first person to be called '*sufi*' was one Abu Hashim of Iraq, who is said to have died in 776. This should not be taken too seriously. It goes against all the evidence from classical Muslim sources, who agree that the term dates from the third century of Islam, which began in 816. Before, as we have seen, ascetics were called by different terms. There is no evidence for a group of people calling themselves Sufis about 776, and indeed it is only around the middle of the ninth century that one finds such groups in Baghdad, the new capital of the 'Abbasid dynasty of caliphs, who had replaced the Umayyads of Damascus.

It has usually been considered that the term *sufi* meant originally 'wearer of wool', the Arabic for wool being *suf*. In Nestorian Christian asceticism before Islam wool was a noteworthy element. The novice, in one ritual, is made to sit on a woollen tunic and is told that it is a grave which declares him dead to the world. In Nestorian Christianity during the Islamic period there is literary evidence (though too late to be conclusive) that a wearer of wool means a monk. Moreover, in early Islam the wearing of wool was characteristic of the very lowest classes of society, and consequently symbolized humility. We know that woollen clothing was adopted by the earliest Sufis, and they themselves accepted this explanation of the name. This etymology might seem, then, to be indisputably and exclusively correct, were it not for a long-neglected counter-argument.

This argument was put forward in 1893, by Adalbert Merx, a man with a remarkable knowledge of both Islam and its antecedents in culture preserved in Syriac sources. He declared that *sufi* could not originally have meant 'wearer of wool', because logically an Arabic word formed in this way would have to mean 'a man made of wool' or 'a seller of wool'. Rather, it must come from the Greek *sophos*, 'wise', rather as Greek *philosophos*, 'philosopher', became Arabic *faylasuf*. To the well-known objection that a Greek *s* is represented in Arabic by the letter *sin* (as in *faylasuf*), not the letter *sad* (as in *sufi*), he responded with a number of counter-examples in which a Greek *s* does correspond to an Arabic *sad*. Furthermore, Sufism is heavily indebted to the neo-Platonist tradition within Greek philosophy. The term *sufi* appeared at the same time as the translation of Greek philosophical works into Arabic. This was heavily patronized by some caliphs of the 'Abbasid dynasty, which reigned in Baghdad from 750 onwards. It was in the first half of the ninth century that this patronage of philosophy was extended. In 847 a change of ruler brought a dramatic fall in the fortunes of philosophy: henceforward it was seen as unislamic and Greek, and to be abhorred. Thus, we might imagine, the Sufis were to find it convenient to suppress the original Greek explanation of their name.

Against Merx one is bound to argue, following Ogén, that *sufi* could have meant 'wearer of wool', as a word formed originally in the spoken, colloquial language, and then transposed into literary Arabic, without being correctly formed in the latter. Other etymologies require exclusion on linguistic grounds, although they were put forward alongside that from *suf*, 'wool', by the Sufis themselves: from *suffa*, 'bench', from *safa'*, 'purity', and from *saff*, 'rank, degree'. There are only three possibilities:

1   from Arabic *suf*, 'wool', alone,
2   from Greek *sophos*, 'wise', alone,
3   a pun, combining 1 and 2 from the outset.

The weight of the evidence would appear to render explanation 2 the least likely. It does not seem feasible to decide which of explanations 1 and 3 is the more probable. In any case, as we have observed, it would be a false question to ask whether Christianity, represented by wool, as opposed to neo-Platonist philosophy, had more influence on the rise of Sufism, since Christian mystical thought was essentially neo-Platonist in inspiration.

Conclusions

The last consideration leads us to a question which is often put: is Sufism Islamic or not? This too is really a false problem. There is no point in asking whether Sufism is Christian as opposed to Islamic, since there was no fully developed religion of Islam preceding Christian influences. Sufism is part of the emerging Christian wing of Islam, not an alien intrusion. Recent scholarship has tended to see the origin of Sufism in the activities of the 'People of the Tradition' (*ahl al-hadith*), who were the most respectable of mainline Muslims, as the collectors and defenders of sayings attributed to Muhammad.

The picture of early Islam which has been given here, that of a religion which tries to steer a middle course between Christian spirituality and Judaic legalism, owes much to Louis Massignon's work. Massignon presented evidence which pointed to the Christian sources of Sufism. This he did in the context of analysing the terms used by Sufis, which he listed under the headings of their apparent provenance. Then he made a statement which has often been accepted and repeated: 'The long inventory above allows us to state that it is from the Koran, constantly recited, meditated, and experienced, that Islamic mysticism proceeds, in its origin and its development.'[7] This is misleading. To collect technical terms and classify them according to origin is an admirable and important method, but to draw such a conclusion is unjustifiable. A mere numerical superiority of words coming from the Koran does not show that Sufism itself comes from it. Scholars have known for a long time that although Christian mystics always use biblical terms Christian mysticism comes from Platonism, not the text of the Bible. It is the patterns of thought and their functioning which are significant, rather than the fragments of discourse themselves. Naturally the Sufis clothe their ideas in Koranic vocabulary: to fail to do so would be to incur censure. But a significant number of Sufi terms are manifestly Christian, being loan-words from Syriac.

There is one last problem to consider: to what extent might the beginnings of Sufism have been influenced by Shiism? This is an extremely difficult question. Answering it has not been made easier by the long hostility of western scholars to Shiism's emotional veneration of Muhammad's family. They have tended to follow mainstream Islam in rejecting Shiite claims. Some specialists have argued, plausibly enough, that the high position given to the figure of Muhammad in Sufism is a late reflection of Shiism's earlier exaltation of its Leaders. Recently it has also been argued that the Shiite conception of the leadership of the Muslim community, which presents the ideal ruler as the source of religious knowledge, is more archaic and closer to the beginnings of Islam than the mainstream view, that of Islam's Sunni majority, in which such knowledge is seen as diffused among a number of scholar-jurists. It has been suspected that the Sufi hierarchies of the 'friends of God' show Shiite influence in their arrangement and the numbers of members assigned to the various grades. In general, however, it would seem that although a Gnostic element was probably present from the beginnings of Islam, and Gnosticism continued to provide a higher knowledge for a Shiite elite, this very elitism prevented Shiism from exerting a great impact on the rise of the Sufi tradition.

THE WRITERS AND THINKERS OF THE NINTH AND EARLY TENTH CENTURY

We now proceed to solid evidence: books composed in the ninth century. Needless to say, these are accompanied by legends of the authors and their contemporaries, and a wealth of anecdotes in later compilations, which have created much confusion. However, ninth-century Islam is rich in its own literary production, and by concentrating on this we can at least follow the gradual emergence of Sufism's components.

Muhasibi
Caution is essential in the case of one great figure often classed among the Sufis, a man called Muhasibi, who died in Baghdad in 857. Although

the Sufis have claimed him as one of their own, the work of Joseph van Ess has demonstrated that he was neither a Sufi nor a mystic, but a moralizing, pious theologian. He is of importance for us, however, as an expositor of a number of themes which the Sufis were to absorb and use. He himself did not belong to any group, and was very much his own man. His independent stance against the Greek-inspired, rationalist theologians of his day brought him into a lot of trouble, since by actually engaging in theology to combat them he placed himself in an unpopular discipline, which many Muslims insisted should be banned.

Muhasibi has no system, not even concerning an upward progression of 'stations' (*maqamat*), as taught in Sufism. Rather, he concentrates on the fear of God and scrupulousness in fulfilling religious duties. Central to his doctrine is the inspection of the lower, carnal soul, the *nafs*. He is at great pains, however, to avoid any ostentatious display of piety. Here he analyses an important technical term much used by Sufis: *riya'*, which means the sycophantic and hypocritical show of religiosity. This idea is of great significance, since the Muslim mystic is usually in society and perpetually observed, unlike the monk or hermit. Other subjects in Muhasibi's writings are predictably paralleled in Christian thinkers: indifference, forgetfulness and sickness of the heart. In analysing the concept of an 'intention' before an action, however, he is developing a liturgical element borrowed by Islam from Judaism. Muhasibi is not concerned with the drunkenness of ecstasy or visionary experiences in this world. He gives graphic descriptions of the terrors of the Last Judgement and the luxurious wallowings of the blessed in the physical pleasures of Paradise. God's friends (*awliya'*), we are told, are companions in heaven because they have loved each other *in their Lord* in this world. They are briefly interrupted in their enjoyment for a vision of God.

In general, Muhasibi has a fairly restrained approach to the Christian roots of Sufism. He refers to contemporary ascetics who dress in wool or patched frocks, but feels that this is rather dubious, as characteristic of Christians. As for the term 'monasticism' (*rahbaniyya*) itself, he is not hostile towards it. He quotes the parable of the Sower in Matthew, and shows no embarrassment at using what he knows to be a Christian source. Muhasibi is indeed important for what he does *not* say. He speaks of 'wearers of wool' from Mecca, South Arabia, Syria and Iraq, but does not give us evidence of specifically Sufi practices. The 'remembrance of God' does not appear in his writings as a special ritual technique. It is only later writers that present Muhasibi and his contemporaries as being familiar with the discipline of 'listening' (*sama'*) to poetry or music in order to produce ecstasy.

Dhu 'l-Nun

We are still without concrete evidence when we approach the almost entirely legendary Dhu 'l-Nun of Egypt, said to have died in 861. Works on alchemy, magic and medicine are attributed to him, but are of doubtful authenticity. Although later Sufis claim him for their own, as a leader and the originator of important concepts, such as the mystic's direct knowledge (*ma'rifa*, gnosis) of God and the stations (*maqamat*) and states (*ahwal*) of the Sufi Path, there is no proof of this at all. At best one can say that here we have a representation of an impact from the Greek philosophical tradition, which included alchemy and medicine, upon the beginnings of Sufism, in contrast to Muhasibi, as the embodiment of Christian asceticism. In portraying these two men as opposite poles in their time, Sufism has perhaps found an appropriate indication of complementary sources in its own beginnings.

Abu Yazid

Very different problems are posed by another early figure, the wild and controversial Abu Yazid, who lived in a village called Bastam in northern Iran and died about 875. A number of sayings are attributed to him, of a type termed the *shath*, the 'ecstatic utterance' in which the mystic gives voice to his most intimate experience. We know that some of these sayings were commented upon in Baghdad less than forty years after his death, and were preserved in a late tenth-century work. More were collected in a book written by a man who died in 1084. In general, it can be said that many of these sayings have strong points of resemblance, and together represent the words of one man or at least a very limited circle of disciples. Debate has centred on the question of whether Abu Yazid was subject to an Indian religious influence: the last writer to claim that he was, R. C. Zaehner, has been vigorously attacked. It is necessary to examine his case.

Zaehner stressed the point that Abu Yazid was said to have a teacher called Sindi. This name would normally be taken to mean that its holder came from the region of Sind, now part of Pakistan. It has been suggested that in this case the holder could have come from a village called Sind, located in the province of northern Iran in which Abu Yazid lived. But it must be said that the combination of external evidence (a report of a teacher of apparently Indian extraction) and internal evidence (the Indian character of Abu Yazid's sayings) is particularly powerful. Moreover, according to our late tenth-century source, Abu Yazid said that he taught Sindi how to perform the obligatory duties of Islam, in exchange for instruction concerning 'realities' (*haqa'iq*) and the affirmation of God's Uniqueness. This suggests that Sindi was originally a non-Muslim.

Zaehner also found, in one of Abu Yazid's sayings, the expression 'Thou art that' applied to God. This is a famous and familiar phrase of the Upanishads, the great Hindu scriptures. Abu Yazid also mentions an encounter, in which he takes the form of a bird, with a 'tree of oneness', its soil, root and branch, and shoots and fruits, and then rejects all this as 'deceit' – just as the Vedanta (the Indian philosophical tradition which develops the thought of the Upanishads) rejects the universe as 'illusion'. In a passage of the Upanishads two birds are presented as clinging to a cosmic tree, the one bound by the 'illusion', the other not. Furthermore, Abu Yazid is celebrated for having declared, 'Glory be to me!' This again is found in the Upanishads. Again, he says, 'I sloughed off my self as a snake sloughs off its skin: then I looked into my self and lo! I was he.' In the Upanishads the body is compared to the sloughed-off skin of a snake, just before a man is envisaged as knowing himself and saying, 'I am he.'

An attempt to disprove Zaehner's case was made by A. J. Arberry.[8] He managed to establish the fact that the idea of God's deceit (to test men) is found in the Koran (4: 142). Arberry then claimed that Massignon's discussion of Abu Yazid's expression 'Glory be to me!' made debate about an Indian origin unnecessary. But if we turn to Massignon's work we find only a list of Sufi comments on the phrase.[9] Arberry then tried to attack Zaehner's rendering of the Arabic words in which he had found the expression 'Thou art that', and argued that the translation should read 'Thou wilt be that' and refer to Abu Yazid's envisaging God as remaining after he himself had ceased to exist. He also observed that the pronoun 'that' is applied to God in the Koran (6: 95 etc.) After this Arberry declined to attack Zaehner's other examples of Indian parallels, on the ground that this would make his paper too long. He concluded by saying that one might speculate that Abu Yazid just instructed Sindi in the interpretation of the verses of the Koran involved in performing his religious duties, rather than teaching him how to perform them.

Arberry's rejoinder, then, is weak, and does not constitute a refutation of Zaehner's argument. We should, however, consider the objections made against Zaehner by a more serious opponent, Molé.[10] Molé claimed, like Arberry, that in saying 'Thou wilt be that' Abu Yazid was declaring that he himself would have disappeared. But there is no statement in the Arabic text that Abu Yazid is disappearing: this is just the usual later Sufi explanation, which the orientalists are projecting back. Molé also claimed that Abu Yazid's image of the bird and the tree was Koranic, not Indian. He did not produce a Koranic example to prove his case. He declared that the 'deceit' was not the universe, but the mystic's experience. The text does not allow us to decide if this is right or not.

Two general observations are necessary here. First: these specialists, whether arguing for or against an Indian influence, made the mistake of assuming that Abu Yazid taught the Sufi doctrine of the 'passing away' (*fana'*) of the mystic. In fact no early source presents him as teaching this. It is late sources that add the element of 'passing away' to the story of Sindi's instructing Abu Yazid. Second: Zaehner, in addition to producing a magnificent and overpowering case for an Indian influence on Abu Yazid, committed the serious error of imagining that this had changed the entire course of Sufism's development – that one man had altered Sufism's natural orientation towards God into a movement towards monism, the doctrine that there is only one entity in the whole of existence. As we shall see, the Sufis of Baghdad were fascinated by Abu Yazid, but realized that what he was saying was not what they wanted, and clearly expressed this feeling. They were to pursue their own path, noting, but not being directed by what Abu Yazid had uttered. My position in this controversy is an independent one: acceptance of the thesis of an Indian influence on Abu Yazid; but rejection of Zaehner's claim for a wider diffusion of Indian teachings through him.

Tustari

That Abu Yazid was a mystic is clear enough; but was he a Sufi? To find clear examples of Sufi figures we have to await thinkers who died in the 890s. One of these, Tustari (d. 896), who taught first in south-western Iran and then at Basra in southern Iraq, is undoubtedly an outstanding personality and one of the founders of Sufi doctrine. Although his works are constituted by the compilations of his students and their successors – who had their own observations to add – the excellent study of Gerhard Böwering enables one to see, in Tustari's commentary on the Koran, a distinctive and original fund of theories which are certainly archaic and represent his own contribution.

God, according to Tustari (and here we have an original doctrine, apparently held only by him at that time), created Muhammad before everyone else, as a light which he caused to appear from his own Light. Muhammad then stood in adoration before him. Much later he created Adam from this Muhammadan light, before creating mankind and making a primordial Covenant with it. The heart of Muhammad is also all-important: it is the mine of God's absolute Uniqueness, of the attestation of that Uniqueness incumbent on all Muslims, and of the Koran itself.

In the next world, says Tustari, the blessed will enjoy 'survival' (*baqa'*) with God. It is noteworthy that he does not, like other Sufis, use this term to denote the aftermath of spiritual experience in this world, where the mystic survives in or through God or with his attributes changed by him. Moreover, although Tustari uses the key concept of theophany (*tajalli*, God's appearing or self-displaying) he does so only in the context of Paradise, not, as later Sufis do, to refer to a terrestrial vision of God.

The soul (*nafs*) in Tustari has a marked ambiguity. On the one hand, to be sure, it is the lower, carnal soul which incites people to commit evil. On the other hand, it is the vehicle for God's secret conversation with man. This is connected with the idea that within the soul there is a secret (*sirr*). Tustari also speaks of the mystery of direct knowledge (*ma'rifa*, gnosis) of God. The secret hidden within man lives through remembrance of God. There is a higher stage of this in which man makes remembrance of God *through* God himself.

Tustari has a personal doctrine of certainty (*yaqin*), which inspires and resembles the one usually found in Sufism, without being identical with it. There is the light of certainty (*nur al-yaqin*) which God makes manifest to man; the knowledge of certainty (*'ilm al-yaqin*); and most importantly, the 'quintessence' (*'ayn*, which also means 'eye') of certainty. This is formally different from the usual Sufi triad of the three types of certainty: the knowledge of certainty; the quintessence of certainty which belongs to the eyewitness; and the 'truth of certainty' (*haqq al-yaqin*) in actual experience. But these three types are reflected in another triad, in which Tustari expresses his view of certainty more clearly: unveiling (*mukashafa*), as in God's interview with Moses on Mount Sinai; visual beholding (*mu'ayana*), as in God's demonstration of his power to Abraham (Koran 2: 260); and contemplative witnessing (*mushahada*), as in Muhammad's ascension.

The light of certainty is perceived in other luminous forms, as the lights of direct knowledge, of guidance and of faith. The light of guidance is part of God's own Light, intervening in a primordial gift. The light of direct knowledge, which is in a man's heart, is clearly related to that of faith. The light of faith enables men to read otherwise invisible lines written in their hearts before their creation.

In Tustari's work the theme of God's Uniqueness is closely bound up with that of the original Covenant, in which men bore witness to this Uniqueness. The attestation to his Uniqueness was deposited at the beginning in their hearts. God's own testimony to it took place before he created creatures. Men's perception of its reality will come to fruition in the vision of God in the next world.

Tustari gives an important presentation of the 'friends of God'. They are different from the ordinary servants of God in that the elite are desired by God, while the common people desire his Face. Again, friendship is conferred on the 'friends' before their creation. Muhammad is the friend of the man whose friend is God. It is significant with regard to the way that much of Islam developed out of the sayings attributed to Muhammad, rather than out of the Koran, that Tustari rejects the Koranic insistence that all men will be questioned on the Day of Reckoning (15: 92) in favour of a Tradition which says that God's friends will proceed directly to Paradise without any questioning. Only the 'friends' understand the Koran. They are ranked in a hierarchy. Tustari says that he has met 1500 'truthful ones' (*siddiqun*); forty 'substitutes' (*abdal*, so called, he asserts, because they keep substituting the mystical 'states' for one another), who are still making progress; and seven 'pegs' (*awtad*), who have reached their goal. As for Tustari himself, he claims to be the 'proof' (*hujja*) of God for his pupils in particular and for people in general. The idea of a man's being the proof of God's presence or will is characteristic of Shiism.

Tustari's teachings in psychology are most peculiar and confused. The ambiguous character of the lower soul leads him to posit a 'lower soul of the spirit' (*nafs al-ruh*) as opposed to the 'lower soul of nature' (*nafs al-tab'*). The former contains a luminous spirit which God takes from man in death. The spirit is joined with the intellect and the heart, both in God's original dialogue with men, to the exclusion of the 'lower soul of nature', and in the beatific vision in the world to come.

It is significant that some Sufi doctrines are absent from Böwering's reconstruction of Tustari's commentary on the Koran. The key concept of 'passing away' is not there, and there is no ordered progression of 'stations' and 'states', although 'states' are mentioned. While Tustari is undoubtedly a mystic, concerned with a 'secret' within man, he is not concerned with the visionary experiences of his contemporaries or their claims to intimacy with God in this world. There does seem to be a Gnostic influence, as shown by Tustari's emphasis on themes typical of Gnosticism: luminosity within men, direct knowledge of God and the importance of the elite. There also appears to be a link with the Greek philosophical tradition: in one early source Tustari says that the four branches of science are religion, medicine, astrology and alchemy. Inevitably, there is unreliable evidence connecting him with the elusive Dhu 'l-Nun, himself seen as an authority on gnosis and the occult sciences.

Kharraz

One contemporary of Tustari, Kharraz (d. 899), who lived in Baghdad, must rank alongside him as one of the two founders of Sufism in their time (as far as the literary sources permit us to judge). Sufi tradition credits him with being the first to speak in Baghdad of 'passing away' (*fana'*) and 'survival' (*baqa'*). Wilferd Madelung has taken the view that this was not really true, since these ideas had been used by Sufis before him and were common in his time. But, as we have seen, there is no reliable evidence of the earlier use of these terms. This is the principal problem with German scholarship as applied to ninth-century Sufism: it is excellent and rigorous when directed towards an individual figure, but at the same time often makes observations which are based on late and unreliable sources about other figures in the background.

Kharraz's *Book of Truthfulness* (*Kitab al-sidq*) reads very much like the treatises of Isaac of Nineveh. He begins by taking the concept of truthfulness (*sidq*), and relating it to those of sincerity and patience. Then he applies the idea of truthfulness to the sequence of 'stations' in the Path. The first part of truthfulness, he explains, resides in repentance (*tawba*). This, as in Isaac and later Sufism, is the first 'station'. After this 'station' are: knowledge of the lower soul, and knowledge of the devil; scrupulousness; 'the lawful and the pure', where Kharraz considers the correct attitude towards material possessions; renunciation of the world (*zuhd*, often translated as 'asceticism'); trust in God (*tawakkul*) (here Kharraz particularly resembles Isaac in speaking of cutting off 'causes', that is to say visible means of support); fear; shame; knowledge of God's bounties and gratitude; love; acceptance; desire; and finally, intimacy.

At the end, joy, rest, direct knowledge of God and nearness to him are attained: 'what no eye has seen'. As in Isaac, we are not given a systematic arrangement of the 'states' which follow the acquisition of the 'stations' or 'virtues'. It is explained that a man reaches a 'state' where he no longer needs to worry about truthfulness, because it is made easy for him by God. But the term 'station' is also used for the higher stages by Kharraz.

The *Book of Truthfulness*, however, is clearly destined for a wider public, not for the elite. The latter are favoured with much more exciting texts in Kharraz's short *Epistles* (*Rasa'il*), which have been finely analysed by Paul Nwyia. Here Kharraz speaks of a superior class of mystics whom he calls the 'people of wanderinghood and perplexitude' (*ahl tayhuhiyya wa hayruriyya*), inventing new abstract words in imitation of the Hellenized philosophers. The highest grade of these mystics reach the essence of God's Quintessence (*'ayn*). Their attributes vanish, joining the attributes of God. This last teaching was to prove particularly controversial and attract a violent attack.

Kharraz himself, in his *Epistles*, mounts an assault on some of the 'people of Sufism' who put the 'friends of God' above the prophets themselves. He explains that the prophets were 'friends' before the beginning of prophethood, and so the gift of prophecy confers an additional superiority upon them. It is significant, however, that there are, in the beginnings of Sufism, some Sufis who were a very long way indeed from acceptable mainline Islamic belief. Obviously, to put the 'friends' above the prophets was to open the gate to rejection of Islamic law, seen as founded by Muhammad. Although Sufism, as it continued, was to insist on respect for the law, it is noteworthy that such Sufis should be attacked by a figure like Kharraz, whom we know to have encountered immense difficulties and powerful enemies because of his audacious teachings.

Man's lower soul, Kharraz teaches, must be made to 'pass away', as must his physical nature and even his heart. It is his direct knowledge of God which will survive, along with his spirit and his friendship with God. These 'stations' of 'passing away' and 'survival' are the highest that man can achieve. It is clear that they are meant to be reached in this world, not just in the next. The 'survival' is linked to the original Covenant, when all the spirits said *Yes* to God. It was only when the lower souls and natures were created that men were divided into friends and enemies of God. But Kharraz also says, in contradiction to this, that the spirits of the believers were created 'from the place of light' and the spirits of the unbelievers 'from the place of darkness'. As Nwyia observes, there is inconsistency, which suggests that Kharraz failed to reconcile different currents of thought.

Kharraz has also given us a striking analysis of the concept of nearness to God. This 'station' is subdivided into three: *finding*, in which man concentrates on God with an inner calm; *stupefaction*, in which mystics cry out wildly, weep and sigh; and *forgetfulness* of what one has been given by God and one's need of him. Then the mystic falls away and only God survives. All questions put to him receive the answer 'God'. If he is asked, 'Who are you?', he cannot reply 'I'. After this he reaches a point where he cannot even say 'God'.

To conclude: Kharraz presents a straightforward enumeration of the lower 'stations' in a recognizably Christian manner, and then emphasizes the fact that the 'people of direct knowledge' are above all this. To them belong 'passing away and survival'. We shall consider the question of the origin of these concepts in the course of looking at leading mystics of the end of the ninth century and the beginning of the tenth.

Tirmidhi

Tirmidhi was born sometime before 835 and lived at least to the age of 65, in the north-east of the Islamic world, what is now Soviet Central Asia. He has been the subject of an excellent study by Bernd Radtke. Tirmidhi is unusual in that he has left some autobiographical information.

He studied jurisprudence and the Traditions until the age of twenty-seven, when, on the pilgrimage to Mecca, he decided to abandon the world. After failing to find a teacher he was encouraged by seeing Muhammad in a dream, and eventually acquired some companions on the Path. Some enemies accused him of 'innovation', of discussing love (between God and man), and of claiming to be a prophet. These denunciations reached the local provincial governor, and Tirmidhi was forbidden to talk about love any more. After a period of working at subduing his lower soul, he had a joyful experience when walking home one night. Dogs barked in his face, but he felt happy. The stars and the moon seemed to come down to the earth. He experienced an inner contraction from the extreme pleasure which he was feeling, and imagined that he was near the throne of God.

Tirmidhi's enemies now besieged him, but he was able to conquer the hearts of the people with his words, and his students could come out into the open. A dream told him to stop starving himself and take a part in the life of the world, helping the poor and the weak. He studied astronomy and learnt to use the astrolabe, but another dream told him to stop pursuing these matters, as they came between him and God. His wife also had illuminating dreams, in which his greatness was revealed: Tirmidhi, among the 'friends of God', was the chief of the forty 'substitutes' needed to save the world.

Tirmidhi is indeed most important for his doctrine of friendship with

God, and in particular for his idea that just as Muhammad is the Seal of the Prophets, so too there is a Seal of the Friends (*khatm al-awliya'*). But for Tirmidhi the expression 'Seal of the Prophets' does not mean that Muhammad is the last prophet, but rather that the gift of prophecy granted to him is provided with a special seal, which protects him from the devil and the lower soul. In the same way, the 'Seal of the Friends' stands in a special position before the rest of the 'friends of God'. These have failed to prevent the contamination of God's friendship by the lower soul. But the Seal absorbs the whole of this friendship without the lower soul's interference. This Seal is the instrument by which God gives life to the hearts of men and directs them on the right path. He is close to the prophets and their rank, and can see the presents which have been given to them. As for the question 'Who is the Seal of the Friends?', Tirmidhi puts it, unanswered, along with 156 other questions designed to test those with claims to superiority. We shall see how centuries later, another thinker rose to the challenge. But it is clear from his account of one of his wife's dreams that Tirmidhi saw himself as having this leading position. In this dream a prince, with his Turkish soldiers, threatens their country. Forty men, led by Tirmidhi, have to go to him. The prince takes Tirmidhi's heart out of his breast (as happens to Muhammad in the legend), shakes him, so that he thinks that all his limbs are being torn apart (another standard shamanistic theme), and confirms his leading position.

Significant distinctions are drawn by Tirmidhi between different classes of the 'friends'. There is (a) the 'friend of the right of God', who by his own efforts watches over the demands of God's law; and there is (b) the 'friend of God', who operates through God's bounty and is either (i) 'enraptured', drawn to God from eternity, or (ii) 'rightly guided', brought to God through his mercy. The Seal belongs to the higher, 'enraptured' type. This distinction between the plodding pilgrim on the Path and the automatic beneficiary of rapture became a major theme of Sufism, as did the question of the relative merits of the pilgrim who eventually attains rapture and the ecstatic who goes from rapture to the Path.

Other aspects of Tirmidhi's teaching resemble what we have already found among other ninth-century masters. He is familiar with the Greek philosophical idea of the Universal Intelligence or Reason, out of which other intelligences proceed to enlighten the intellects of men (here the Arabic term *'aql*, 'reason', will be translated as 'intelligence' when referring to a supraterrestrial entity, and 'intellect' when referring to the human mind). He knows the saying attributed to Muhammad, apparently of Gnostic origin, that Reason is the first created thing, but quotes it in a diluted form: since for him the Spirit was first to be created, Reason is not the first, but the most loved creature of God. He presents different pictures of the heart, divided into three, four and seven organs. The heart is the king, and the intellect its chief minister.

Tirmidhi's doctrine concerning the role of the teacher is unusual. He himself did not have one, and learnt from what he read. He does not openly advise one either to take a teacher or to do without, but he does warn a correspondent not to make himself too dependent upon another man. His own portrayal of the Path starts conventionally enough: the stages begin with repentance, abstinence and disciplining the lower soul, and lead to God's self-displaying (*tajalli*, theophany). That does not mean, however, that the mystic actually sees God in this world: it is the consciousness of God's Uniqueness, and this is the highest stage that man can reach. Here the lower soul disappears, and the heart is granted 'stability'. This seems to correspond to some extent to the usual Sufi idea of 'passing away and survival'.

There appear to be a number of different currents of thought in Tirmidhi, as in other ninth-century mystics. On top of the usual Christian Path we have a superimposition of 'direct knowledge', with light imagery suggesting Gnosticism: in particular, the attributes of God are presented as kingdoms of light. There is a possibility of shamanistic inspiration from the north-east: the 'friend' flies through the air. It is not surprising that in the century after Tirmidhi there was considerable disagreement as to whether he was a Sufi or not. This is largely anachronistic: as Radtke observes, Sufism, as we have it in the classic manuals, is a tenth-century construction which pushes its early history further back than is justified.

Junayd

Junayd of Baghdad (d. 910) is often regarded as the greatest of all Sufis, and invariably seen as the most respectable. Sufi tradition portrays him as the chief upholder of sternness and caution, surrounded by wild ecstatics, whom he rebukes with evident distaste. We shall concentrate on his own few and short epistles, in which he emerges as a subtle and sharp thinker, with an extremely obscure style and some daring ideas.

Junayd's doctrine is built around two pillars: the Covenant and 'passing away'. These are closely connected. He says in his opuscule on the Covenant that originally God made his friends exist when he called them and they replied. 'He was speaking to them when they were not existing except through his existence for them, since they were existing for God without their existence for themselves.' Junayd then goes on to say that God created them in the start of their 'passing away' (*fana*'). Here he is evidently using the term 'passing away' to mean man's impermanent, temporal existence in this world. He is able to play upon the paradoxical ambiguity of the term: when someone passes away in mystical experience he escapes from that impermanent, temporal existence, and returns to his original, real existence with God. Consequently Junayd says in his brief treatise on this term that God makes the mystic pass away by originating him as God originated him in the beginning. Then there was a perfect mode of existence, in which God 'encompassed' men. So, Junayd explains elsewhere, in a short fragment which has been preserved from one of his lost works, his 'passing away' is his survival. Moreover, God then makes one pass away a second time, by taking one away from one's personal 'passing away and survival' into the ultimate reality of 'passing away', where there is no interference from the individual.

This seems a suitable point at which to pause and consider the source of the concepts of 'passing away' and 'survival' in Sufism. Here is a familiar and recognizable theme in Christian mysticism, found in the works of Meister Eckhart and Angelus Silesius: man first realizes, both intellectually and in experience, that his apparent, individual and temporal existence is really non-existence (since it is borrowed from God and not really owned by man), and then turns away, abandoning this negation of his existence, to the positive apprehending of real existence in God. In this one can see the celebrated 'negation of the negation', which is one of the distinguishing characteristics of dialectical thought and finds its ultimate development in the works of Hegel and Marx, while having its earliest roots in neo-Platonism.[11] The New Testament had already emphasized the importance of 'dying' to the world in order to find true life (Colossians 3: 3), and the theme of dying in anticipation of one's eventual physical death continues, albeit without much clarity of definition, in patristic literature. One hears of early Christian monks in North Africa and the East who took the idea of 'annihilation' literally, and committed suicide. This motif continues in early Sufi legend, accompanied by disapproval. On the spiritual level, Muhammad is credited with the saying 'Die before you die!' The Koran also provides justification for the terms 'passing away' and 'survival': 'Everyone who is on the earth passes away, And there survives the face of your Lord with grandeur and glory' (55: 26–7). From this to the Sufi use of the terms seems quite some way. It would appear that we have a natural development, not out of the Koranic text, but out of the

Christian theme, generated by the dynamism inherent in neo-Platonist thought.

To return to Junayd: he is much concerned with the idea of the spiritual 'states', which are transient and succeed one another, but does not seem to set out explicitly the classical Sufi distinction between them and the permanent 'stations'. He sees the ultimate stage of 'survival' as equivalent to 'sobriety' after the overpowering drunkenness of ecstasy. It is for this doctrine of sobriety that he has become best known in Sufism, as standing in opposition to Abu Yazid. Junayd himself wrote comments (which have been preserved) on a few of Abu Yazid's sayings. He finds these insufficient. In particular, he rejects the expression 'a million times' in Abu Yazid's description of his flight as a bird. Junayd felt that if Abu Yazid had been further advanced he would not have thought of such things as birds, bodies, atmospheres and so on. He reached only the beginning of the Path.

Junayd also shows an overt political conformism. The true mystics, he says, never criticize the leaders of the Islamic community, but believe that one should obey them. Rebellion is the sign of ignorance and sin. It is to be noted, however, that Junayd's own correspondence was opened without his permission and, he complains, subjected to misleading interpretations. He found it difficult to extricate himself from the resulting trouble, and the episode led him to be careful about writing again. One can judge from this how suspiciously the whole Sufi network was regarded in its earliest phase.

Hallaj

The need for caution was graphically illustrated by the case of Sufism's most famous martyr, Hallaj, who was executed in Baghdad in 922. Here we encounter an extremely important episode in the history of Islam, and also an extremely obscure one. This is partly due to the nature of the sources, in which Hallaj is presented as eager to die, performing miracles, and maintaining an exemplary attitude in the face of imminent death. It is also partly due to the imaginative contribution made by Massignon, the principal specialist in this field, whose prodigious learning was counteracted by a proneness to introduce his own religious ideas into historical reconstruction.

The biography of Hallaj which was transmitted by his son provides reasonably firm ground with which to begin. He was born in southern Iran (probably around 860) and there became a student of Tustari. He got to know Junayd and his circle in Iraq, but quarrelled with him and returned to Iran. There he became popular, but upset the Sufis and stopped wearing their distinctive clothing. He preached in public in Iran and travelled to India and Central Asia. Eventually he installed himself at Baghdad and again preached in public. Some accused him of magic, while others saw him as a performer of real miracles. He was arrested, imprisoned and eventually executed.

The official reason for Hallaj's execution, as we know from the account of his trial which was preserved by the clerk of the court, was that he taught that the pilgrimage to Mecca could be performed while staying at home. There were, however, other accusations: that he was an extremist Shiite agent, and that he claimed divinity for himself. The evidence does indeed point to extremist Shiism, with Hallaj being assigned an important role, in which God manifests himself through him. Hallaj's son says that letters came to his father from India calling him 'the Succourer', and from Central Asia calling him 'the Nourisher'. It would seem that evidence that Hallaj belonged to the extremist Shiites was rejected by Massignon out of personal hostility towards them (he equated them with communists and freemasons).

As for the 'miracles' supposedly worked by Hallaj, it must be said that there is a hard core of early evidence, sometimes from his own lifetime, that he was working wonders, such as appearing to fill an entire room with his body and producing fruit from out of thin air. It is not just a matter of later legend. Unfortunately, Massignon believed that Hallaj was working real miracles with supernatural intervention. The obvious explanation is that Hallaj was operating in the well-known tradition of producing visual illusions by hypnosis. This was firmly established in the Middle East before Islam and has always flourished there up to our own time. It was familiar enough to his opponents.

Hallaj composed some short prose texts, and a few of these have survived. They present Tustari's doctrine of Muhammad's primordial light. But Hallaj goes further than his teacher in what might be taken to mean self-identification with God. He says, 'Leave created nature, so that you may be he, and he may be you, from the standpoint of reality.' Hallaj seems to speak dismissively of Abu Yazid, however, when he refers to a bird with two wings which fails on the way to God. Hallaj continues with a famous piece of verse (misread by Massignon, and thus often misquoted):

> I saw my Love with the eye of my heart,
> And He said, 'Who are you?' I said, 'You!'

In one passage, which has obviously been inserted by someone else, since in it Hallaj is made to describe the details of his execution, we find the saying for which he is best known: 'I am the Truth' (or 'I am the Real', *ana 'l-haqq*), which has often been taken to mean 'I am God'. But there is good and early manuscript authority for the variant 'I see the Truth' (*ara 'l-haqq*). In any case, there is no firm evidence that Hallaj ever uttered the expression for which he is most notorious. Massignon, however, after himself coming to this conclusion, nonetheless asserted that Hallaj must have said it, for the dubious reason that everyone agreed that he had. Whether he said it or not, it is certainly of interest: one thinks of the phrase attributed to Jesus, 'I am the Way, the Truth and the Life' (John 14: 6), and the frequent occurrence of the phrase 'I am the Truth' in Greek magical papyri of the first few centuries CE.

Hallaj has also left us some most peculiar Traditions. Instead of the usual lists of the names of men as transmitters and guarantors of authenticity, he gives a colourful variety of intermediary entities, such as the Spirit, heaven and earth, the 'ruby of light', the 'crescent of the Yemen' and so on, before God himself is made to speak, saying such things as:

> God casts 360 glances during each day and night. In each glance he brings closer to himself the spirit of one of his loved ones, and replaces him with one of his sincere ones. And with his looking at his loved one he gives mercy to 70,000 of those who profess friendship for that friend.

One of these Traditions reads:

> From the quintessence of the balance of the year 902, from the age of the announcer of the year seven of the call, from the friend of nearness: God says, 'My attribute succeeds my attribute, and my looking my looking, and lights and spirits are linked to one another until the Day of Resurrection. Whoever understands the work of attesting that God is Unique utters God's supreme name and reaches a glorious station after he has left this world.'

In the mention of the year 902 we can see a reference to an extremist Shiite uprising.

A number of verses are attributed to Hallaj. The authenticity of these is extremely doubtful, as is that of the anecdotes which present him as anticipating his execution. Since he was crucified, there were, inevitably, stories calqued on Christian models, and some short poems in which he is made to ask to be killed or to say that he will die in the religion of the cross. From this there has been a natural development to modern academic reconstructions, in which Hallaj appears as a deeply Christian figure, dying to redeem the Muslim community or be united with Jesus. It seems most unwise to try to build any theological system out of the poetic fragments. The prose texts show us a man mainly concerned with God's Uniqueness, and able to explore this theme with a formidable command of arguments drawn from grammar and mathematics. Their terminology resembles (but is not identical with) that of the Hellenized philosophers.

Conclusions

One can exclude Muhasibi as neither Sufi nor mystic; Dhu 'l-Nun as a legend; Abu Yazid as a representative of Indian ideas with no real impact; Tirmidhi as an independent, tutorless figure separated from the mainstream; and Hallaj as someone who cut himself off from the Sufis and was largely rejected by them in his own time. That leaves Tustari, first in south-western Iran and then in southern Iraq, and Kharraz and Junayd in Baghdad. These mystics did, to be sure, have friends and correspondents, some of whom wrote short texts that have survived. But we are left with only a tiny group of sophisticated leaders in Iraq, above the great mass of 'wool wearers' in the wider Muslim world.

These leaders were extremely talented, but they were not professional philosophers or systematic thinkers, nor were they concerned to express their beliefs in a clear and ordered manner. The exception is Kharraz's enumeration of the 'stations' or virtues. The Sufis had taken over the Christian mystics' Path, with repentance leading, through other stages, to 'what no eye has seen'. They had also inherited the ideas of the Covenant and God's friends. To all this they tacked on Gnostic teachings about primordial lights and their own development, presumably from Christian and neo-Platonist sources, of the theme of 'passing away and survival'. Here – one might think inevitably – there were differing views about what is made to 'pass away': the lower soul, man's attributes, or man's entire individual personality? So too it is not clear what survives: God alone, man with God's attributes, or man as an original idea in the mind of God?

The principal doctrines of Sufism are here, but they will need plenty of structuring, rephrasing and clarification. Moreover, great dangers had already arisen. Some thinkers had assumed that they were the most important people in the universe, with the exception of the prophets, and indispensable to it. Others had uttered what seemed to be blasphemous expressions of self-identification with God.

2 FROM CONSTRUCTION TO SYSTEMATIZATION (c. 922–c. 1240)

CONSTRUCTION AND SPECULATION (c. 922–c. 1020)

By the beginning of the tenth century Sufism's principal doctrines had already been formulated. But Sufism itself, as a recognized tradition or discipline, did not yet exist (contrary to what used to be believed). However, by the end of the tenth century it was firmly in place, with its classic, standard manuals composed at that time.

How did this happen? We are not in a position to say, for various reasons. Scholars have only just begun to realize that Sufism is a tenth- rather than a ninth-century construction: this was not yet understood in the 1960s, and has been appreciated only by a few specialists in the 1970s and 1980s. Thus essential research into the tenth-century materials has yet to be done. Sufism has presented itself as being in place before it actually was. There is also a peculiar gap in the middle of the tenth century. For a period of some fifty years, between Hallaj and Tirmidhi on the one hand, and the figures whose deaths are placed in the last quarter of the century on the other, no mystical writer of note is recorded as having died (the dates of death are used, since normally there is little, if anything, else).

To understand the reasons for this gap it is necessary to look at the historical background. The 'Abbasid caliphate, whose capital was Baghdad, had, in its heyday in the ninth century, represented an extraordinarily rich chapter in cultural history. Urban life in Iraq reached the ultimate heights of sophistication. But the flowering of the arts was paid for by a correspondingly horrific over-exploitation of the peasantry. The sources of the time agree with the severe judgement of modern economic historians: the robbing of the country to subsidize the town, a common enough practice throughout history, was done here on a scale and with a cruelty unusual in the extreme.[1]

It was previously imagined that the earliest manifestations of Sufi thought were part of a reaction against worldliness and self-enrichment. Now, however, the evidence suggests that these ideas were an expression of the view of people within the privileged and comparatively wealthy urban elite, and, in their intellectual transcending of simple-minded asceticism, reflected a desire to protect material advantages. It should be added that books, since they were copied by hand, were extremely expensive. When, in the tenth century, the economy collapsed, and the splendour of the cities of Iraq turned to desolation, this was bound to affect literary production. That is one reason for the gap in the history of mystical literature during this period.

The economic disaster that occurred in the tenth century was accompanied by political and religious developments. The century saw the fall of the 'Abbasid caliphate as a ruling temporal force. From 945 it continued only as a religious institution, reigning, not ruling in Baghdad, while the government of Iraq and western Iran was left in the hands of a new Iranian dynasty, the Buyids, who were moderate Shiites. Indeed, throughout the tenth century the victory of Shiism was widespread: in Egypt part of its extremist wing, the Isma'ilis, took over and established a counter-caliphate. Moreover, in the eastern Islamic world there was plenty of extremist Shiite propaganda, with constant pressure for the overthrow of existing rulers, and some isolated successes. The decentralization of Islam was further increased by other new dynasties in the east, dynasties which were not Shiite, but represented the tendency of local governors and military leaders to claim sovereignty for themselves and revive regional (most notably Iranian) traditions.

This mixture of revolutionary and non-Islamic ingredients in the background helped to produce a peculiar secret society, based in southern Iraq, called the Brethren of Purity (*Ikhwan al-Safa'*). These Brethren took Greek philosophy and Iranian and Indian lore and combined them in a collection of treatises, often seen as an encyclopaedia. They revived the ancient Pythagorean obsession with numbers, and frequently preferred Christian doctrines to Islamic ones. Although their eclecticism has often incurred contempt (for example in their self-contradictory espousal of free will and astrological determinism at the same time), they had an immense influence on the mystics of Islam.

Perhaps esoteric and political manifestations of Shiism diverted energies from the production of important Sufi literature in the mid-tenth century. Probably the execution of Hallaj also had a sobering and inhibiting effect: it showed the Sufis that there were limits beyond which they could not go, and they doubtless felt obliged to maintain caution and silence.

The successors of Junayd and Tustari

It seems that after Tustari's death in 896 a number of his pupils left Basra for Baghdad. There they lost their identity as his disciples and some became followers of Junayd. Junayd's students were not particularly distinguished: they are known for collecting biographical information about their predecessors, and appear as actors in didactic anecdotes, constructed to illustrate edifying themes such as the importance of caring for the dying. But those of Tustari's pupils who stayed in Basra developed a striking and exceptional school of thought known as the Salimiyya, after Muhammad ibn Salim (d. 909) and his son Ahmad (d. 962). The Salimiyya aroused much condemnation, both among theologians and lawyers and among some other Sufis. A number of teachings attributed to them were formally denounced, notably ones relating to the vision of God in the next world. They allegedly taught that God would be seen in human form by men (even the unbelievers) and in animal forms by animals. They also maintained, we are told, that certain secrets, if revealed, would destroy the functions of those who keep them: God's his Providence, the prophets' their prophethood and the scholars' their knowledge. Not surprisingly, Ahmad is shown as being very secretive when not speaking to his own associates. We may observe that the idea of a secret doctrine or doctrines in Sufism continues to have great importance up to our own time. In particular, it is often repeated that God's attribute of Lordship (*rububiyya*) has a secret which, if revealed, would nullify that Lordship itself.

One Sufi who attacked the Salimiyya was Ibn Khafif of Shiraz in southern Iran. He died at a great age around 982. What little survives of his works bears witness to his severity and sobriety, in which he resembles Junayd. He says that one cannot reach God except through service, nor can one see him in this world. One cannot escape from the condition of being God's slave, but one can free oneself from the lower soul. The mystic's attributes can be made to 'pass away', and he can return to normality after joining God. He can walk on water and disappear before men's eyes. The drunkenness of ecstasy is permissible for the novice, but not for the mature mystic. Oddly enough, Ibn Khafif sees 'stations' as the preserve of the latter, while 'states' are only for those who have reached an intermediate level. Thus some of the more elevated aspects of the Path, such as direct knowledge of God, are not to be reckoned among the 'states'. There is no limit to the 'states', but each individual 'state' does have a limit. The practice of *sama'*, listening to music or poetry, is to be denied to the novice, and is in any case better avoided, because of its unfortunate consequences. Finally, Ibn Khafif says about Sufism itself that it is not a science or a practice, but an attribute through which the essence of the Sufi displays itself.

We have a biography of Ibn Khafif, written by his pupil Daylami (date of death unknown). This consists largely of the master's reminiscences of his predecessors; it is to be noted that they were usually in some form of paid employment. We are also told that they would repent of words uttered in ecstasy that were contrary to the law. Ibn Khafif is shown as particularly touchy on the subject of controversial figures. He lost his temper when told that Abu Yazid was called an infidel. When young he had met Hallaj, whom he presents as someone who engaged in magic in order to call people to God. Ibn Khafif saw Hallaj as a true believer in God's Uniqueness, and cursed the author of certain verses attributed to him:

> Glory be to Him whose Humanity manifested
> The secret of His piercing Divinity's radiance
> And who then appeared openly in His creation
> In the form of the eater and the drinker

These verses look very like an expression of the Christian teaching of incarnation. By contrast, Ibn Khafif's doctrine seems to have been that God adorns the mystic with some of his attributes before returning him to society.

A mystic of a different type was Niffari (so named because he came from the ancient town of Nippur in Iraq), who died sometime after 977. Niffari has received very little attention, but is undoubtedly one of the greatest of Muslim mystics. Almost nothing is known about his life. He has, however, left writings which are absolutely extraordinary. Chief among these is his *Book of Stayings* (*Kitab al-mawaqif*). In this, at the start of every chapter, Niffari begins with the words 'He [God] stayed me [usually this is followed by an expression such as 'in Nearness', 'in His Majesty', etc.] and said to me'. Then God speaks in the first person.

The concept of 'staying' (*waqfa*) is peculiar to Niffari, and the crowning point of his personal system. This system is composed of three levels. At the bottom of the hierarchy there stands formal or theoretical knowledge, the learning to be found in books. Above this is the direct knowledge of the mystic. But this too is a veil, a barrier between man and God, and so one must pass on to the third level, that of 'staying', where the mystic is made to stand immediately before God and is granted the vision of him, so that no obstacle of 'otherness' remains. This is the main theme of Niffari's work: the various means of proceeding towards God (the skills needed for progress on the Path and the gifts acquired therein) must be discarded as objects of his jealousy. As for the vision of God, he tells Niffari, 'You may not describe how you see me.' God and his interlocutor have secrets which must not be divulged.

The mystic, according to Niffari, will be given the creative power of God described in the Koran, so that he can bring things into temporal existence just by saying 'Be' (see for example Koran 2: 117). God even says to Niffari, 'You are the inner meaning of all temporal existence.' Not surprisingly, just as the mystic approaches God in his power and importance, so too God acquires very human traits. These are most notable in passages which anticipate the end of time. God describes himself as passing across the earth and taking off his cuirass and breastplate. He refers to the Second Coming of Jesus and a 'true monasticism'. Most strikingly, he speaks to his addressee in the feminine; or rather, one might say, he addresses the feminine part (perhaps the lower soul, the *nafs*, feminine in Arabic) of the mystic.

Niffari's teachings, then, resemble doctrines attributed to the Salimiyya: that God will appear in human form, and that there are secrets which must not be divulged. The idea that the mystic will be given God's power to create by oral commands is also ascribed to Hallaj. Niffari's views, sometimes shocking to mainline legal and theological thinking in Islam, prefigure later expressions of Sufism in poetry, and especially prefigure the Sufi poets' constant rejection of the stages of the Path in favour of the pure love of God for himself.

The first classic manuals of Sufism

Composed in the late tenth century, the first classic manuals of Sufism may be seen as part of a cultural renaissance which followed the mid-century decline. This renaissance has been linked to the tolerant rule of the Buyids, who did not impose their Shiism on their subjects, but permitted a great diversity of opinion.

Böwering calls these Sufi books 'treatises' and reserves the term 'manuals' for eleventh-century compositions. He says that the point of the former was to prove Sufism's legality. Here they will be called 'manuals', since they always seem to have functioned as such, whatever the expressed intentions of their authors.

Sarraj

Sarraj was born in north-eastern Iran and died in 988. His work, the *Book of Flashes* (*Kitab al-luma'*), consists largely of the sayings of his predecessors: he rebukes his contemporaries for seeking fame in pretentious and prolix discussions of their own. Sarraj gives a clear enumeration of the 'stations' and the 'states'. The 'states', unlike the 'stations', cannot be gained through ascetic and devotional practices. The 'stations' begin with repentance, followed by scrupulousness, renunciation of the world, poverty, patience, trust in God and, lastly, acceptance. This is followed by the 'states', of which the first is watchfulness, followed by nearness, love, fear, hope, longing, intimacy, tranquillity, contemplation and, finally, certainty, which is both the beginning and the end of all the 'states'. Later, however, Sarraj admits that there are other 'states', such as drunkenness and 'passing away'.

Sarraj shows himself to be a stern and rigorous follower of the 'sober' school of Junayd and his pupils. However, he takes a very favourable view of the practice of listening to music or poetry and defends it as lawful (even for novices), if there are no forbidden musical instruments or corrupt intentions. Moreover, like Ibn Khafif, he defends Abu Yazid against charges of being an infidel for uttering 'Glory be to me!' and other apparent blasphemies. It is noteworthy that he engaged in a controversy with the Salimiyya (who were also attacked by Ibn Khafif) on this very subject. His personal relations with the Salimiyya, however, were entirely amicable, and he used them extensively as sources. On the other hand, at the end of his book Sarraj gives a survey of errors connected with Sufism. Some people falsely maintain that everything is permitted, and that prohibitions refer only to excessive self-indulgence. Some wrongly think that men can lose their human nature; but 'passing away' cannot bring the destruction of the lower soul. Certain people in Baghdad, in their belief that they have passed away from their own attributes, and entered those of God, have gone so far as to believe in incarnation (*hulul*) or what Christians believe about Jesus. The earlier Sufi doctrine of leaving one's attributes for God's just means abandoning one's own will to God's will, and in any case God is not identical with the divine attributes. Finally, some err in speculating about the spirit or higher soul, imagining for example that the spirits of the elite are uncreated.

Kalabadhi

Kalabadhi (the name indicates that he came from a district of Bukhara, in what is now Soviet Central Asia) died in 990 or 995. In the manual he composed, Kalabadhi begins by saying that Sufism is in decline, but then contradicts himself by declaring that contemporary Sufi writers know as much as their predecessors. He devotes a large part of his treatise to a statement of mainstream Muslim belief. His Sufi teaching is unusual in that he thinks that the 'states' are to be found between the beginning and the end of a given 'station'. Moreover, some of his 'stations' would normally be seen as 'states': for example, intimacy, nearness, and the last, love. Again, he is unusual in asserting that a lot of 'states', such as 'passing away', 'survival', absence and presence, are considered by some Sufis as being one single 'state', even when they are apparent opposites: the man who passes away from what belongs to himself survives through what is God's, and so on. Kalabadhi gives a long analysis of these themes of 'passing away' and 'survival'. For him, as for Sarraj, the idea of 'survival in God's attributes' means subordination to God's will. The 'passing away' of human attributes does not mean that they cease to exist: rather, man's bad qualities are submerged in pleasure at the victory of God's knowledge and justice. But Kalabadhi recognizes the diversity of Sufi opinion regarding 'passing away', as well as the question of whether the mystic can return from it to his own attributes. Here Kalabadhi declares that he cannot: he will either appear to be mad or will be a leader for other men, in which case he will govern his affairs through God's attributes and be controlled by them.

Abu Talib (Makki)

Abu Talib was brought up in Mecca and thus acquired the surname Makki. He moved to Iraq, where he joined the Salimiyya, and died in 996. His best-known book is his massive Sufi manual, the *Food of Hearts* (*Qut al-qulub*). As might be expected in a handbook for a wider public, Makki reproduces respectable, mainstream opinions, and does not proffer the dubious tendencies of his school. This is a treatise of conventional piety, in which the account of the Sufi Path itself is limited to the description of nine 'stations of certainty': repentance, patience, gratitude, hope, fear, renunciation of the world, trust in God, acceptance and love. Here the 'stations', as being lasting, are seen as more important than the thousands of fleeting 'states'.

By contrast, a description of Makki's real opinions, those destined for the elite, is to be found in his *Knowledge of the Hearts* (*'Ilm al-qulub*). It gives us texts attributed to Tustari about primordial events: here the lower class of 'disciples who desire God' (*muridun*) are said to be created from the light of the higher class of 'masters who are desired by God' (*muradun*).

Daylami

The texts Makki ascribed to Tustari are also found in the work of Daylami (the surname means that he came from a province of northern Iran), the pupil and biographer of Ibn Khafif. Daylami associated with members of the Greek philosophical tradition and incorporated their ideas in a book on love.

He naturally confronted a problem which Sufism inherited from classical antiquity: can one say that God experiences passionate love (*'ishq*) as opposed to a restrained love or affection (*hubb*)? Here, says Daylami, the Sufi elders were divided, but he himself considered that this was permissible, and quotes a saying in which God speaks through Muhammad to declare that he reciprocates the passionate love of certain servants. After examining the views of various Sufi masters on the origin of love, such as the opinion that God begins with a love for some men in his primordial knowledge of them, before creating their bodies, Daylami puts forward his personal position: love is an eternal attribute of God, in which he originally loved only himself. Then this attribute divided itself into the triad of Love, Lover and Beloved. The Christians, with their Trinity, come close to affirming God's Uniqueness.

Daylami distinguishes between a pure, Platonic love, with a 'permitted looking' at a human beloved, and a blameworthy carnal love. The Sufis teach that the natural love of humans for each other is necessary to show one the way to the love of God. The lover who 'passes away' has no carnal soul left (here Daylami agrees with the view of his teacher, Ibn Khafif). Daylami also develops the theme of the witness (*shahid*) in love: the friends of God, by loving one another, bear witness to the reality of love, as do animals and the works of the Divine Artist, which manifest universal Beauty. The lovers of God reach either unitive fusion with him (*ittihad*, a concept condemned in later Sufism), or the 'station' of experiencing God's Uniqueness (*tawhid*), which means reaching him, so that he seems both to be and not be in and through everything. There are higher things of which the author refuses to speak.

Sulami

Daylami's contemporary, Sulami, who came from north-eastern Iran and died in 1021, is by contrast an unoriginal and uninspiring writer. A wealthy man, he was educated by his grandfather, who belonged to the grouping of mystics called the *malamatiyya*, because of their devotion to bringing 'blame' (*malama*) upon themselves. Unfortunately, although

Sulami wrote a treatise about them, his method of abstaining from expression of his own beliefs, while repeating respectable, isolated quotations from earlier Sufis, prevents us from obtaining a real picture of the 'people of blame'. The same is true of the rest of his work, as of much early Islamic literature: the atomistic and disorderly presentation of materials hinders us from seeing the continuity of patterns from late antiquity. Although Sulami wrote a treatise about the tradition of 'youngmanliness', which comes from pre-Islamic Iran, it contains nothing but a succession of banalities about the ethical implications of sacrificing oneself for others. Sulami is important mainly for putting Sufi interpretation of the Koran firmly on the map, with others' opinions arranged in the commentary which bears his name, and for compiling a collection of Sufi biographies. But the collection of biographies is overshadowed by the much larger collection of Abu Nu'aym, of Isfahan in central Iran, who died in 1038. Both biographers are concerned to ensure that the sayings attributed to their subjects are accompanied by lists of the people who transmitted them – an attempt to guarantee authenticity which may strike the modern western student as tedious pedantry but is all-important for the Muslim sense of history as a living process of preservation.

REACTION AND POETIC EXPRESSION (*c*. 1020–*c*. 1130)

In the tenth century the Shiite sect was victorious, the Muslim world was split up, and Iranian features became prominent. The eleventh century witnessed an opposite trend: the Sunni majority returned with spectacular successes, regaining political supremacy and, thanks to the advent of Turkish rulers, uniting vast areas of Islamic territory.

The Turks, coming from Central Asia, conquered much of north-west India for Islam, overran the whole of the eastern Islamic world as far as Syria, and began the conquest of what is now Turkey. They were to influence Sufism in two opposite ways: on the one hand their rulers tried to impose strictly rigorous Sunni norms, using Sufi institutions to protect the state against enemies; on the other hand the influx of nomadic, tribal elements imbued Sufism with shamanistic, ecstatic and often subversive tendencies.

Kazaruni

The Turkish conquerors found some aspects of Sufi organization and administration already in place. These are most evident in the life of a

Sufi leader called Kazaruni, named after his home town in southern Iran, who died in 1035. A biography of Kazaruni was written by his successor's son, who died in 1109, and this has been preserved in a later, expanded version. Fritz Meier has succeeded in stripping away a lot of legendary accretions in order to isolate a historical core.

Kazaruni was a preacher, operating among adherents of Iran's old national religion, Mazdaism, and under Shiite rulers, who appointed a Mazdean to govern the town of Kazarun. The Sufi elder himself was not an abstract thinker. He has left a strictly mainline Sunni profession of faith and some firm moral precepts. However, he is presented as speaking of God's eternal love for the believers and his being one with them, so that their words and actions are his. But what is most important is Kazaruni's organizational activity, notably in developing the Sufi institution of the lodge. 'Lodge' is probably the best translation for the various Arabic words used to denote this institution, notably *ribat*, which might also be rendered 'hospice'. *Ribat* is often the equivalent of the Persian word *khanaqah*, used in the tenth century to designate a Manichaean building, perhaps a meeting place for lay members. In any case the Sufi lodge is linguistically distinguished from the Christian monastery, which is called *dayr* in the Muslim world. Such lodges had existed before: in the tenth century Ibn Khafif had one, in which visiting Sufis could stay. Kazaruni's was used to shelter and feed travellers and the poor. It was attached to a mosque. Guests were given bread, meat and fruit, without any obligation to pay. Kazaruni's disciples founded sixty-five of these lodges, mainly in the villages of southern Iran. He himself collected funds (notably from wealthy patrons) and distributed them to the lodges.

Modern western writers have called this organization an 'order'. This involves both an anachronism and a mistranslation, since the Arabic term in question did not yet have the connotation of 'brotherhood', and in any case should never be rendered as 'order'. The word *tariqa*, which we have already encountered as meaning the Sufi Path, was used at this time, and later, to mean also the Sufi way of life: in effect, Sufism itself. Later it was used to mean an individual Sufi brotherhood, with a 'chain' of masters and disciples down the generations, constituting a school of thought and practice, which might or might not have an administrative framework. This must not be confused with the Christian institution of the monastic orders, as we shall see below. The concept of the Path is one of linear progress, not one of internal or external structure (as in the case of a Christian monastic order's interior framework, fixed within an exterior ecclesiastical one).

Kazaruni's initial organization was no more than a network of disciples whose main purpose was presented as serving the poor. His successors as leaders of the network had the titles 'deputy' (*khalifa*) or 'preacher' (*khatib*). He had no wife or children. There was hereditary succession after him, however, in that his first four successors all belonged to one family. The members of the network were called 'companions' (*ashab*). We have no evidence of any special method used by Kazaruni to train them. They would rise at crack of dawn to perform extra worship and recite the Koran. During the day they would serve the poor, listen to sayings attributed to Muhammad and engage in the repetition of formulas containing God's names. By the fourteenth century the network had spread to Turkey and China; it had then come to be seen as one of the 'paths' or brotherhoods.

Abu Sa'id

A very different figure of this period was Abu Sa'id of Mayhana (now in Soviet Central Asia), who died in 1049. We have some early information about him in the manual on Sufism composed by the Iranian Hujwiri (d. *c*. 1075). Abu Sa'id took the view that wealth was preferable to poverty. The Sufi ideal of poverty was to be understood in a metaphorical sense, as meaning 'being rich in God'. He lived in luxury, dressing in fine Egyptian linen, and explained that since he saw God in all things, he was indeed 'rich in God'. In any case, he said, the true mystic has 'passed away' from all 'stations' and escaped from all 'states', so that he is exempt from reproach. Hujwiri says that Abu Sa'id abandoned the study of books entirely, apparently in order to cut himself off from worldly ties and concentrate on God.

Late and legendary accounts of Abu Sa'id have been much used by modern writers, as have Persian quatrains attributed to him in late anthologies of poetry. In these anthologies it is normal for the compiler to give the label 'Abu Sa'id' to verses of a libertine character. Such attributions of early quatrains to 'authors' should often not be taken seriously: the name of the 'author' usually indicates only a certain style. Thus sceptical quatrains are attributed to the philosopher and mathematician 'Umar Khayyam (d. 1131), who became famous as a poet in nineteenth-century England, thanks to the popular translations of Edward Fitzgerald. Modern writers then imagined that Khayyam was not only a leading poet but also a Sufi, although the quatrains ascribed to him express distinctly irreligious, not mystical sentiments. Abu Sa'id has also been credited with a brief list of precepts, which has been seen as a rudimentary monastic 'rule'. It was normal for a Sufi leader of this time to give his followers a few injunctions regarding morality and devotional practices. But the drawing-up of an extended catalogue of regulations is a twelfth-century development.

Avicenna and Biruni

There are two great Islamic thinkers of the period who do not belong to Sufism, but are nonetheless extremely important for Sufi studies. The first is the best-known of Muslim philosophers, Avicenna, who came from a village near Bukhara and died in 1037. There has been much debate as to whether he should be counted as a mystic or not. He speaks with sympathy of the ideal figure of the mystic (the gnostic, the knower, *'arif*), while expressing his contempt for conventional piety and asceticism when pursued for celestial rewards. He sees the true Path as passing through 'moments' in which the light of God dawns upon one, each moment being preceded and followed by experiences of ecstasy. Eventually one finds oneself looking at God: that is the arrival (*wusul*).[2]

Avicenna is also important for his short symbolic narratives. Here we find the idea of a journey to a Great King (God) across the heavenly spheres of the medieval universe. The terms 'East' and 'West' are used, not in a geographical sense, but to indicate the light of true being and the darkness of ignorance and deprivation. Avicenna saw himself as developing a higher type of philosophy, that of 'Oriental Illumination' (*ishraq*), destined for an elite, as opposed to the ordinary philosophy to be found in his books, which represents the sober, Aristotelian wing of neo-Platonism as it passed from the Greeks to their successors in the Muslim world. Unfortunately, there is not enough surviving evidence to show that he did succeed in creating such a higher philosophy, although, as will be seen below, this project was carried out after him.[3] The Sufis were to mock Avicenna in their poetry as the chief representative of the Greek philosophical tradition, which they hated, for being mainly concerned not with God, but with the series of supernatural 'Intelligences' believed by the philosophers to emanate from him and to constitute the source of knowledge. The Sufis nevertheless did not refrain from borrowing ideas from neo-Platonism when it suited them.

The other great Muslim thinker is the Iranian scholar Biruni, also born in what is now Soviet Central Asia, who died sometime after 1050. His prodigious knowledge of many languages and disciplines enabled him to make a lot of comparative judgements. Biruni believed the word *sufi* was derived from the Greek *sophos*, 'wise'. He drew a number of parallels between Greek, Christian and Indian ideas on the one hand and Sufi teachings on the other. Like some Greek philosophers, the Sufis think that only the First Cause (God) has real existence. As in neo-Platonism, the Sufis believe that this world is a sleeping soul, while the next world is a soul which is awake. Some Sufis believe that God is immanent in certain places in heaven; others that he is immanent in the whole world. The Sufis, like some Indians, consider Paradise an unimportant distraction. They also maintain, rather in the manner of Hindus and Christians, that man has two souls: one eternal, one human. Like Indian writers, they believe that one can move where one likes, for example through mountains. Biruni, in trying to show the similarities between Sufi and Hindu beliefs about abandoning one's terrestrial existence to reach God, quotes Abu Yazid on sloughing off one's skin to find that one is God – a saying which, as observed above, indicates a direct Indian influence. The important point, however, is not the degree of resemblance between Sufi ideas on the one hand and Indian and Christian ideas on the other, but rather the fact that an extremely well-informed writer sometimes presents the Sufis as holding opinions which are more daring than what they themselves put in their own writings.[4]

Avicenna and Biruni belong to the cultural renaissance of the late tenth century. But the tolerant government which permitted that renaissance, the Shiite dynasty of the Buyids, was now to fall. In the 1030s the Turkish family of the Saljuqs moved across north-eastern Iran, and in 1055 they reached Baghdad, deposing the Buyids and 'liberating' the Sunni caliphate, somewhat against its will, from the disgrace of Buyid domination. There was now a return to traditional norms, and the eclecticism and openness which had prevailed during the past decades were abandoned.

Qushayri

The Sunni revival was already in full swing by the mid-eleventh century. One of its leading representatives was a Sufi called Qushayri, who lived in north-eastern Iran and died in 1074. As a pupil of the tedious Sulami he was naturally to provide the sober respectability that was now in demand; but he has the merit of describing some theoretical frameworks which are lacking in his master's writings. This he does in a manual of Sufism, which is largely devoted to an exposition of the stages of the Path. After a conventional enumeration of 'stations' from repentance onwards, he explains that there is a controversy about 'acceptance' (*rida'*, 'satisfaction'). The Sufis of north-eastern Iran regard it as a 'station', won by man, but the Iraqis call it a 'state', given by God. Obviously, the term can mean man's accepting or being satisfied with God, or God's accepting or being satisfied with the mystic. Finally, we reach the highest point: direct knowledge of God. Some, however, say that above this comes love. But elsewhere Qushayri, as Richard Hartmann pointed out, provides a different perspective, in which the highest stage is 'passing away', first through 'survival' in God's attributes, then through the vision of God and lastly through God's own existence. It seems, then, that although there is a considerable degree of theoretical classification there is no single unified system in Qushayri.

One important aspect of Qushayri's work is his insistence on the need for an 'elder' (*shaykh*) to guide the Sufi and teach him to recite a given formula of 'remembrance of God'. Qushayri is particularly concerned that the novice should be prevented from falling into the practice of pederasty, though he himself uses the love of boys as an image for the love of God. It is also noteworthy that, writing in 1046, he does not speak of Sufis meeting in special 'lodges', although, as we have seen, they already existed to some extent, but rather of their assembling in mosques. It would seem that the spread of the lodge, like that of the 'college' (*madrasa*, a school for the teaching of Islamic law and other religious disciplines), was due to the new Saljuq dynasty, in the late eleventh and early twelfth century, and its desire to use these institutions both as bulwarks against external enemies and as instruments of social control.

Hujwiri

A writer similar to Qushayri is his contemporary from Ghazna in Afghanistan, Hujwiri, who died about 1075. His manual also shows different patterns in the descriptions of the end of the Path, without adequate systematization. Indeed, Hujwiri has been severely criticized for his indecisiveness. He is unable to provide a coherent verdict on whether poverty should be preferred to wealth.

As in Qushayri, one finds a standard enumeration of 'stations', before being told that 'acceptance' represents the end of the 'stations', which are permanent, and the beginning of the 'states', which are temporary. Beyond the 'states', we are told, is 'passing away'. This cannot mean the loss of one's essence; nor can one pass away from all of one's attributes: all that happens is that one human attribute is replaced by another. Elsewhere, however, Hujwiri presents a conflicting picture. The 'state' is portrayed as permanent, as opposed to the temporary 'moment' (*waqt*), which it renders stable. After the 'states' there is 'fixity' (*tamkin*), the highest grade; 'fixity' is divided into a lower part, in which one experiences 'passing away', while retaining one's attributes, and a higher part, in which one has no attributes.

Hujwiri speaks of twelve groupings of Sufis, ten of which are praiseworthy, and two of which are to be condemned. There has been much uncertainty among modern scholars about whether these groupings really existed, or whether they are arbitrarily delineated for Hujwiri's exposition of aspects of Sufi doctrine. The answer is that sometimes they existed and sometimes they did not: when he speaks of Sufi followers of Muhasibi, clearly there was no such group; when he speaks of followers of Tustari other than the Salimiyya, they no longer existed as a distinct group at this time; when he speaks of followers of Junayd (including his own teacher), there was a school of thought in Sufism in Hujwiri's time which could trace its ancestry back to Junayd; when he speaks of followers of Abu Yazid in the latter's native Bastam, these were people whom Hujwiri met and who preserved sayings attributed to Abu Yazid; and sometimes when he speaks of contemporary followers of ninth- and tenth-century figures, we do not know enough to judge.

In any case, Hujwiri's standard procedure is to isolate one concept (for example, in the instance of Junayd, sobriety), rather than to describe the range of ideas in a given group. Writing in Persian, he says that a group (*giruh*) has a method or 'path' (*tariqat* or *tariq*) in spiritual endeavour, such as, in the case of Tustari's followers, the mortification of the lower soul. (We are still a long way from the clearly defined brotherhood (*tariqa*) of later centuries.) The two condemned groups, the supporters of incarnation and people who claim to follow Hallaj, he lumps together as one, and fiercely attacks them continually. Some people on the fringes of Sufism, he says, declare that nothing can ever be known, and this position has been commonly attributed to Sufism as a whole. There are plenty of ignorant frauds, who have never had an 'elder' to teach them. They spend their time listening to idle quatrains. Listening to poetry and music is permissible under certain conditions, but not dancing. The term 'dancing' should not be applied to the legitimate physical agitation produced in the listener by ecstasy. It is forbidden to look at youths and keep company with them. Hujwiri is unusual in counselling celibacy (which, he asserts, was the original Sufi practice) and praising abstinence from sexual intercourse in marriage.

Ansari

To these last two writers there must be joined a third, Ansari of Herat in Afghanistan, who died in 1089. He belonged to the Hanbalite school of Sunni law, renowned for its ferocious hostility to theology and philosophy. His work also presents contrasting sketches of the Sufi Path.

We have notes taken by a disciple of lectures which he gave in 1056 describing a hundred stages. The ninety-ninth is 'passing away' and the hundredth 'survival', but after these is love, which encompasses all of them. Ansari was later to produce a book, entitled *The Stages of the Travellers* (*Manazil al-sa'irin*), which is also divided into a hundred parts. There is no distinction between a 'stage' (*manzil*) and a 'station' (*maqam*). 'Stages' 61–70 are the 'states' (*ahwal*), of which the first is love. Numbers 91–100 are the 'endings', which begin with direct knowledge, 'passing away' and 'survival', and conclude with attesting to God's Uniqueness, which was sixty-ninth in the earlier version. Each stage is divided into three. In the last are the attestation by ordinary men that God is Unique; the attestation by the elite, which consists in abandoning reason and argument; and the attestation by God himself, part of which he has revealed in a flash to a smaller elite. One can see how Ansari's mysticism goes hand in hand with his school's rejection of philosophical speculation, and expresses itself in a simple piety, that of short rhyming invocations of God and pieces of moralizing advice, for which he is best known.

Muhammad Ghazali and Ahmad Ghazali

The contrast between what have been called the 'sober' and 'drunken' schools of Sufism in the generation after Ansari is sharply exemplified in two brothers, called Ghazali, from north-eastern Iran. One of them, Muhammad Ghazali (d. 1111), representing the 'sober' school, has received a vast amount of attention in the West, which he hardly deserves since his work has neither the spirituality nor the philosophical rigour with which it has often been credited. Many western writers have accorded a naive acceptance to his autobiography, in which he portrays himself as searching for true certainty among theologians, philosophers and extremist Shiites before finally finding it in Sufism. Recent research has demonstrated that this is just an apologetic device, which bears little relation to Ghazali's real life story (an establishment figure's continuing involvement with powerful political patrons).

Earlier western writers imagined that Ghazali's enormous *Revival of the Religious Sciences* (*Ihya' 'ulum al-din*) was a work which conveyed profound mystical experience. It has been pointed out, however, that it is really a book on ethics and conduct, which owes a lot to the popular manual written by Makki in the late tenth century.[5] In the past it was often claimed that Ghazali reconciled Sufism with orthodoxy. But there is no such thing as orthodoxy in Islam, and the word should not be used in the history of religions. There were plenty of safely respectable Sufis before Ghazali, and plenty of disreputable and outrageous ones after him. He himself gives every indication of holding personal views that directly contradict his public attacks on philosophers and speculative theologians. Indeed, he is unable to express himself without self-contradiction on the problem of whether the spirit in man is created or not.

The source of his fame is presumably to be found in the massive spread of new colleges and Sufi lodges, founded by the Saljuq empire at the height of its power. The empire's rulers were anxious to purvey conventional banalities about morality as an alternative to the extremist Shiites of Egypt and their propagandists in the eastern Islamic world. Ghazali does not really belong to Sufism, and the Sufis themselves do not usually give him much respect: they omit him from their lists of masters.

 Ghazali's brother Ahmad (d. 1126) is, on the other hand, a leading figure of Sufism's ecstatic or 'drunken' wing. He wrote a treatise on love, in Persian, which shows an important development in the Iranian tradition of discussing this subject (already well analysed by his fellow-countryman Daylami a century before). He begins and ends by insisting on the interconnection and reciprocity between love and the Spirit, in a way which makes one think of the Greek antecedents of Eros and Psyche. Since reason cannot reach the Spirit, it cannot find its way to love, which is concealed within it. Ahmad Ghazali declares that the most perfect form of love is represented by the discipline of incurring 'blame' in one's complete devotion to the Beloved. He links this with the idea of the *qalandar*, a type of wandering, libertine mystic who had now appeared on the fringes of Sufism, and also with the figure of the 'rogue' or brigand (*'ayyar*), whose name also means an adherent of the 'youngmanliness' tradition. The mixture of these elements is typical of north-eastern Iran. Ahmad Ghazali's use of the popular, anonymous quatrain is also Iranian:

> This is the ball of blame and the field of destruction
> And this the road of gamblers who stake their all
> A *qalandar*-like man is needed with torn robe
> So that he can pass over like a brigand and without fear[6]

As with Daylami, we find in Ahmad Ghazali the triad Love, Lover and Beloved, and the assertion that since the last two are derived from the first all three are one. Audacious paradoxes arise. The lover is closer to the Beloved's beauty than the Beloved is, and even thinks that he himself is the Beloved. When one passes away from one's self, one can go beyond a famous black light which tells the mystic that his journey is almost at an end. Ahmad Ghazali also uses the classic image of the moth which is burnt in the candle: for one moment the moth becomes his beloved. Love itself, however, is in its essence above communion and separation.

Ahmad Ghazali not only had a vast influence on the evocation of love in later Persian literature, but was also perceived as a teacher, to be included in the spiritual pedigrees of the Sufi brotherhoods which were soon to emerge. His importance for Sufism is therefore far greater than that of his celebrated brother.

'Ayn al-Qudat

The dangers implicit in Ahmad Ghazali's ideas were tragically illustrated with the execution of his most brilliant pupil, 'Ayn al-Qudat of Hamadan in western Iran (d. 1131). 'Ayn al-Qudat was accused of being an unbeliever and claiming to be a prophet. His reply to the accusations survives. His enemies attacked him for saying that God is 'the All' and the only real existent; he answered that he just meant that God is the creator of all things. He was accused of being an extremist Shiite, because he insisted on the need for a spiritual instructor; he replied that he meant a Sufi elder, not the Shiites' infallible Leader (*Imam*). He was criticized for expressions in which he referred to the 'passing away' of creatures; he answered that he did not mean the passing away of things in their essence, but their disappearing from the view of the observer.

'Ayn al-Qudat's books and letters, however, show that he held opinions formally condemned by Muslim lawyers and theologians. He believed that the Koranic depictions of a physical resurrection of the dead and heaven and hell were to be taken symbolically – although he made a desperate declaration of his belief in their literal truth at the end. In his earlier compositions and letters he speaks of unbelief as being the necessary foundation of faith, and an important 'station' on the Path. He glorifies the devil as a mad lover of God, and even goes as far as to quote the saying, 'The Sufi is God.'

Persian Sufi poetry

The earlier mystics of Islam had made extensive use of Arabic poetry, whether by seeking inspiration in the recitation of love poetry, which could be taken as directed to either a human or a divine beloved, or by composing verses of their own. It was in Persian poetry, however, that Sufism was now to find its greatest and most widespread expression, producing what the eastern Islamic world from Turkey to India regards as the highest peaks of its cultural heritage.

We noted the attack, in the eleventh century, by the eastern Iranian writer Hujwiri on pseudo-Sufis who spent their time listening to 'idle quatrains', and, in the work of Ahmad Ghazali, the use of the popular, anonymous Persian quatrain in a distinctively Iranian context. From the early twelfth century we find expressions of Sufism in other forms of Persian verse: the ode and the long didactic composition in rhyming couplets. The first master of both was Sana'i, a court poet of Ghazna in Afghanistan, who died in 1131. Like Hujwiri, he attacks the local fake dervishes there, and in particular the sexual misconduct of the women mystics. His work reveals him to be a pronounced misogynist, whose love lyrics are often directed to boys, as is normal in classical Islamic poetry. Here western writers have worried about the distinction (which, as has been argued above, is imaginary) between 'the sacred' and 'the profane'. The introduction of these terms has caused much confusion, especially since they have been used, when referring to love, to mistranslate the words *haqiqi*, 'real', and *majazi*, 'metaphorical'. From the Sufi standpoint the beauty which is visible in this world is a metaphor for the real Beauty of God. This view of things goes back to Plato, as does the 'metaphorical' love of boys, which a modern western critic would see as only too rooted in the 'real world'.

Sana'i's odes contain not only the praise of wealthy patrons and straightforward exhortations to piety, but also the language of libertinism: he extols wine-drinking, handsome cupbearers and also, in contrast to his attack on their terrestrial self-manifestation in Ghazna, the dervishes who go against the religious law, the *qalandars*. The *qalandars* are used to represent the higher flights of ecstasy and truth, as opposed to ordinary religiosity:

> Cupbearer give wine since wine alone shatters abstaining
> So that I may lose awhile this specious world renouncing . . .
> For a time the religion of Zarathushtra and the custom of the
>   *qalandar*
> Must be made the provisions for the spirit which takes the road[7]

Sana'i also composed an extended narrative and didactic poem, called *The Journey of God's Servants* (*Sayr al-'ibad*), which has often been compared to Dante's *Divine Comedy*. In it the narrator acquires a guide, an old man who is evidently the Active Intelligence of the Greek philosophical tradition, that is to say the tenth and lowest of the immaterial manifestations of Reason which, the philosophers believe, emanate from God. Together the poet and the guide journey through the material world and then the heavens, before reaching the Universal Soul of the neo-Platonists. The highest emanation, the First or Universal Intelligence or Reason, is hidden by veils, which cover different classes of dervishes. Eventually the poet finds a superior rank of these, and in it a dominating light, which represents his patron, a local judge, whom Sana'i asks for money at the end.

Sana'i is best known, however, for a longer didactic poem, the *Enclosed Garden of Reality* (*Hadiqat al-haqiqa*). In this he begins with an exposition of God's Uniqueness, before tackling the subject of asceticism, and then the teachings of the Greek philosophical tradition: the human body is a city with the heart as its king. Reason is the king's minister, supported by Anger (the chief of the garrison) and Desire (the tax gatherer), who rule over the limbs (the artisans). Again, the Active Intelligence appears as an old man, who gives the poet spiritual guidance: he must join the Sufis. The rest of the poem is largely taken up with the praise of the Sultan of Ghazna.

BROTHERHOOD AND THEORY (*c.* 1130–*c.* 1240)

Two major themes will soon engage our attention: the rise of the Sufi brotherhoods (often wrongly seen as the equivalent of Christian monastic orders); and the systematization of Sufi theory (largely the work of one leading thinker). These themes, however, belong mainly to the early thirteenth century, since, as will be shown below, the mid-twelfth-century Sufis who are supposed to have founded the earliest brotherhoods did not really do so, while Sufism's chief systematizer of doctrine, Ibn 'Arabi (1165–1240), wrote his most important books after the turn of the century, when he moved to the Muslim East from his native Spain. Spain has hitherto been neglected in our survey, but now requires special consideration, as the scene of political and philosophical innovations which are particularly important for Sufism's later development.

Spain
Since its conquest by the Muslims in the early eighth century the political and dynastic history of Spain had been separate from that of the

other areas under Muslim rule, with the exception of North Africa, with which it was closely connected. Of the early history of Sufism in Spain, there is really no important evidence before the twelfth century. There were pious ascetics, and there was one notorious figure, called Ibn Masarra of Cordova, who died in 931. He had some disciples, but his books have not survived, and all that can be said with confidence is that he aroused much hostility on account of his opinions. Extremely dubious attempts have been made to reconstruct Ibn Masarra's teachings and alleged influence on later thinkers. What is known about Islamic Spain up to the early twelfth century is that there was immense intolerance on the level of ideas: even the works of the sober Muhammad Ghazali were burnt.

In the mid-twelfth century, however, the emergence of a new school of mystics in Spain had dramatic political consequences. One Ibn Barrajan of Seville was apparently recognized by his followers as the rightful leader (*imam*) of the Muslim community. He was arrested and died in prison in 1141. His follower Ibn al-'Arif, who was also imprisoned, and also died mysteriously in 1141, wrote a short treatise on the stages of the Sufi Path, in which he shows considerable daring. For although the enumeration of the stages is conventional enough, Ibn al-'Arif dismisses each one as vulgar: the elite must concentrate on God himself. In 1142 another mystic of this school, called Ibn Qasi, started a revolt in southern Portugal (then also under Muslim rule). Using his disciples as an army, he was able to establish himself as ruler of a small kingdom, before being assassinated in 1151. A treatise by him survives, in which he speaks of a man who is placed after Muhammad as the 'one who stands upright at the highest'. This man is also the leader of the Muslims: a position which Ibn Qasi claimed for himself, as is evident from the coins which he had struck.

Apart from these eventful political developments, twelfth-century Spain and North Africa saw an important continuation of the Greek philosophical tradition. Within this tradition there was one noteworthy attempt to incorporate Sufi teachings. This was made by Ibn Tufayl (d. 1185), who wrote a remarkable story about a child who grows up on a desert island. The child, by careful reflection, evolves a philosophical system identical with that of the neo-Platonists of the Muslim world. By means of fasting and concentration he reaches the ultimate level of 'passing away'. In this he has a vision of the universe, which corresponds to the description given by the philosophers. Then another ascetic joins him on the island, and discovers that his philosophical system is identical with the inner truth of all the revealed religions.

Together they leave the island for human society, but find that ordinary mortals do not appreciate higher realities, and require the outward vestiges of religion instead. So they return to the island to live the spiritual life reserved for the elite.[8]

A striking picture of Sufi activity in Spain during the late twelfth century has been left by the great Sufi theorist Ibn 'Arabi, whose teachings will be considered later in this section, since they belong mainly to the period between his departure for the Muslim East in 1202 and his death in 1240. The Spanish mystics whom he describes were often lower-class urban artisans, such as potters and smiths, and also included in their ranks workers in even humbler occupations, such as henna-sievers and tanners.[9] Some of the ascetics respected by Ibn 'Arabi were illiterate, and some were women. It was unusual, he said, for a man to be both a jurist and an ascetic. However, this remark may reflect Ibn 'Arabi's ambiguous attitude to the Muslim jurists in general. He was not inclined to see them as world renouncers, but speaks with evident high regard of several who were also mystics. Even when he gives first-hand accounts of the Spanish Sufis whom he had known, his stories are highly coloured with the intervention of the supernatural (dishes mysteriously refilled with honey, etc.), and must be treated with caution.

We must now leave Spain for Iraq, the centre of Sufism's development in the middle of the twelfth century. In the eastern Islamic world the empire of the Saljuq Turks was by this time in decline. Already, at the end of the eleventh century, the Crusaders had appeared on their western frontiers, taking Jerusalem and other important cities. During the early twelfth century the Saljuqs had dissipated their energies by fighting one another. Now, in Iraq, the 'Abbasid caliphate was able to re-establish its temporal authority, against a background of widespread brigandage. To the east new invaders were moving through Central Asia into north-eastern Iran.

'Abd al-Qadir and Abu 'l-Najib: two figures who did not found brotherhoods

In Baghdad itself one encounters two figures who have been wrongly hailed as the founders of international brotherhoods, which in fact were created later. One of these, 'Abd al-Qadir (d. 1165), who came from the northern Iranian province of Gilan, is venerated as the founder of the Qadiri fraternity, which is now found as far afield as North Africa and Indonesia. However, Jacqueline Chabbi has pointed out that in the oldest sources he seems to be just a jurist and a preacher, with a certain reputation for asceticism. On the other hand, his discourses are full of Sufi teaching: they are in effect sermons, but they expound the mysticism of the Hanbalite school of law, which, as we have seen before, avoids abstract theorizing. 'Abd al-Qadir frequently refers to the Sufi hierarchy of grades. He says that the 'states' belong to God's friends, while the 'stations' belong to the higher rank of the 'substitutes' (*abdal*). Members of 'Abd al-Qadir's school were often accused of having anthropomorphic tendencies, and he himself is not exempt from these: he presents an image of God as a king, sitting on a throne, and heavily armed with arrows and spears, with which he bombards a helpless man.

The other alleged founder of a brotherhood at this time, Abu 'l-Najib of Suhraward in north-western Iran (d. 1167), was a pupil of the ecstatic Ahmad Ghazali and also an academic lawyer. He did in fact have an influence on the Suhrawardi brotherhood, but this was really founded after his death by his nephew, and has been (and is still) particularly important in what is now Pakistan. Abu 'l-Najib's influence, however, would seem to have come mainly through a book of his, which is unique in that in it Sufism is surveyed only from the standpoint of rules of conduct. This book is remarkable for its section on dispensations (*rukhas*, relaxations of strict rules). These dispensations allow one to have an income, visit rulers and eat delicious food. It is interesting that, although the Suhrawardi brotherhood became noted for its emphasis on severity, some of its members were also conspicuous for their self-enrichment, collaboration with temporal rulers and enjoyment of worldly pleasures.

The emergence of brotherhoods

Soon such Sufi brotherhoods actually did begin to come into being. During this period the 'Abbasid caliphate in Baghdad, after its previous recapture of temporal power over Iraq, reasserted itself on an international level. This was largely the work of one caliph, Nasir, who ruled from 1180 to 1225. His reign saw first of all the end of the great empire of the Saljuq Turks, and later the first disastrous invasions of the Mongols. It also saw the recapture of Jerusalem from the Crusaders by the famous ruler Saladin (1169–93), who had earlier put an end to the extremist Shiite domination of Egypt. Nasir's long reign also coincided with a massive Muslim push in the north of the Indian subcontinent, which now fell completely under Islamic rule. A number of minor dynasties surrounded the caliph, who apart from his temporal rule over Iraq was also the spiritual leader of Islam.

Nasir's religious activities included the persecution of the Hellenized philosophers, whose books were publicly burnt. He does not seem, however, to have been involved in the martyrdom of Islam's most colourful philosopher, Yahya Suhrawardi (whose surname indicates that he came from the same town in north-western Iran as the family after which the Suhrawardi brotherhood is named). This thinker was put to death, for reasons which remain obscure, in Syria in 1192. His work constitutes another attempt to integrate Sufism within neo-Platonism, of a kind which we have already seen in Spain at the same time. Suhrawardi, however, inaugurated a new school, that of 'Oriental Illumination' (*ishraq*). He saw himself as reviving the higher wisdom of the ancient Greek and Iranian sages, and thus carrying out the project which had been conceived by Avicenna. This higher wisdom, he claimed, had also been possessed by the early Sufis. He presents the usual neo-Platonist view of the universe as a series of emanations from God, but clothes it in Gnostic language: God, as the Light of Lights, gives rise to ranks of angelic and human lights, and the latter are entangled in the darkness of matter. Suhrawardi speaks of Sufism as offering the means of escape, but he sees this escape as essentially directed by the Active Intelligence, identified with Gabriel.[10]

One participant in the attack on Greek philosophy was the caliph Nasir's main religious adviser, 'Umar Suhrawardi (d. 1234), the nephew of Abu 'l-Najib (they should not be confused with the philosopher Yahya Suhrawardi). Here we have a leader of the greatest importance in the history of Sufism. For by his activity as a teacher, and by his rigorous insistence on expanding his uncle's rules of conduct to cover every possible detail of Sufi behaviour, 'Umar Suhrawardi effectively founded an international brotherhood, and was one of the very first to do so. To understand the significance of this it is necessary to examine the Sufi institution of the *tariqa*, or brotherhood, and the mistranslation of this term as 'order'.

A *tariqa*, in the new sense which the word acquired from the thirteenth century (as opposed to the general meaning of 'the Sufi Path'), may be defined as a brotherhood of Sufis who have a common pedigree of spiritual masters, and in which elders initiate disciples and grant them formal permission to continue a common school of thought and practice. This brotherhood sometimes does and sometimes does not have an organization. An international administrative structure has usually proved impossible to achieve, but there is organized activity at a local level.

Now this is very different from a Christian monastic order. Islam, in theory, at least, has no monasticism, nor does it have the institution of a church, which is indispensable for the government of the Christian monastic orders. The latter are necessarily constituted as fixed organizations within an ecclesiastical framework. There are, however, certain parallels in the historical development of Christianity and Islam here. In Christianity, up to the end of the eleventh century the Latin expression *ordo monasticus* had meant the monastic life in general.[11] From then on the word *ordo* was used to designate any one of a number of monastic 'orders' in the modern sense. This was because it was from this time that these institutions appeared in western Christianity (in eastern Christianity they never did). Their rise was due to changes associated with Pope Gregory VII (1073–85), which were intended to unite Christianity around the papacy. In some ways Gregory and Nasir are alike: both tried to give their office immense powers (in this they both had limited success), and to install themselves above temporal rulers. Was the rise of the Sufi brotherhoods influenced by, or conceived in conscious imitation of the Christian monastic orders? This isn't something that the Muslims could admit, at least not in the sources available to us. In any case, on the Christian side the documents show organizations with fixed constitutions. Although modern specialists have spoken of the 'organizing of orders' in early thirteenth-century Islam, there is no evidence of such organization. To be sure, in major cities one finds the office of 'elder of elders', the senior Sufi leader appointed by the local ruler. Nasir gave the position in Baghdad to 'Umar Suhrawardi. But it had existed in Baghdad long before, retained in one family since the second half of the eleventh century.

Moreover, 'Umar Suhrawardi's manual of behaviour, which formed the basis of his brotherhood's teaching, is not linked to a legal constitution, although it is imbued with the spirit of Islamic law and is firmly directed against libertine dervishes. It is an expansion of his uncle's rules for novices into an all-embracing collection of instructions, covering behaviour in the 'lodge', travelling, listening to poetry, the Sufis' forty-day retreat, the details of ablutions, fasting, vigils, conduct towards one's elder and fellow Sufis, the 'stations' and the 'states'. The manual initiates the practice for which the Suhrawardis were best known, that of perpetually reciting the formula 'There is no god but God', until the 'remembrance of the tongue' becomes a 'remembrance of the heart'. Then the heart is emptied of everything, and God manifests himself within it. In the thirteenth century, in the Middle East and what is now Pakistan, this constant 'remembrance' was a noteworthy feature of affiliation to the Suhrawardi brotherhood, in particular among women, who engaged in it while performing tasks such as grinding flour.[12] One difference between 'Umar Suhrawardi's manual and earlier ones is that it is not just a collection of different people's opinions, but an integrated programme orientated towards real practice: it is the expression of a *tariqa*, a method, literally a 'path' to God.

The emergence of the brotherhoods in reality meant the emergence of 'elders' with specific programmes of instruction, linked to a founder who is believed to have instituted their method. 'Umar Suhrawardi had disciples and successors who reflected his insistence on severity and used his rules as guidelines. We know that at the beginning of the thirteenth century a founder of a brotherhood like him would formally designate people as 'deputies' (*khulafa'*). But there is no evidence that these 'deputies' were intended to operate together in any kind of organization. In the event, the degree of mutual co-operation would depend on them, and they might simply go their own ways. As time went on a few very well-organized brotherhoods came into existence, and at the beginning of the sixteenth century, as we shall see, one fraternity had enough control of its resources to overthrow existing rulers and establish a mighty empire. This, however, was to be the exception, not the rule.

Brotherhood 'chains'
One important aspect of a brotherhood is its 'chain' (*silsila*), that is to say its pedigree of masters going back to Muhammad. So essential a feature is this that to a large extent the brotherhood *is* the 'chain': a living expression of continuity down the generations. Modern western scholars reject the authenticity of the parts of these 'chains' which refer to the beginnings of Islam, and twelfth- and thirteenth-century Muslim jurists have also attacked them as unhistorical. The Sufis needed to have these guarantees of authority, partly because in Islam knowledge has to be transmitted from sound teachers, and partly because the Traditions, the sayings attributed to Muhammad with pedigrees of transmitters, constitute the foundations of Muslim doctrine and practice. Consequently the appearance of Sufi 'chains' mirrors the development of lists of Tradition collectors.

First of all, from the tenth century onwards, lists of Sufi masters had gone back only to the Followers (*tabi'un*), the generation of Muslims who came after that of Muhammad's Companions, and who were seen as possessing a form of collective authority. It was only after these Followers that individuals were mentioned by name. In sources of the twelfth century and later, however, one finds that the lists are made to extend back to Muhammad himself, through one of his first successors. Since the pedigrees of the Traditions had evolved in this way, and given the rise of the veneration of Muhammad in the twelfth and thirteenth centuries, this is not surprising. Sometimes the 'chain' goes through 'Ali, the first Leader of the Shiites; sometimes through one of Muhammad's other successors, either Abu Bakr or 'Umar, who are respected by the Sunni majority as the first two caliphs. That Sufis who belong to mainstream Islam should have the first Shiite Leader as their link to Muhammad might be thought remarkable, but this also needs to be seen in the twelfth- and thirteenth-century context: along with the increased veneration of Muhammad came greater reverence among Sunnis for the Leaders of his family. The caliph Nasir himself went to great pains to institutionalize respect for the Shiites' early heroes and to integrate this into Sunni Islam.

The subject of the Sufi 'chains' has been finely analysed by Richard Gramlich. He points out that in the past there was much confusion in Sufism concerning the exact nature of the transmission of authority: it was often not clear whether a disciple had just studied with a master; whether he had obtained a certificate (*ijaza*) giving permission to continue one or more lines of teaching or aspects of practice; or whether he had been given the Sufi patched frock (*khirqa*) by the master (and if so, whether this was given as a form of blessing, which might be bestowed by a hundred masters on one Sufi, or as a way of designating a successor to carry on teaching more disciples). It is noteworthy that Gramlich, with his extraordinarily impressive knowledge of Sufism in Iran, should say that nowadays both confusion over the 'chain' and (contrary to what is often asserted) its personal significance for the individual have disappeared among Iranian Sufis: investiture with the frock is no longer usual, and it is belonging to the brotherhood that counts, not the pedigree of masters taken in isolation. Thus it is not the disciple's 'chain', but rather that of the brotherhood's leader which is all-important, as validating the authenticity of the membership's collective teaching and practice (most notably in instruction concerning the 'remembrance of God', which was previously seen as a jealously guarded and inherited prerogative of individual elders).[13]

Within the 'chain' of a given brotherhood a particularly strong and effective personality may well produce a sub-brotherhood. His forcefulness may provide a new series of teachings, or a revival of old ones. Alternatively, it may be his organizational activity which gives the parent brotherhood a significantly increased membership in one area of the Muslim world. We, in the hope of achieving greater clarity, shall continue to use the term 'sub-brotherhood', but the Sufis themselves use the same word as for 'brotherhood': *tariqa* (path). For the sub-brotherhood is a 'path' within another 'path', and most commonly this will be reflected in a double-barrelled label embodying the names of the two founders. But the sub-brotherhood may later achieve such great importance that the name of the original brotherhood is lost.

Although in the present survey we shall speak of brotherhoods and sub-brotherhoods, and of local branches of both of these, it should be borne in mind that this is the perspective of a western student who has to divide the materials up and then try to arrange them in a systematic manner. The viewpoint of the Sufi is very different: there is the one Path (*tariqa*) to God, Sufism itself, and there are different individual 'paths', which all belong to this greater Path. Sometimes these individual 'paths' are major ones, and sometimes they are minor subdivisions. In later centuries it is common for a Muslim to belong to two or more 'paths' at the same time, and engage in practices which are forbidden in one (such as listening to the flute) but permitted in another. What seems self-contradictory to the westerner is, seen from a Sufi angle, entirely natural: to travel on different 'paths' to the same destination. One must avoid the error committed by nineteenth-century French scholars based in Algeria, who imagined that the Sufi 'paths' were all perfectly drilled armies or political parties, led by Masonic conspirators in a deliberate campaign of obstruction of European progress.

The relative absence of organization within Muslim associations and of sharply defined boundaries between them is evident in another activity of the caliph Nasir's, in which 'Umar Suhrawardi, as his chief adviser, was involved: the reform of the 'youngmanliness' tradition. Previously this had been characterized by unruly urban bands, composed of 'rogues' or brigands. They had had some influence upon Sufism, as they exalted the ideal of altruism; and some influence was exercised by Sufism upon them, as the bands acquired 'elders' in the Sufi manner. Nasir decided that he alone would be the chief of the 'youngmanliness' tradition, and that he would initiate the kings and judges of the Islamic world as his subordinates. 'Umar Suhrawardi duly obliged by integrating the rituals of 'youngmanliness' (initiation by investiture with trousers, and drinking from a cup) within Sufism. We shall find the tradition later, continuing in the Sufi brotherhoods, with unmistakable evidence of its Iranian, non-Islamic origins.

The Persian poet 'Attar

The changes brought about by Nasir are reflected in the works of the most famous Persian Sufi poet of this period, 'Attar (the name means that he was a pharmacist) of Nishapur in north-eastern Iran, who apparently perished in 1221 in the massacres committed by the Mongol followers of the notorious Chinggis (Genghis) Khan. 'Attar's long didactic and narrative poems are usually dominated by the figure of the Spirit, which is seen as God's caliph, his deputy on earth. The most famous work of 'Attar, however, *The Language of the Birds* (*Mantiq al-tayr*), concerns a search for a king, made by a number of birds. The book has an elaborate structure. Eleven species of birds are presented as discussing the journey ahead. They keep reappearing in the debate as symbols of types of men: the nightingale is the passionate lover, the duck the pious ascetic, and so on. The eleventh, the sparrow, represents Jacob, blinded with grief for his lost son Joseph. When the thirty birds (in Persian *si murgh*) who survive the journey come for the great confrontation with their king, the fabulous bird called the *simurgh*, they are unable to distinguish themselves from him. They are also compared to Joseph's ten guilty brothers. In an epilogue 'Attar tells a story about a king who condemns his boy friend to death: the ten slaves who are ordered to execute him are persuaded not to, and tell the king that he is dead. In the end the king and boy are reunited.

'Attar's *Book of Affliction* (*Musibat-nama*) also has a complicated structure. In it a pilgrim runs away from his elder and asks Gabriel (who represents the Spirit) for help. Since he has presumptuously sought assistance from the very summit of creation he has to descend through the universe before reascending to find the Spirit again. He learns that the parts of the universe are attributes of the Spirit, which is derived from the light of Muhammad.

Another work by 'Attar, the *Book of the Divine* (*Ilahi-nama*), begins by invoking the Spirit as God's caliph. It has six sons: the lower soul, the devil, the intellect, knowledge, poverty and the realization of God's Uniqueness. In the body of the work a caliph instructs his own six sons. These sons fall into three pairs, which correspond to the triad of the lower soul, the intellect and the heart (which is transformed into the Spirit); the three pairs also correspond to the neo-Platonist triad of Soul, Reason and the One; and also to the hierarchy of ascetics, philosophers and Sufis. Thus the lower soul is linked to the devil (in the instruction of the first pair of sons) and the intellect to knowledge (in the instruction of the second pair). Above these stands the dialectical process in which the mystic negates and passes away from his own existence (recognizing that true poverty is understanding that one is poor in lacking true being in comparison with God), and then (in a negation of this negation) has his heart transformed into the Spirit, which is absorbed into the light of God, whose Uniqueness is thus affirmed. This tripartite structure has been anticipated by Sana'i, as we have seen above, in the form of asceticism, philosophy and Sufism, in his *Enclosed Garden of Reality*. It corresponds to part of a Greek philosophical work (not older than the first century BCE), which was available in Arabic translation by the early eleventh century, and in which three stages of progress are outlined: in the first are allegories of the lower passions; in the second unsuccessful philosophers; in the third the blessed elite who find true knowledge.[14] So we see the indebtedness of 'Attar to the Greek philosophical tradition, on which he nonetheless makes violent attacks: the ambiguity of the Sufis' position is reflected in that of the philosophers themselves, with their exaltation of a stage beyond ordinary reason.

'Attar was also an important lyric poet, who in one of his shorter compositions expressed the current tendency in the direction of monism, the doctrine that there is only one entity in the whole of existence. It is important to realize that hardly any Sufi writers actually profess this doctrine itself (those who do, the occasional prince and minor poet, do not seem to have understood their teachers). But in the thirteenth century Sufism moved to a position which was perilously close to monism, so that we can legitimately call it 'monistic'. So 'Attar writes:

> Whatever is other than you is mirage and appearance
> Since there neither a little nor a lot has come
> Here incarnation is unbelief and so is unitive fusion (*ittihad*)
> Since this is a unity but come in repetition . . .
> How should otherness show itself when everything which exists
> Is identical with another one come into appearance?[15]

Kubra and his disciple Daya

It seems that the Mongol massacres of 1221 also claimed as a victim Kubra of Khwarazm in what is now Soviet Central Asia, the founder of a brotherhood to which he gave his name. The Kubrawiyya, who spread to Iran and India, are, like their founder, noteworthy for an emphasis on visions and coloured lights. Here Kubra, as is clear from his writings, had a distinctive method, which he imparted to many disciples. His ideas obviously go back to the Gnosticism of late antiquity, although, as we shall see below, there is also evidence of Indian influences. He insists that one can know only that which is like unto oneself. The believer is a light, which comes from God's light. One can pass away in God's attributes, which exist in different 'locations' (or levels, *mahadir*, like the Gnostic *topoi*), and then in his Essence. To do so one must purify one's created nature, which appears as a black cloud, reddened by the devil. 'Our method (*tariq*)', says Kubra, 'is the method of alchemy.' It is to extract the luminous part of one's being from beneath the mountains of the physical body. You may visualize yourself as rising from the depths of a well, and find yourself seeing deserts and cities. Eventually, you see the colour green, as representing the life of the heart. A green light constitutes the atmosphere of the heaven of God's Lordship. This theme of a vision of emerald green has its source in the famous Hermetic tradition of late antique Egypt, in which Gnostic teachings were attributed to the god Hermes Trismegistus, notably in a work called *The Emerald Tablet*.

Eventually, according to Kubra, the mystic encounters his other self: one's heavenly 'witness' (*shahid*), the 'elder of the invisible world', who appears in a luminous form. (Once, says Kubra, he fell in love with a girl, and did not eat for days. He breathed flames, and more flames came to meet them from the sky. Finally he realized that his heavenly 'witness' was in the place where the flames met.) When you encounter this witness he will not leave you: indeed you are this witness, with whom you have become one. The jewel of light has been extracted. Here we see a close correspondence with the Hermetic *Emerald Tablet*, in which the narrator's 'perfect nature' appears to him as an old man in his own image.

One of Kubra's disciples, Daya of Rayy (now a suburb of Tehran), who died in 1256, was able to escape from the invading Mongols and take refuge in Turkey. There he encountered 'Umar Suhrawardi, who advised him to dedicate a book about Sufism to a temporal ruler, a king. This was a course of action which would previously have seemed improper for a Sufi, but was now, they felt, justifiable because of the danger to Islam posed by the Mongols. The book, *The Path of God's Servants (Mirsad al-'ibad)*, presents an odd combination of Sufi and monarchist elements. Most of it is cast in the form of a description of the transition from the original act of Creation to the eventual resurrection of the dead, in the Semitic tradition of Judaism, Christianity and Islam, with its emphasis on a history with a beginning, a middle and an end. But the last part of the book deals with the various classes of society and their duties in a manner which goes back through the royal

Iranian tradition to the Indo-European past. Thus Sufism is used to call on men to fit into a society dominated by temporal rulers, in which everyone has an ordered place. The pursuit of agriculture is fixed in a threefold hierarchy of farmers, village headmen and peasants, who are told to rely on God for next year's crop instead of storing up a surplus of this year's, and to engage in constant 'remembrance' while they work. The world is compared to a Sufi lodge: God corresponds to the Sufi elder; Muhammad to his steward; and the inhabitants of the world to the Sufis in the lodge, who are divided into labourers with individual duties on the one hand, and those who are totally engaged in worship and acts of devotion on the other. So most men fall into the category of those who work, whether kings or merchants, in order to serve the other category, those whose time is entirely taken up by the religious life.

The Arab poet Ibn al-Farid

The monistic tendencies which have already been noted as characteristic of this period, and which appear in the poetry of 'Attar, also find expression in the verses of the most famous of all Arab Sufi poets, Ibn al-Farid of Cairo (d. 1235). As his name indicates, Ibn al-Farid was the son of a leading legal administrator, but he lived a hermit's life. In his long, didactic *Poem of the Way* (*Nazm al-suluk*), he affirms, like 'Attar, the self-manifestation of one Essence in the universe. The mystic adores himself: he realizes that the Divine Beloved has existed in all the beauties of legend.

> That was none other than She showing Herself in appearances
> And they thought it was another than She while She displayed
>   herself therein
> She showed Herself in veils and concealed Herself in appearances
> According to the tints of changing colour every time She came out

As is also common in this period, Ibn al-Farid gives increased exaltation to the supernatural figure of Muhammad, with which he identifies himself, notably in a verse seen as scandalous:

> My spirit is spirit to all the spirits and all you see
> Beautiful in the universe is from the emanation of my clay

Like other thirteenth-century poets, Ibn al-Farid accepts the worship of God in religions other than Islam:

And if the Mazdeans worshipped fire and it was not extinguished
As is said in the reports in a thousand years
They did not aim at another than Me even if their aim
Was else than I and if they did not manifest a binding intention

However, it seems that the mystic's ultimate achievements can be attained only via Muhammad, through whom the poet speaks to affirm the Prophet's unity with God:

And from His Light the niche of my essence lit up
Upon me and through me my evening shone as my dawn
And I was made to see my being here and I was He
And I saw that He was I and the light was my splendour[16]

Ibn al-Farid's celebrated Wine-song (*Khamriyya*) finds him expressing a standard theme of Sufi poetry, the ecstasy which recalls the primordial drinking bout with God as the cupbearer:

We drank in remembrance of the Beloved a wine
With which we became drunk before the vine was created

In contrast to 'Attar, he extols unitive fusion (*ittihad*):

And my spirit fell in love with that wine so that they mingled in
Unitive fusion and not as a body permeated by another
So there is a soul (*nafs*) and no wine when Adam is my father
And wine but no soul when its vine is my mother[17]

The meaning here is perhaps that when the mystic's terrestrial existence as a son of Adam is considered his carnal soul is there, but when he rejoins his primordial state it vanishes.

Ibn 'Arabi

Sufism's greatest systematizer, Ibn 'Arabi, fully developed the monistic tendencies of this period. Already mentioned for his descriptions of the mystics of Spain where he was brought up, Ibn 'Arabi was born in 1165 to an influential family which claimed noble Arab ancestors, and he obtained a formal education in Seville. He spent some time alone, in cemeteries, and studied with a number of Sufis. He tells us that he had many visions and supernatural encounters during visits to North Africa. In 1202 he went to the Muslim East. He says that in Mecca a vision showed him that he was the ultimate Seal of God's Friends in the period inaugurated by Muhammad. Here he began the longest of his many works, the massive *Meccan Revelations* (*al-Futuhat al-Makkiyya*), which provides an account of his new system. Later, he moved to Cairo, where his teachings encountered much hostility and his life was threatened. In both Turkey and Syria, however, he was to find royal protectors, and he settled in Damascus, where he died in 1240.

Ibn 'Arabi's system (which has been well analysed by A. E. Affifi) is really a combination of classical Sufism with neo-Platonism and Islamic theology. Such a synthesis was certainly overdue. Sufis had long attacked the neo-Platonist philosophers while taking over many of their ideas, and had often written books upholding mainline apologetic theology while also expressing mystical opinions at variance with it. Some Hellenized philosophers had tried to incorporate Sufi teachings in their own thought, but it was really time for the Sufis to try to produce a coherent mixture of their own. Moreover, mainline theologians, after a long history of making peremptory remarks without a philosophical foundation, were now realizing the need to acquire one. But it was obvious that a serious amalgamation of all three of these elements would have to be radically different from what had gone before.

Ibn 'Arabi declared that there is only one ultimate Reality in the whole of existence. This is certainly monistic, but not the same thing as pure monism, which maintains that there is only one entity. So we should call his theory by its own title: 'the unity of existence' (*wahdat al-wujud*). The one ultimate Reality is sometimes seen as 'the Truth' (*haqq*, the Real, one of God's names), the Essence of all things; sometimes as 'creation' (*khalq*, created things), the manifestation of the Essence. The Truth is the One, the Lord. Creation represents the many, the slaves. So paradoxes arise: the Truth simultaneously is creation and is not. In helping God to reveal himself, and in knowing him, the mystic in fact creates him. The One appears in images in mirrors, as colours in substances, and as food permeating bodies. Thus the various objects in the universe are God, but he is not limited to being identical with any one of them taken in isolation. Nor is he identical with the universe taken as the sum total of its constituent parts: the doctrine of Ibn 'Arabi is not pantheism (the belief that all is God and God is all), and does not incline towards pantheism in such a way as to deserve to be called pantheistic. The term is grossly over used, and often applied too loosely to be helpful.

The ultimate and highest Reality in Ibn 'Arabi's system is the Divine Essence, revealed through a number of God's names. These names are manifested as his attributes in this visible world. The mystic cannot reach the supreme level of Oneness (*ahadiyya*), which belongs to the Essence. He can attain only the level of Uniqueness (*wahidiyya*), which belongs to the names. God reveals himself to the mystic by being present to him through a given name in its absolute form, as opposed to its terrestrial manifestation. So the One is known through self-revelation (*tajalli*, theophany or irradiation), which must not be confused with the incarnation of a spirit in a body. Moreover, there can be no question of unitive fusion (*ittihad*), since, as Ibn 'Arabi's followers observe, that would require two essences to join together, and there is really only one Essence, that of God.

Ibn 'Arabi also has an important theory about the figure of Muhammad. This figure plays a part akin to that of the Logos in Christianity, as the most privileged instrument of God's self-manifestation. The First or Universal Intelligence of the Greek philosophers is identified with Muhammad's inner reality (*haqiqa*), with the Spirit, and with much else besides. For the Muhammadan Reality is also the 'Perfect Man' (*al-insan al-kamil*), the mystic who is perfected not in an ethical sense but as encompassing all of God's attributes. Such a man unites God with the world, not as a bridge but as an interface (*barzakh*), the imperceptible border between a shadow and the light. It is for the sake of such a Perfect Man that the universe has come into being. So the Perfect Man alone preserves the existence of the universe.

Now this theory is combined with a detailed development of the Sufi doctrine of friendship with God (*walaya*), which has been well studied by Michel Chodkiewicz. The friends of God who come after a given prophet, says Ibn 'Arabi, are inferior to that prophet. But the prophets themselves are also friends of God, and this aspect of theirs is superior to their external, specifically prophetic functions. Ibn 'Arabi went much too far for the taste of some Muslim jurists, who attacked him violently for this idea. He says that on the one hand there is a *general* cycle of God's friends, which is brought to an end by Jesus, as the Seal of that general cycle, who – being the last of God's friends as Muhammad was the last prophet – will return for the end of the world. On the other hand there is a *particular* cycle of God's friends, which belongs to the period of history inaugurated by Muhammad.

Ibn 'Arabi, replying to the challenge and questionnaire issued by Tirmidhi four centuries earlier, claims that he himself is the Seal of this particular cycle. From a certain point of view, he says, this Seal is inferior to Muhammad, as subject to Muhammad's revealed law; but from another point of view the same Seal is superior to Muhammad, since Muhammad's prophetic activity is strictly limited in time and can find its inner fulfilment only through the Seal's continuing spiritual involvement. There will be friends of God after Ibn 'Arabi, but they will be subordinated to his function as Seal, as will be even Jesus himself, when he returns, since then he will have to obey Muhammad's law.

Such, in its briefest outline, is Ibn 'Arabi's system. He is undoubtedly one of the greatest thinkers in the history of ideas, with a talent that ranks him alongside Spinoza and Hegel, whom he to some extent resembles. But his thought contains great dangers, and not only in its exaltation of the mystic as the Perfect Man, which has encouraged many others to claim for themselves an importance open to question. His presentation of the human condition as the manifestation of contrasting names of God – such as the Compelling (*al-Jabbar*) on the one hand, and the Pardoning (*al-Ghaffar*) on the other – excludes all possible freedom, just as it leads to a passive resignation in the face of injustice. His connection with the rulers of his time seems to represent a tendency to collaborate, and this has had grave consequences in the later history of Islamic thought, which has been dominated and often overwhelmed by his doctrines.

3 ELDERS AND EMPIRES (*c.* 1240–*c.* 1700)

RULERS, COLLABORATORS AND REVOLUTIONARIES (*c.* 1240–*c.* 1500)

One period in Sufism's history almost defines itself, the one which stretches from the death of Ibn 'Arabi to the division of the Islamic world between three great empires in the early sixteenth century. It seems best to consider this period in successive stages: the domination of Chinggis Khan's successors; the years which lead up to the death of a new great Central Asian conqueror; and the aftermath of the new conqueror's victories.

Mongols, Jews, Christians and Iranians (c. 1240–c. 1320)

The decades which followed Ibn 'Arabi's death were marked by increased Mongol power. From the early 1250s the Mongols pressed westwards from north-eastern Iran, and in 1258 sacked Baghdad itself, putting an end to the 'Abbasid caliphate. Henceforth only a pale shadow of the caliphate continued under the protection of the rulers of Egypt.

The Mongols were prevented from conquering Syria, but had suzerainty over Turkey. One part of their vast empire was the old combined domain of Iran and Iraq. Until 1294 this was subject to the ultimate authority of the Mongol emperors in China, but in 1295 the conversion of the viceroy in Iran to Islam meant that this branch was now independent. Previously the Mongols had adhered to the old Central Asian religious tradition of shamanism, though some became Buddhists or Christians. Meanwhile other Mongols, known as the Golden Horde, had conquered Russia. They too became Muslims. The Mongols were not interested, however, in conquering India, which now experienced its first real period of extended Islamic rule and culture, under the sultans of Delhi.

At the same time Egypt and Syria came under the control of the

Mamluk dynasty, whose name means that they were slaves (as were the Muslim rulers in India): according to a peculiarly Islamic practice, slaves would be the leading officers in the army, and were consequently able to gain supreme power. As is indicated by this level of success, 'slavery' in medieval Islam did not have the connotation of collective forced labour that it has today, but was the condition of people whose lives were not exceptionally uncomfortable and who could rise to positions of wealth and influence.

In the west, the Muslims had to abandon most of Spain (apart from the small kingdom of Granada) and retreat to North Africa. These political events brought about considerable contacts between adherents of different religions.

Sufism's influence on Judaism and Christianity

Previously the lack of significant mystical teachings in Judaism had led some Jewish authors to adopt Sufi doctrines virtually unchanged. In the eleventh century, in Spain, the Jewish writer Bahya ibn Paqudah wrote a book in Arabic entitled *The Book of Guidance to the Duties of Hearts* (*Kitab al-hidaya ila fara'id al-qulub*), which is mainly a repetition of Sufi instructions, and similar works were composed by Jews in Egypt in the thirteenth and fourteenth centuries. But the rise of the main Jewish mystical tradition, the Kabbalah, in southern France around 1200 seems to be a purely independent phenomenon. Besides, the Kabbalah is not concerned, as Sufism is, with losing oneself in God, but with an esoteric comprehension of the universe. Abraham Abulafia (d. after 1292), who left his native Spain to travel in Syria and Palestine, appears to have adopted Sufi meditational techniques which themselves had come from India (bodily postures and control of the breath), but is careful to subordinate 'passing away', which he views with disdain, to the discipline of concentration upon the letters of the alphabet, which is most characteristically 'kabbalistic'. Similarly, a pupil of his, who wrote in 1294, speaks of the Muslim mystics as a low and vulgar group who, by 'remembrance' of God's name, attain only 'effacement' (*mahw*, a synonym of *fana'*, 'passing away'). Above them is the path of the philosophers, and above them is that of the letter-symbolists, the Kabbalists.[1] Here we must observe that the Muslims had a long history of attaching esoteric significance to the letters of the alphabet, but it is really only in the late fourteenth century that the subject acquires a special importance in Sufism, so that (as will be seen below) a Muslim writer will place the 'people of the letters' above the philosophers and ordinary Sufis in a hierarchy of seekers after truth.

With regard to the influence of Sufism on Christianity, claims have been made for a Sufi impact upon the Catalan theologian and philosopher Ramón Lull (1232–1316). He himself says that he wrote his *Book of the Lover and the Beloved* (*Libre d'amic e amat*) in the manner of the Sufis. But the similarities are in effect confined to the form of expression. Lull's comparison between the Trinity and the Love, Lover and Beloved triad had already been made by both Augustine and Daylami, and the idea that this triad constitutes a unity was a commonplace in both Sufism and the Greek philosophical tradition in Islam – the philosophers equated it with the neo-Platonist doctrine of the identity of the act of knowing, the knower and the object of knowledge. Lull's combination of these themes is natural enough. In his other works, his use of the new term 'dignities' (*dignitates*) to designate the modes of God's self-manifestation would appear to come from the Sufi employment, begun by Ibn 'Arabi, of the term *hadarat*, 'presences'. But Lull does not seem to have understood or continued the Sufi uses of this expression. His indebtedness, it has recently been argued by Dominique Urvoy, is to the theologians and philosophers of Islam, not to the mystics.[2] This is generally the case with Islamic influences upon western Christian thinkers, who preferred to borrow from the dogmatic theologians and the representatives of Greek thought, rather than from the Sufis.

In the fields of organization, practice and popular beliefs it is difficult to find concrete evidence of Sufi influence. René Brunel, whose superb work on libertine dervishes in North Africa will be summarized in the chapter on modern Sufism, took the view that there was a great mixing of ideas of western Christianity and Islam in the twelfth and thirteenth centuries, in which the figure of the wandering mystic would have been central. But his own evidence showed that such wanderers had flourished in Christianity before continuing in Islam. The relationship between these disreputable travellers and the respectable religious fraternities is much the same in medieval Christianity and Islam: a combination of hostility and mutual association. But that could represent parallel development – a similar picture is found in Chinese monasticism at the same time.

It is certain that eastern Christianity, on the other hand, borrowed extensively from Sufism, and this is not surprising, since it had provided the original inspiration. Now Muslims were giving doctrines to the Christians: the last important Syriac writer, Barhebraeus of Malatya in eastern Turkey (d. 1286), slavishly repeats Islamic discussions of the legality of listening to poetry recited by youths, but does so by rewording them to apply to the ethics of listening to Christian hymns sung by choirboys.[3] Modern specialists in the study of eastern Christianity are agreed that the original Christian 'remembrance of God', which, as we have seen, was taken over by Sufism, was now influenced by it. Here again, we have details of bodily postures and breath control, which must have come via Sufism from India, and are part of a later development, attested from the late thirteenth century onwards.[4] Moreover, it seems possible that the phenomenon of the 'elder' – which is represented by such words as the Greek *geron* before Islam – may after influencing Sufism have been influenced by it before reappearing, beneath the term *starets*, in Russian Christianity, as the type of spiritual director best known through Dostoevsky's depiction of Zosima in *The Brothers Karamazov*. The importance of this phenomenon in Russia resides largely in its independence from an ecclesiastical framework, and its consequent appeal to society at large: here, as in the emphasis on absolute obedience to the elder, one suspects a reinforcement from Sufism.

Rumi, the greatest Sufi poet
The most highly regarded of all Sufi poets is Rumi (d. 1273). The name means that he lived in Turkey, where his family (originally from northern Afghanistan) had taken refuge from the Mongols. Rumi became the dominating element in the spiritual life of Konya, then Turkey's most important city, and was closely associated with its ruler, who was a protégé of the Mongols and also in sympathy with their Muslim opponents. In the records of Rumi's discourses to his entourage we find the Sufi leader discussing political problems with this ruler and expressing his own hostility towards the Mongols. However, he says that it is lawful to accept property from them.

In Rumi's correspondence there are numerous letters of introduction in which he asks influential personages to help his disciples. His role is presumably that of 'God's friend', which he puts forward in his discourses: if men befriend him, they befriend God too. The world has been created for God's friend, and other mortals have the functions of carpenters and weavers, who make a tent in which he contemplates God. Here Rumi is echoing not only the teachings of his father (himself a leading Sufi), but also those of Daya, noted in the last chapter.

Rumi says that there is a great man who is the caliph of his time, and who is like the Universal Intelligence of the philosophers. Of particular interest is a conversation between Rumi and a Christian, who says that some of the disciples of Sadr al-Din of Konya (d. 1274; Ibn 'Arabi's main pupil) drank wine with him and declared that Jesus was God. Rumi is naturally shocked. In Ibn 'Arabi's system Jesus (like everyone else) is God, but God is not Jesus in the sense of being Jesus to the exclusion of anyone or anything else.

Rumi wrote one massive didactic work, the *Poem in Rhyming Couplets* (*Mathnawi*). In the past this was seen as a disordered collection of stories and themes chosen at random. The present writer has pointed out elsewhere that on the contrary the poem has a plan, extremely similar to that noted above in the analysis of 'Attar's *Book of the Divine*. Rumi's work is also divided into six sections or books, which fall naturally into three groups of two. The first book is principally concerned with the subject of the lower soul; the second book continues with this, while bringing in the figure of the devil, and concentrates on the themes of deception and evil. The Sufi elder, we are told, stands above the devil's power. Later it is explained that the lower soul is really identical with the devil. The third and fourth books are joined together by their common content: Reason and Knowledge. Reason is personified by Moses, and opposed by Imagination in the form of Pharaoh. The figure of the devil is replaced by that of the angel. The fifth and sixth books are united by the idea that man must first deny his own existence in order to affirm that of God. 'Passing away' is linked to the heart, the Spirit and light. But, in contrast to 'Attar's work, the position of the Spirit as God's 'caliph', his deputy, is partly taken over by the Sufi elder, and in particular by one of Rumi's close friends, who (after the effective ending of the Baghdad caliphate in 1258) is addressed as God's caliph in the present age.

Rumi's lyric poetry is also permeated by his love for leading fellow Sufis, notably the wild and ecstatic Shams al-Din of Tabriz in north-western Iran (d. 1247?) Thus Rumi often puts Shams al-Din's name at the end of his poems, indicating that one can reach God only by rising to the level of an ideal Sufi master, who is identified with the Universal Intelligence: Reason itself.

> At daybreak a moon appeared in the sky
> Came down from the sky and gazed at me
> As the falcon that snatches a bird when hunting
> That moon snatched me and started running over the sky
> When I looked into myself I did not see myself
> Because in that moon my body through grace became as spirit
> When I travelled in spirit I saw nothing but the moon
> So that the secret of the pre-eternal theophany was all revealed
> The nine spheres of heaven all went down into that moon

The ship of my being was all hidden in that ocean
That ocean surged in a wave and Reason rose again
And cast out a cry So it happened and so it became
That ocean foamed and in every fleck of that foam
A picture of someone came and a body of someone was made
Every foam-fleck of body that received a sign from that ocean
At once melted and in that ocean became spirit
Without the ruling power of Shams al-Din of Tabriz
One cannot see the moon or become the ocean[5]

Rumi is also important as the supposed founder of the brotherhood of the Whirling Dervishes (called the Mawlawis, after his title *mawlana*, 'our master'), which was apparently brought into existence by his son. Why do these Sufis engage in their distinctive whirling dance? It has often been imagined that the original intention was to reproduce the movements of the heavens. Rumi himself, however, says that this is just the interpretation offered by the Hellenized philosophers.[6] Elsewhere he puts the question and answers it:

Why do I have to dance in the glow of His sun?
So that when the speck of dust dances He may remember me[7]

For him the Sufi rises above all the concentric spheres, intelligences and souls of neo-Platonism to view God himself from the standpoint of the Universal Intelligence. Although from one perspective this seems to be achieved through the 'mediation' of the ideal master, in fact by rising to the ideal master's level the mystic acquires unmediated access to God, unlike what is found in the Greek philosophical tradition.

The 'youngmanliness' tradition of Iran

One text in particular will demonstrate the Iranian, and indeed Indo-European origin of the 'youngmanliness' (*futuwwa*) tradition. It is by a gold-beater, called Najm al-Din, of Tabriz (d. 1312), and belongs to a set type of treatise, that of the 'book of youngmanliness' (*futuwwat-nama*), which gives ethical and initiatory instructions. This tradition is noteworthy above all for its rituals of initiation, and this text provides details which, as its author observes, had never been divulged before.

He says that the members of the tradition belong to three classes, arranged in an ascending order: (3) 'of the saying', linked to Adam; (2) 'of the sword', linked to 'Ali, the son-in-law of Muhammad; (1) 'of the drinking', linked to Muhammad himself. In the ritual of drinking from the 'cup of youngmanliness' three bindings for the loins are placed round the cup, corresponding to the three classes: cotton, leather and wool respectively, It is evident that there is a hierarchy of three grades, with three kinds of activity: (3) at the bottom, the saying of 'Yes' in the primordial Covenant between God and the sons of Adam, and also (here the text refers to Adam as the founder of agriculture and weaving) agriculture and the making of trousers – which symbolize chastity (as covering the genitals) – out of cotton; (2) at the intermediate level, the activity of the warrior, of whom 'Ali is the ideal type, and for whom leather, we are told, is particularly suitable; (1) at the top, the drinking from the cup, here associated with Muhammad, in a gesture of obedience to a leader credited with knowledge – here wool represents Sufism, and the drinking itself is a well-known symbol for mystical experience.

This threefold arrangement is anticipated in the literature of Mazdaism, Iran's main pre-Islamic religion, in a text in which we are told of three classes – agriculturalists, warriors and priests – and the triple pattern of duties proper to each of these: the agriculturalists till the soil, fight off thieves and worship; the warriors act as agriculturalists in producing arms, fight and worship; the priests act as agriculturalists in preparing the sacrifice, fight as warriors against the Lie, and worship.[8] Thus the continuity from Iran's pre-Islamic past to the Islamic 'youngmanliness' tradition can hardly be doubted. We have here a striking confirmation of the validity of Georges Dumézil's view that Indo-European ideology centred on an articulation of three concepts: fertility, with its agricultural and sexual aspects; strength, notably in war; and sovereignty, with its aspects of religion and knowledge. This triad appears among the ancient Scythians (who belonged to the Iranian family of peoples), in their legend of objects falling from the sky: agricultural equipment, an axe (or an arrow and a lance) and a cup for pouring libations to the gods. It is found also in the old Iranian ritual in which the new king has to eat a fig cake, chew terebinth (living off which was part of the military training of Persian boys) and drink from a cup.[9] Its best-known occurrence is in Plato's *Republic*, where the pattern Desire–Anger–Reason is put in parallel with the parts of the state. We have already seen this last structure, transmitted from the Greek philosophical tradition, in Sana'i's *Enclosed Garden of Reality*. It must not be confused with the neo-Platonist triad of the One, Reason and the Soul, which in Sufi poetry is put in parallel with that of the mystics, the philosophers and the ascetics (also encountered in Sana'i's *Enclosed Garden*, as observed above).

Sufism and philosophy

Meanwhile, Spain had continued to produce men who tried to combine philosophy with Sufism. The leader of these was Ibn Sab'in of Murcia (d. *c.* 1270), who, in a remarkable example of interaction between Christianity and Islam, composed replies to philosophical questions sent by the Emperor Frederick II of Hohenstaufen. Here again we see that the Christians were interested in the Greek philosophical tradition rather than in Sufism itself. Ibn Sab'in was forced to leave one Muslim country after another to avoid persecution, which, it may be noted again, was directed against philosophers rather than Sufis. He was attacked by later writers either for teaching the doctrine of 'unitive fusion' (*ittihad*) with God, or for teaching monism itself. His main successor in Syria, the Spanish prince Ibn Hud (d. 1297) read the work of the Jewish philosopher Maimonides (d. 1204) with Jewish pupils.[10]

These Sufi philosophers were a principal target of someone who is today highly regarded and a great influence on Muslim writers: the lawyer Ibn Taymiyya of Damascus (d. 1328). It is now widely imagined that this jurist was a violent opponent of Sufism itself: this was not the case, and he did in fact belong to a Sufi brotherhood. He was against only certain aspects of Sufism, as was common among lawyers: the monistic trend of the early thirteenth century; and the rise, at the same time, in the veneration of individual mystics, involving visits to their tombs. As regards the latter tendency, it has been observed that Ibn Taymiyya, although condemning the customs of the lower classes, addressed his criticisms to the rulers of his time. The rulers seem to have been happy to work with new trends in Sufism, and did not like Ibn Taymiyya's violent expression of his opinions: he was persecuted and imprisoned.

Collaboration with princes (c. 1320–c. 1405)

A questionable complicity between Sufis and temporal rulers is characteristic of this period. The vicissitudes of these princes should be briefly mentioned. Mongol sovereignty in Iran collapsed after 1335 and was succeeded by a number of local dynasties. In India, after the supremacy of Delhi in the first half of the fourteenth century, in the second half its power declined considerably. In Turkey a new empire was appearing, that of the 'Ottoman' Turks, so called after their first leader, 'Uthman (d. *c.* 1324). This empire spread to the Balkans. Meanwhile, in Central Asia, another great conqueror had been born: Timur the Lame. He rose to power in the 1360s. By the 1390s he was able to beat the Mongol masters of Russia, the Golden Horde, and to sack Delhi. Before his death in 1405 he also managed to defeat the Ottoman Turks at Ankara.

'Ala' al-Dawla Simnani: a collaborator

The collaboration of Sufis with rulers is reflected in the life of 'Ala' al-Dawla Simnani (the title means Height of the State, while the surname means that he came from a town in north-eastern Iran). Born in 1261, into a family of leading administrators, he entered the service of a Mongol ruler at the age of fifteen. In 1284 he had a mystical experience in the middle of a battle. An inner light showed him the next world and its contents as previously described to him by scholars. After two more years in his master's service he abandoned it for a life of piety, separating from his wife and son and giving his land and wealth to the Sufis. He did not, however, break off his relations with princes and court officials, but remained in contact with them until his death in 1336. In his writings he maintained that one must obey a Muslim ruler and not revolt against him, even if he is a tyrant. In the same way that God does not leave the earth without a ruler to order men's lives, so too he does not leave it without a 'friend', who gives outward and inward guidance for this world and the next.

Modern writers have debated at length whether Simnani did or did not have tendencies of a pro-Shiite character. This is a somewhat pointless question, since scholars agree that he was explicitly opposed to Shiism, and also that there are signs of Shiite influence upon him. Such influence is evident when he asserts that 'Ali (the first Leader of the Shiites) has pride of place among God's friends, and was a secret companion of all the prophets who appeared before Muhammad. Given that in the Sufism of this period the personality of the mystic received greater emphasis, and given the inclination within the Sunni majority to show much more respect for the Shiites' early Leaders, it is not surprising that Sunni Sufis of the time should see these Leaders as having an important mystical role.

Simnani had contacts with Buddhist ascetics in the entourage of his Mongol master, and some knowledge of Buddhism itself. One wonders how much importance should be attached to this. His accounts of his relations with the Buddhists show the habit, usual among Sufis in India at this time, of using anecdotes to show that the degree of spiritual development of the Sufi master was superior to that of his non-Muslim counterpart. On the other hand, Simnani's meditational practices may demonstrate a direct Chinese influence, from Taoism, on bodily posture and expulsion of breath.[11] It is more probable, however, that they represent an impact from India, inherited from his Sufi predecessors, and perhaps renewed by further contacts. As regards Buddhism itself, Simnani attacks it for teaching the doctrines of reincarnation and unitive fusion (*ittihad*). Similarly, in spite of an early enthusiasm for Ibn 'Arabi's monistic theories, Simnani was to reject them, and also what he saw as the illusion of ecstasy, in favour of what he thought was the highest stage: man's enslavement (*'ubudiyya*) to God.

As a member of the Kubrawi brotherhood, Simnani was particularly preoccupied by visions of coloured lights, and he is the most important systematizer of this aspect of Sufi experience. According to him these lights, seven in number (grey, blue, red, white, yellow, black and green), correspond not only to 'subtle organs' (*lata'if*) inside the mystic, and to the parts of the universe, but also to the various 'prophets of your own being' and the various types of man (primitive, pre-Muslim, Muslim, true believer, friend of God, prophet and Messenger), so that one has to rise through an internal hierarchy to the level of Muhammad within oneself. Now this systematic sevenfold arrangement of colours, 'subtle organs' and parts of the universe is paralleled in Hindu Tantrism (in the degree of structuring, though not in the actual detail).[12] Other sevenfold patterns of colours are found in the works of Kubra himself and his pupil Daya. It seems that here again Simnani is the heir to an influence which was originally Indian, and to which he may have introduced more Indian inspiration.

There are very few sources before this period for the study of Sufism in the Indian subcontinent. Earlier modern writers painted a rosy picture of thirteenth-century Hindu and Muslim mystics mingling their doctrines into a common synthesis. This picture has been destroyed by the penetrating analysis of Simon Digby, who has shown that the 'evidence' is merely hagiographical, and that genuine syncretism was to come only much later. The hoary myth of massive Sufi-inspired conversion to Islam in India has also been shown to be based on late and legendary materials.

The Suhrawardi brotherhood in Multan

In the fourteenth century, however, we have one informative text concerning the branch of the Suhrawardi brotherhood in Multan, in what is now Pakistan. This is the *Legal Judgements of the Sufis* (*Fatawa 'l-sufiyya*), written about 1350 by one Fadl Allah Majawi. The author is determined to clarify regulations by reference to the practice of his teachers. He says that visitors came to the lodge in Multan from many lands, and sometimes numbered a thousand at a time, apart from the permanent inhabitants of the lodge and the workers therein.[13] The lodge, we are told, has roofs, a courtyard, cells and terraces. All its parts have doors opening on to the courtyard, so that everyone can follow the leader of worship. It is like a mosque, being built for prayer and worship, and open to local residents and travellers. But it offers additional possibilities for the service of God and other advantages: the perpetual recitation of the Koran from beginning to end; the distribution of food; continuous 'remembrance of God'; and the granting of an allowance to the Sufi's family and dependants.[14]

Majawi enables one to reply to the question, 'What actually happened in a Sufi lodge?' Books were read, either in an academic setting, with a tutor instructing the students in the correct transmission of the text to posterity, or in a devotional framework, with the Sufi elder weeping profusely as he listened to literary evocations of the love of God. Extra prayers would be said, corresponding to the occasions of the liturgical calendar, and prescribed by the brotherhood's local leaders; there was a special recitation of the Koran on Thursday nights, with public prayers and distribution of a sweet (*halwa'*); once a year food and drink would be distributed as well; feast days with public prayers were limited to ten a year. On Thursday nights some disciples would also keep a vigil, performing the prayers of the rosary in great quantities. A Sufi might recite the whole of the Koran on his own, in his cell. Every year a fast of six months would be observed, in seclusion. Special food of good quality was served to those undertaking the discipline for twenty days beforehand, to give them strength. These disciples were also given clothes or the money to buy them, as well as a separate cash incentive. The Sufis would also assemble to listen to poetry, and would become agitated by it. Their leader would call out to them, and they would calm down. The leader himself would not participate in the dancing or forms of ecstatic or automatic motion that accompanied the recitation of poems, but would supervise affairs from a distance.[15]

One visitor to Multan was the celebrated North African traveller Ibn Battuta (d. *c.* 1370), who has left an account of Sufi activities there. He portrays the leader of the Multan branch of the Suhrawardi brotherhood, Rukn al-Din (d. 1335), as enjoying very close relations with the Sultan of Delhi. Rukn al-Din's brother was killed in battle taking the sultan's place, whereupon the latter gave the family a hundred villages. When Rukn al-Din died the sultan intervened in the quarrel over the succession to the leadership in Multan (which was in practice hereditary) and supported his grandson. His grandson shocked the North African visitor by riding in a litter when honoured by the sultan, who eventually executed him for amassing riches.[16]

Other sources for the study of the Suhrawardi brotherhood in Multan are the records of conversations between masters and disciples of the rival Chishti fraternity in north-western India. The fraternity is named after a village called Chisht, in eastern Iran, where its earliest masters are said to have lived. Its members did not have the academic character of the Suhrawardis, and accused the Suhrawardis of excessive formality, self-enrichment and snobbishness. One feels, however, that the two brotherhoods had more in common than they were prepared to admit: both were pillars of temporal authority, and both also functioned with the help of libertine elements around the leaders.

Nizam al-Din of Bada'un and the relation between elder and disciple

The conversations of the Chishti leader Nizam al-Din of Bada'un (d. 1325) give plenty of information about the relationship between the elder and the disciple. Nizam al-Din recalls that his own teacher, Farid al-Din of Pakpattan (d. 1265), had told him that the elder is the disciple's 'bride-dresser' (*mashata*); then he had invested him with special clothes. On another occasion he had given Nizam al-Din a staff: this, along with a prayer-mat, clothes and shoes, formed part of the elder's insignia, transmission of which indicated that the recipient was to take the master's place after his death. Nizam al-Din used a hair which had fallen from Farid al-Din's moustache as a charm. When he is told that, according to one opinion, the pilgrimage to Mecca is performed only by someone who has no elder to guide him, Nizam al-Din relates that personally he found visiting his teacher's tomb an adequate substitute for the pilgrimage. Once, when a visitor had raised his voice in an argument with Farid al-Din, Nizam al-Din physically intervened.[17]

On the subject of prostration before the elder, which was challenged as contrary to Islamic law, Nizam al-Din says that he is following the example of his predecessors in not forbidding it. A visitor who has come from the Middle East is shocked to see one of Nizam al-Din's disciples placing his head on the ground before him. The master explains that the ancient practice of prostration before kings and teachers had been stopped by Muhammad, but is still permissible. The Indian character of the practice seems evident enough. Nizam al-Din says that he personally would like to stop it, but Farid al-Din had told him a story about an elder's making a disciple kiss the ground beneath his horse. A similar problem is whether disciples should interrupt their supplementary prayers (that is, those said in addition to the obligatory acts of formal worship) when the elder appears, in order to obtain the spiritual reward for kissing his foot. Nizam al-Din thinks that the practice of interrupting one's prayers for this purpose should be rejected, but avoids condemning it outright.[18]

Steadfastness in allegiance to one's elder, declares Nizam al-Din, brings forgiveness for past sins. He tells a story about a disciple who, when about to be executed, refused to face in the direction of Mecca, as Islamic law demands, but insisted instead on facing in the direction of his master's grave. When Nizam al-Din was distressed he would call out: 'Elder! elder! (*shaykh! shaykh!*)' He says that love for one's Sufi instructor is better than any amount of formal worship. The pupil must make his teacher his governor. When the teacher forgives, God forgives. But the elder must not be worldly, or he will be unable to restrain his disciple from love of the world. Nor should he expect gifts from his disciple, or be in any way dependent upon him.[19]

This picture of the relationship between the elder and the disciple is corroborated by other Indian sources of the period. Majawi, the Suhrawardi author, tells us that Rukn al-Din once said to him,

> The elder has tied a rope to the disciple's foot, and holds the other end in his hand, so that the disciple may go where is necessary; but, when he is attracted to a place of deadly danger, the elder can stop him, pull the rope and bring him back.[20]

It would be wrong, however, to imagine that the elder monopolized the task of instructing the disciple in Sufism. Majawi, in addition to his elder, had an academic tutor (*ustad*), who taught him not only law but also Sufi regulations, and would read the text of 'Umar Suhrawardi's manual of Sufism with him.[21] In fact, Nizam al-Din indicates, a Sufi master of this period might well have so many disciples that he would be unable to remember who they were. Nor would his transmission of authority to a disciple necessarily be a matter for himself to decide alone, as Nizam al-Din makes clear: some elders would consult a colleague before investing someone with a patched frock, and would refuse to go through with this investiture if there was an objection.[22]

Qalandars

In the conversations of Nizam al-Din's successor, Nasir al-Din of Delhi (d. 1356), mention was often made of the libertine dervishes called *qalandars*. His disciple Hamid Qalandar, who wrote down the conversations, seems to have oscillated between Sufism and the independence indicated by his surname. Eventually Nasir al-Din was attacked by a *qalandar* with a knife and sustained several wounds. Such violence was typical. He tells a story about a *qalandar* who visited Farid al-Din, spilt some cannabis (consumption of which was typical among these dervishes) on the master's prayer-mat and threatened to hit a Sufi who objected. On one occasion Nasir al-Din, putting some *qalandars* up for the night, remarked that dervishes had become few in number; in the time of his predecessor they came in groups of twenty or thirty, but in those days prices had been low, money plentiful and hospitality easy.[23]

Listening to poetry

Nizam al-Din tells us that once a poet brought a long panegyrical poem to his own predecessor. The latter then asked the poet what he wanted. The poet said that he had an old mother to support. The Sufi master told him to bring an offering, which was duly given in the form of a sum of money, and was distributed among the Sufis present. The poet then obtained a post in the service of the Sultan of Delhi's son.[24]

Nizam al-Din has much to say about listening to poetry, and sets out an important doctrine of what he calls 'relating' (*tahmil*). He declares that every time he listens to poetry he 'relates' the descriptions of human beauty to his own elder's qualities and nature. Similarly, one must 'relate' every line of verse that one hears to God's attributes. At first poetry is 'attacking', that is to say it makes a violent onrush: someone hears a voice or a line and is brought into movement. Then the line is 'related' to God, one's elder, or some spiritual concept. The joy obtained in listening to poetry comes in three parts: first, lights come down from the world of divine sovereignty (*malakut*) to the spirit; then 'states' come down from the world of divine compulsion (*jabarut* – here in an intermediary position, not, as often, above the world of sovereignty) to the heart; finally, effects such as weeping, movement and agitation come from this visible world to the parts of the body.[25]

The conversations of Nizam al-Din's successor give important indications of the early shamanistic role of listening to poetry (the evidence suggests influence from Central Asia). We are told that this is the cure for all pains, and notably those of love. One legend tells how the dismembered body of a prince was reconstituted by organized listening to poetry and music. We are told a story of how an early thirteenth-century king decided to end a drought by telling the Sufi dervishes to hold an organized session of such 'listening' (*sama'*) to bring rain: inevitably, a leading mystic produces the desired effect. These three elements of magical medicine, reconstituting a dismembered body and rain making are all highly characteristic of Central Asian shamanism. Nasir al-Din also says that previously 'listening' was much more common, since prices were lower, and recalls the large-scale 'listening' parties of the time of his predecessor.[26] It should be explained that in this period it was normal for a wealthy individual to invite Sufis to his house for such parties, an important component of which would be the dinner. Naturally, it was common for such occasions to be attacked as manifestations of gluttony providing entertainment more suitable for the tavern.

The Persian poet Hafiz of Shiraz

As we move on to the second half of the fourteenth century, one figure requires attention, since he is often regarded as the finest of all Persian poets: Hafiz of Shiraz (d. 1389 or 1390). There has been much disagreement over the question of whether his poetry is Sufi or not. As observed above, there is a tendency to produce false problems here, with the unfortunate introduction of the opposition 'sacred–profane'. There is also the introduction of the misleading idea of 'orthodoxy'.

Recently one talented historian, Angelika Hartmann, has produced new evidence to refuel the debate: a Persian paraphrase of 'Umar Suhrawardi's attack on Greek philosophy and libertinism, composed in Shiraz by one of Hafiz's contemporaries, known as a bigoted and fanatical influence on the local rulers. From this she has argued that Hafiz's poetry, with its libertine language, would not have been seen as mystical by his contemporaries, at least not by the 'orthodox'.[27] This is an untenable line of argument. We have early evidence that Hafiz used to attend the meetings of a Sufi master, and was seen by an Indian Sufi visitor as an *Uwaysi*, that is to say a mystic who obtains guidance from physically absent or dead teachers.[28] Moreover, the Suhrawardi brotherhood, in spite of the severity affected by its leaders, had always tolerated poets and the symbolism of wine and handsome boys. Certainly, some of Hafiz's compositions are straightforward pieces of court poetry, and celebrate temporal joys in a way which cannot have been intended as symbolic. But in others Hafiz is merely continuing a well-established Sufi tradition, and himself makes his intentions explicit:

> The vats are all boiling and shouting in drunkenness
> And that wine which is in there is reality [*haqiqat*, spiritual truth]
> not metaphor [*majaz*, earthly image][29]

One problem is whether, in addition to the straightforward celebrations of the pleasures of court life, and the use of libertine language to convey the heights of Sufi ecstasy, there is also a third level. Gilbert Lazard has argued that there is: not only do the conventional symbols refer to well-known objects such as the Divine Beloved and spiritual 'states', but behind these can be seen a variety of noble feelings, such as sincere friendship and inner freedom. This looks like an anachronistic injection from modern rationalism, with its vision of eternal truths undefiled by religion. Lazard's argument is founded largely on Hafiz's habit of putting the praise of a temporal patron into the endings of short odes which have some Sufi symbolism. Though this is a new technique, it is perhaps a natural development: Rumi, at the end of poems in which the language of human love is used to express the love of God, had put the praise of leading fellow Sufis. Although the presence of the temporal patron makes him a third beloved in the poems, alongside a handsome boy cupbearer and God, the praise of a benefactor obviously indicates mercenary motives, rather than a third level of noble ideas. If what is symbolized itself becomes a symbol, it is only to reflect the original image.

> Last night I happened to drink a cup or two near dawn
> And from the cupbearer's lips wine spilt on to my palate
> In drunkenness again with the beloved of my youth
> I wanted a reconciliation but divorce had come
> In the stations of the Path wherever I travelled
> Separation had arisen between ogling and safety
> Cupbearer keep giving the cup for in the journey of the Way
> Whoever has not become like a lover has sunk into hypocrisy
> Interpreter of dreams give good news for last night the sun
> In thankfulness for its morning sleep became my companion
> At that hour when Hafiz wrote these scattered lines
> The bird of his thought had fallen into the snare of longing
> If Nusrat al-Din Shah Yahya had not generously done
> The work of the kingdom and the religion it would have fallen out
> of order and harmony[30]

Amuli: marrying Sufism and Shiism

The author of the greatest importance for the combination of Sufism with Shiism was Amuli, named after his home town in northern Iran. Born in 1320, Amuli served a local prince until he was murdered in 1349, and then devoted himself to a religious life. He had extraordinary visions, in which he saw the names of Muhammad and his family in the sky. He used these visions to support his arguments in his literary output, which he continued until 1385, when he disappears from view (the date of his death is unknown).

His writings had one sole aim: to demonstrate that whoever professed Sufism professed Shiism, and vice versa. He himself admitted that hitherto the adherents of the two doctrines had engaged in unparalleled mutual vilification: the Sufis had been the firmest supporters of the mainline Sunni positions. But Amuli argued that Ibn 'Arabi, in his systematization of Sufi teaching in the previous century, had insisted on the importance of the Perfect Man as the interface (*barzakh*) between God and creatures. Shiism had shown who the ultimate Perfect Men were: the Twelve Leaders of Muhammad's family. Referring to his own visions, Amuli declared that the Seal of the universal cycle of God's friendship could not be Jesus, as Ibn 'Arabi had asserted, but could only be 'Ali, as the First Leader. Similarly, the Seal of the 'particular' cycle of God's friends, the cycle inaugurated by Muhammad's prophetic activity, could not be an individual outside his family, such as Ibn 'Arabi (as he had claimed), but had to be the Twelfth Leader, with his final messianic role.

This argument of Amuli's has been violently attacked by recent writers in the West (such as Michel Chodkiewicz and Hamid Algar), who have also taken exception to the view of Henry Corbin that here Shiism was merely reappropriating what had been its own property in the beginning. Such debates are futile. Obviously, from the point of view of Ibn 'Arabi's own system (which he expounded with insulting remarks about the Shiites), this is a betrayal of his original intentions. However, from the standpoint of the external inquirer the Shiite doctrine of the Leader is not particularly different from that of the Perfect Man, and one might reasonably suspect that the latter had arisen under some influence from the former, or from some common pre-Islamic source first represented in Shiism.

The Hurufi movement

Similar problems surround the origins, in the late fourteenth century, of the peculiar Hurufi movement, so called because of its concentration on the letters (*huruf*) of the alphabet. Mystical letter-symbolism had always existed in Islam, notably in Shiism, and the techniques of Hurufism are sometimes identical with those used in the Gnosticism of late antiquity and the Jewish tradition of the Kabbalah. The mystics select a word or name as the object of analysis and speculation. The word or name is divided into its letters, and the numerical values of these are added up. Another method is just to count the number of letters. One can also combine the totals produced by these methods. Alternatively, the name of each individual letter is written down, thus producing more letters; repeated letters are eliminated; and the rest, each counted as equalling one, are added up. A total will be found to correspond to some aspect of man or the universe.

The Hurufi movement was founded by Fadl Allah of Astarabad in north-western Iran. He was put to death in 1394, at the order of a son of the conqueror Timur, with whom he had taken refuge. (This tendency to look for protection from princes and then fall foul of them was to prove characteristic of sympathizers of his school.) The movement was in effect originally intended as a new religion, in which Fadl Allah was identified with God. He was familiar with the start of John's Gospel ('In the beginning was the Word . . .') and taught that God was revealed through his speech. The Arabic language of Muhammad had given an incomplete revelation, since its alphabet possessed only twenty-eight letters; but Fadl Allah was able to perfect it, since he wrote in Persian, which had thirty-two. In practice what had been meant as a new religion was to end up as just a set of doctrines, surviving mainly in Sufism as practised in Turkey.

The poet Nesimi

Nesimi, a follower of Fadl Allah, is one of the most important poets of the Turkic languages. He was also executed, at Aleppo in Syria, probably in 1405. In his poems Nesimi repeatedly declares the identity of man, and himself, with God, in a way which cannot be excused on the usual grounds that God is speaking through a mystic who has passed away. Admittedly, the theory is still one of theophany, of God's self-manifestation, not one of incarnation, but Nesimi's repeated and explicit evocations of the privileged status of man as being none other than the Truth (here evidently God) amply reflect the danger which he was putting himself into.

> Your eye is sedition and your face is the sun and the moon
> It seems you are the sedition in the turning of the moon
> Your face is the Truth This is news from the Truth
> He who says it is the Truth but his name is Man[31]

Moreover, Nesimi claims identification with God not just for man in general, but for himself in particular.

Since I am surviving from pre-eternity to post-eternity
I am the created and the Creator of *Be and it was* (cf. Koran 2:
117, etc.)
Since I am the Cupbearer of the banquet of unity
I am the signs and horizons of souls[32]

Reaction to radical changes in Sufism

Meanwhile, in North Africa and Spain (where political power was now
divided among local dynasties), the Muslim West was seeing the
expression of a reaction against daring Sufi theorizing. One Ibn 'Abbad,
who was born at Ronda in Spain, but spent his adult life in Morocco,
where he died in 1390, is an extreme example of this reactionary
tendency. He was a preacher who presented himself as a Sufi. He left
letters in which, as well as his repetitious and monotonous moralizing,
he expresses his hostility to new ideas. He says that when, while
reading a book, one encounters disagreement between Muslim
thinkers, one should simply move on to another chapter, maintaining a
deferential attitude towards religious scholars. He thinks that the
pilgrimage to Mecca is more likely to be acceptable to God if one is
from the more educated classes. What is most striking in these letters
is the lack of progress made by Ibn 'Abbad's chief correspondent, who
complains that he is not notably moved when chanting the Koran, and
would like very much to cry but cannot; and also that he spends his time
reading a great variety of books, but not in a concentrated manner.

Another example of reaction to radical changes in Sufi thought is
provided by the great historian and sociologist Ibn Khaldun (d. 1406).
Born at Tunis, he served several princes in the Muslim West before
leaving for Egypt, where he was a judge, a teacher of law and also an
administrator at the main Sufi lodge. In his autobiography he praises the
policy of previous rulers and dignitaries, who had founded such lodges,
along with colleges, and endowed them with rich properties for the
maintenance of ascetics and students, leaving the possibility that surplus
revenue might be available for the founders' poorer descendants.

These intentions of the founders of pious institutions are made
clearer in Ibn Khaldun's celebrated 'Introduction' (*Muqaddima*) to his
Universal History (*Kitab al-'ibar*). The founders had been afraid that
their descendants would have their property confiscated by the
arbitrary use of royal power, and consequently arranged for them to
participate in the endowments (sometimes as administrators). Ibn
Khaldun also has a lot to say about Sufism itself in his Introduction. Like
Ibn 'Abbad, he shows himself to be a supporter of the old, sober piety

of Muhammad Ghazali. He dislikes more recent Sufis, whom he accuses of teaching the doctrines of incarnation and absolute monism. Here, he says, their teachings are identical with those of the Shiites. Even earlier Sufis, however, had been influenced by (just as they had exercised an influence upon) the extremist Shiites, notably in the Sufi doctrine of the Pole (*qutb*), according to which there is one chief mystic in the world at any one time. This, says Ibn Khaldun, was apparently taken from the extremist Shiite view of the Leader, as was the Sufi theory of the rest of the hierarchy of God's friends. Shiite influence is seen in the Sufi construction of pedigrees of masters who invest their disciples with the special frock (*khirqa*), since such pedigrees sometimes go back to 'Ali, the first Shiite Leader. Ibn Khaldun attacks recent Sufis for confusing the problems of philosophy with those of their own discipline. He also criticizes them for wasting their lives on producing new and ever-unfulfilled predictions of the coming of the messianic ruler, the Mahdi. He says that no would-be ruler can win power unless there is group solidarity (*'asabiyya*) to support him.

The nature of Ibn Khaldun's own Sufi beliefs is not clear. There is manuscript evidence that in the text of the Introduction he deleted an earlier expression of belief in an original unity of man with the rest of the universe. A short treatise on Sufism is attributed to him, but its authenticity has been challenged, as yet inconclusively. Its author is replying to the question of whether Sufism can be learnt from books alone, or requires the teaching of an elder. He replies that an elder is not absolutely necessary for the practice of simple piety, but is usually necessary for the acquisition of higher virtues, and is indispensable for the pursuit of ecstasy. The question had originated among the Sufis of Spain, where it occasioned much debate: this shows how different things were in India, where the strict insistence on the need for an elder was universal.

Subversion and erudition (c. 1405–c. 1500)

The fifteenth century contains sharply contrasting elements in Sufism: on the one hand there is revolutionary political activity; and on the other there is a period of literary virtuosity and erudition. There are both messianic expectations, linked to Shiism, and unoriginal, academic commentaries upon (and imitations of) what has gone before. Accordingly the historical background is very difficult to study, since Sufism itself is deeply imbedded within it, and the secrecy which surrounds Sufi doctrines complicates the task still further: politics and mysticism combine to draw the veil. Although there is plenty of literary evidence, it is not easy to evaluate, and modern scholars have yet to reach conclusions about the underlying patterns.

After the death of Timur the Lame in 1405 his family ruled over most of what is now Iran, Afghanistan and Soviet Central Asia, though they could not hope to govern all the areas of his victories. The period was characterized by great splendour in the visual arts. In Egypt and Syria slaves continued to rise to become rulers, while in Iraq and north-western Iran Turkish tribal leaders engaged in internecine warfare, and one such leader eventually conquered almost the whole of Iran. In Turkey and the Balkans the Ottoman Empire, which Timur had almost destroyed, had to spend the first half of the century pulling itself together, and also had to cope with a Sufi revolt. Once re-established, the Ottomans obtained their greatest triumph, the capture of Constantinople in 1453, and thereby ended the Byzantine Empire. The old Christian capital was now to be the centre of Islam's temporal power, with the name of Istanbul. In India there were a number of independent Muslim dynasties, corresponding to a variety of regional and ethnic factors. In North Africa there was also a lack of strong centralized rule. In Spain the last remnant of Muslim sovereignty came to an end in 1492.

'Ali Turka's hierarchy of thinkers

The political background of Shiite revolutionary activity is particularly important when considering Sufism after Timur. One figure in particular stands out: 'Ali Turka of Isfahan, who died at the Timurid capital of Herat in 1427. It seems that he may have been connected with an assassination attempt in that year on the son and main successor of Timur, made by a member of the Hurufi movement.

At any rate, Turka was deeply involved in the political history of his time, and did borrow Hurufi ideas. These appear in his fascinating depiction of the hierarchy of the various classes of religious thinkers. At the bottom he puts the jurists and collectors of sayings attributed to Muhammad. Above these he places the theologians and the ordinary adherents of the Greek philosophical tradition, and above them the members of the school of 'Oriental Illumination', the philosophico-mystical movement founded by Yahya Suhrawardi in the late twelfth century. Above these he puts the Sufis themselves: in effect the followers of Ibn 'Arabi, with their emphasis on the role of the Perfect Man. In the next position we find the Hurufis: the masters of the science of letters (*huruf*), who concentrate on speech, as being for them the most important source of God's self-manifestation. Above these, at the very summit of his hierarchy, Turka puts the family of Muhammad.

This reveals his strong pro-Shiite sympathies, as well as a graduated respect for a variety of schools of thought. The difficulty here is that Turka, like other writers of the period, is unable to attempt the task of a grand synthesis of them all, and consequently has to maintain contradictory positions as he moves from one to another: instead of a new system in which inconsistencies are removed, there is just a vertical arrangement of different theories. Turka's hierarchy may be compared with the one, already noted, that was developed in a late thirteenth-century Jewish text: Sufis at the bottom, philosophers in the middle, letter-mystics at the top.

Jili
At this time Ibn 'Arabi's ideas were being popularized by many people, of whom the best known is Jili of Baghdad (d. *c*. 1428). We have little information about Jili's life: it is known that he spent some time in South Arabia and visited India. He is most interesting for his accounts of his own visions, into which Ibn 'Arabi's system is integrated. Thus he explains that the Perfect Man is the Prophet Muhammad, who reappears in every age. Jili says that he once met him in the form of his own elder. This is because Muhammad has the power to assume every form. Jili relates that he also met the Spirit, who explained that he was the Muhammadan Reality (*al-haqiqa al-Muhammadiyya*), symbolized by the legendary beautiful women of early Arabic poetry. The author also relates how he visited the various heavens, and the prophets therein, and describes the seven earths, which are arranged in layers: our own possesses a blessed northern region, inhabited by the 'men of the unseen' (*rijal al-ghayb*), while immediately beneath us is the earth inhabited by the monotheists in the race of genies (*jinn*). Most of the latter envy the Sufis, and sometimes lead them astray. Jili also asserts that he visited hell, the torments of which he does not believe to be eternal. On the contrary, hell contains some excellent people – put there in order to have God revealed to them – such as Plato, whom Jili saw irradiating light from a position of great distinction.

Badr al-Din, Ottoman chief jurist
Meanwhile, a colourful and dramatic episode was taking place in the Ottoman Empire. In the confusion following the conquests of Timur the Lame, one Ottoman prince, Musa, assumed control of the European part of the empire and declared himself independent in 1411. He

appointed as the chief jurist of his dominions the Sufi Badr al-Din of Simavna (near Edirne in the European part of modern Turkey). Badr al-Din had extraordinary political opinions, both regarding property, which he held should be owned in a communistic manner, and regarding the Christian subjects of the empire, who he said should be put on an equal level with the Muslims. These doctrines were based on the views of Ibn 'Arabi, who had indeed shown an openness to other religions in theory, while advocating severity towards Christians in practice. The idea of the common ownership of property has been seen as a natural extension of Ibn 'Arabi's doctrine of the 'unity of existence', although one doubts whether he would have approved of it. In any case, although Badr al-Din's teachings won popular support, they antagonized other jurists and the Turkish notables of the Balkans, who engineered the fall and death of his royal patron in 1413. The new ruler of the united empire, Muhammad I (1413–20), dismissed him, but his supporters rebelled. They found plenty of sympathizers among the poor, Muslim and Christian alike, whose poverty had been rendered more extreme by war, and also among the Turkomans, the nomadic Muslim Turks, who tended to favour radical ideas. The revolt was put down, and Badr al-Din was hanged (probably in 1420), but his followers continued their subversive activities in Shiite Sufism, as will be seen below.

Two Sufi biographies

If we return now to the empire of the Timurids, we find valuable information about Sufism in the small town of Bam in south-eastern Iran. A Sufi master called Shams al-Din (d. *c.* 1432) and his son and successor Tahir al-Din (d. 1456) were to be the subjects of revealing biographies, composed by their immediate disciples. These biographies have been brilliantly analysed by Jean Aubin, who paints a disturbing picture. The Sufi leaders were extremely rich, with plenty of servants and fine horses. They would pay for enormous feasts on the main occasions of the liturgical calendar, as well as for all the local weddings. Their wealth brought them into conflict with the governors and agents of the temporal authorities, who tended to meet with violent deaths, sometimes evidently at the hands of the Sufi leaders' disciples, although the biographers usually attribute such fates to the masters' supernatural intervention. Compared to the relatively sympathetic character of Shams al-Din, the portrait of his son drawn by his biographer shows a sinister development, at least in the mentality of the disciples. The master is presented as using his miraculous powers in particularly unpleasant ways: first, as a child, to kill a younger brother for saying something to their father; later, to murder a girl because he prefers to marry her younger sister; and finally, to execute a boy whose poor mother (who operated a mill belonging to Tahir al-Din) did not have the heart to bring him to be beaten. These Sufi elders were Shiites and themselves proudly claimed descent from the early Leaders of Muhammad's family, but they were on good terms with the Timurid princes (as opposed to their underlings) and were certainly no revolutionaries.

Muhammad Nurbakhsh

One Shiite Sufi who was a revolutionary was Muhammad Nurbakhsh, born at Qa'in in north-eastern Iran in 1393. A member of the Kubrawi brotherhood, he was designated as the messianic Mahdi (the ideal ruler) by his teacher, who made his pupil declare himself to be the leader (*imam*) of the Muslim community, and provided him with the title 'Nurbakhsh' (giver of light). The aim was to attack the tyranny of the ruling Timurid dynasty, which reacted by killing Nurbakhsh's teacher. The claimant himself had an eventful life, being repeatedly arrested, released and exiled. At one point he was obliged to renounce his claims, but his writings show that he continued to believe that a further attempt would be successful. He died in 1465. His works naturally refer to the visions characteristic of the Kubrawi school, which now have the purpose of confirming his mission. Nurbakhsh's teacher had visions demonstrating to him that his own master was now manifested in the person of Nurbakhsh; another adherent believed he saw Jesus come down from the sky as a light and enter the claimant. Nurbakhsh also argued in defence of his claims that he had disciples from Turkey to Kashmir. It was in Kashmir that his movement was later to survive.

The synthesis of Shiism and Sufism

A revolutionary mixture of Shiism and Sufism found its ultimate military and political triumph at the beginning of the sixteenth century. It was achieved by a family of hereditary Sufi masters called the Safavids, after the original founder of their brotherhood, Safi 'l-Din of Ardabil in north-western Iran (d. 1334). He was neither a Shiite nor a social revolutionary, but a man of respectability, wealth and power. It appears that in the fifteenth century some of his successors, like many other Sufis of the period, adopted a radical form of Shiism. A distinguished modern specialist in this field, H. R. Roemer, has counselled caution with regard to accepting this version of affairs, but we have a fair amount of evidence from various sources (Italian visitors, and Ottoman

Turkish as well as Iranian historians, both Shiite and Sunni) which indicates that this is what did happen.

One leading member of the brotherhood, called Junayd, was killed in battle after a life full of political and military adventures. He married the sister of a chief of the nomadic Muslim Turks (the Turkomans), called Uzun Hasan (d. 1478), who was later to establish his rule over most of Iran. Junayd himself had a lot of supporters, who, as Roemer observes, gave a new meaning to the word 'Sufi'. It now meant not just a committed devotee of the mystic Path, but a fighter in the holy war. Moreover, in the Turkoman support henceforth enjoyed by the Safavids we find a phenomenon still widespread in the Muslim world: away from the urban students of Sufi exercises there exists, outside the towns, a tribal loyalty to families of hereditary Sufi masters. It is in the intensity of such loyalty that one is to see the reason for the large following obtained by Junayd's son Haydar, who was also killed in battle, in 1488. As leader of the Safavids' brotherhood he militarized it still further and even brought in a uniform. After his death the Turkoman tribesmen disappeared from the scene of political events, until, eleven years later, his own son was to mobilize them again (see below).

The combination of Sufism with Shiism naturally brought with it considerable theoretical problems. Earlier, at the start of the thirteenth century, Ibn 'Arabi had evolved a synthesis of Sufism, theology and philosophy. But after him the difficulty of mixing these three disciplines remained, since at the same time there was an independent philosophical development of theology, while the continuation of the school of 'Oriental Illumination' meant that the philosophical tradition itself had a new and more mystical wing. Besides, Ibn 'Arabi had been adapting mainline Sunni theology, whereas in Shiite theology there was a separate, rationalizing school of thought. Some Muslim thinkers would simply indulge in inconsistency, writing books in different disciplines and contradicting themselves, in a manner which seems ludicrous to the modern western student. Systematization of a kind was obtained by arranging the various disciplines in a hierarchy of levels, as Turka did in the early fifteenth century.

In the late fifteenth century, however, the task of combining Shiite theology with Sufism and the philosophy of 'Oriental Illumination' was undertaken by one Ibn Abi Jumhur, from al-Ahsa' in Bahrein. He was born about 1433 and visited Iraq and Iran. He was still writing in 1499: the date of his death is unknown. In his work the twelve Leaders of the early Shiites are given a primordial and cosmic role in God's original self-manifestation. It is from them that proceed the intelligences and souls of the philosophers, which govern the celestial spheres. The cosmic Leaders manifest themselves through heavenly spirits and angels, who guide their terrestrial, bodily counterparts: the Leaders as men on earth. In the hidden Twelfth Leader, the one of our own time, all twelve come together, just as in the twelve are manifested all the religions of mankind: so he is the Pole (*qutb*, the Axis) of the Sufis, around whom the spiritual life of the world revolves, and the Perfect Man. He is the Paraclete announced by Jesus and the self-fulfilment of Muhammad. Ibn Abi Jumhur's synthesis does not seem to have achieved much popularity, perhaps because it is just too mechanical: to combine the various elements properly with true philosophical rigour a radically new perspective was needed, and this was to come only in seventeenth-century Iran.

Jami

The revolutionary Shiite Sufis were attacking an empire whose Timurid rulers often enjoyed Sufi support. We have already seen what was happening in the small provincial town of Bam, where Sufi leaders were on good terms with Timurid princes, though not with local administrators. But what of the Sufis at the court of Herat itself? Here one finds the ultimate depths of decadence: literary activity took the form of slavish imitation of past models, along with the multiplication of trivial artifices. The best-known representative of this period is the Sufi poet Jami, who was born in the town of Jam in north-eastern Iran in 1414 and died at Herat in 1492. His praise of his royal patrons contains revealing thoughts on tyranny. Why are the prayers of its apparent victims not answered? Because, says Jami, they are really tyrants themselves.[33] The tyranny of the king is like the welcome blow of the Beloved, but the tyranny of others is unbearable.[34] Here Jami seems close to the Sufi lords of Bam.

Jami was a member of the Naqshbandi brotherhood, founded by Baha' al-Din Naqshband of Bukhara (d. 1389). This is characterized by its emphasis on a silent 'remembrance of God' as opposed to the usual practice of repeating a formula aloud. In Sufi theory Jami belonged to Ibn 'Arabi's school, and set out its positions in reply to a request from the Ottoman Sultan Muhammad II (1451–81), simply presenting them as superior to those of the theologians and philosophers. But his long didactic poems belong sometimes to Sufism and sometimes to the Greek philosophical tradition: his leanings in the direction of the latter are typical of poets in the entourage of kings.

Trimingham's reconstruction

We should not leave the fifteenth century without considering the influential socio-historical reconstruction put forward for this period by J. S. Trimingham. He claims that at this time the Sufi *tariqa* (brotherhood) was transformed into the *ta'ifa*, the so-called 'order' as found today. Trimingham himself admits that the Sufi use of these terms does not support his argument. He says that the tendency for leadership within a brotherhood to become hereditary is one aspect of the alleged transformation. But such hereditary leadership is already found in the thirteenth century (for example, in Multan). Trimingham thinks that a huge rise in the importance of the Sufi elder began in North Africa in the fifteenth century. As we shall see, in our discussion of sixteenth- and seventeenth-century Morocco, this famous idea of a 'Maraboutic Crisis' is just an illusion. He imagines that the complete integration of a so-called 'saint-cult' with the brotherhood is characteristic of the change which he reconstructs. But the veneration of leading Sufis at their tombs is already closely bound up with the brotherhoods in the thirteenth century, as are other elements put by Trimingham in the fifteenth – transmission of an allegiance and a popular following. Nothing remains to support his theory.

THE AGE OF THE THREE GREAT EMPIRES (*c.* 1500–*c.* 1700)

The sixteenth and seventeenth centuries, taken together, represent a special period in the history of Sufism. Islam was effectively dominated by three empires in their heyday and the beginning of their decline: the empire of the Ottoman Turks, the Safavid Empire in Iran and the Timurid or Mogul Empire in the Indian subcontinent.

In 1517 the Ottomans conquered Egypt and Syria. From 1520 to 1566, during the reign of Sulayman the Magnificent, they reached the peak of their achievements, ruling from Hungary to Arabia and from Algeria to Iraq. After this the Ottoman Empire gradually decayed, and lost Hungary and some of its other European provinces in 1699. In Iran a member of the Safavid family and Sufi brotherhood, Isma'il, the son of Haydar, took over at the start of the sixteenth century and imposed Shiism upon the population. In 1694 the last real Safavid ruler, Husayn, acceded to the throne, and brought about the collapse of his empire through religious persecution: it effectively fell to the Afghans in the 1720s. The Timurids, who had been ruling in what is now western Afghanistan and Soviet Central Asia, were forced to move south, and conquered India, where, from the 1520s, they established what is usually called the Mogul Empire (from the Persian *mughal*, meaning Mongols, as they claimed to be descended from Chinggis Khan). Their last great ruler, Awrangzib (1658–1707), also resorted to religious persecution (against the Hindus), and thereby brought about lasting decline. Meanwhile, from the start of the sixteenth century, new Muslim polities were installed in Central Asia (that of the Uzbeks); in Morocco (that of the Sa'dis, extended to West Africa); and in parts of what is now Indonesia (with the establishing of the power of the Acheh kingdom in North Sumatra and the fall of the Hindus in East Java).

This period presents new problems, for two main reasons. First, appreciation of cultural developments now presupposes extensive knowledge of what has gone before, and it is not easy to distinguish between lack of originality on the one hand and sophistication of allusion to the past on the other. Secondly, changes in Sufism are closely bound up with political ramifications peculiar to each of the major empires. Consequently, instead of looking at the Muslim world for short spans of time, we shall examine the three empires separately, across the period as a whole.

The Ottoman Empire

The Ottoman Empire, surveyed at the peak of its glory in the first half of the sixteenth century, offered a remarkable example of administrative expertise imposed upon every aspect of life. Beneath the sultan stood a ruling class, composed of soldiers, civil servants and religious educators and lawyers. Beneath this was a subject class, consisting of the various religious communities: Muslim, Jewish, Eastern Orthodox and Armenian Christian. The problem is: how did Sufism fit into all this?

Important work on the Sufi brotherhoods in the Ottoman Empire has been done by H. J. Kissling, largely in the 1950s. He made some general observations, which are still widely accepted, and also engaged in detailed pioneering studies. The latter do not really support the former, as he himself admitted, and his sociological concepts and presuppositions seem old-fashioned and untenable today. Kissling viewed the Sufi brotherhoods as 'men's societies' (in fact we have evidence of women visiting Sufi lodges and participating in Sufi activities there). He was also concerned with the false question of 'orthodoxy', and saw all Sufi brotherhoods as 'unorthodox' and 'pantheistic'. He thought that Sufism, as opposed to an 'orthodox Islam', represented the primitive, lower religion of the common people.

But some of Kissling's own research suggested a different picture.

He discovered that the Khalwati brotherhood, apparently founded in the fifteenth century, and so called because of its concentration on the Sufi practice of a solitary retreat (*khalwa*) of forty days, was linked to the very summit of the state. Muhammad II had greatly offended the Sufis by wholesale confiscation of religious endowments. Modern writers have suspected the Khalwatis of murdering him in order to facilitate the accession of his son Bayazid II (1481–1512), who was a fervent supporter of their brotherhood. Now they enjoyed many advantages, and in the reign of Sulayman the Magnificent they also had followers in the most important government posts. Royal patronage also meant the subsidized founding of lodges, sometimes attached to new mosques (in a way which makes contemporary Soviet sociological descriptions of Sufism as 'out-of-mosque religion' unconvincing).

In contrast to the extremely respectable Khalwati brotherhood, that of the Bektashis seems as disreputable as might be imagined. Allegedly founded around 1300 by a man called Bektash from north-eastern Iran, its practices in the twentieth century have been extraordinarily shocking to mainline Muslim opinion, and have included the consumption of alcohol and dancing with unveiled women, along with evident Christian elements (such as the confession of sins), Shiite teachings (such as near-deification of 'Ali) and shamanistic survivals from the Turks' Central Asian past (such as the tabooing of the hare). It is not clear, however, whether all this was characteristic of the Bektashis in the sixteenth and seventeenth centuries.

Suraiya Faroqhi, in her magnificent work on the documents in the Turkish archives, has established that there is a strong correlation between the geographical distribution of Bektashi lodges and that of denunciations of Safavid Shiite propagandists. However, these denunciations do not mention the Bektashi brotherhood as such. In this due to the brotherhood's concealing its Shiite teachings? One problem is that Faroqhi uses the word 'heterodox' to cover Sufi, Shiite and shamanistic activities. She is inclined to agree with the view that the brotherhood developed its dubious tendencies gradually. It has been suggested that the Bektashis were corrupted by the Turkoman tribes which the Ottoman government wanted them to reform. The Bektashis also had an official responsibility, given to them at the end of the sixteenth century, for the celebrated Janissary soldiers (so called from the Turkish *Yeni Çeri*, 'New Troop'), who were recruited from Christian boys and made to accept Islam. The Bektashis were formally attached to this corps through its ninety-ninth batallion, of which their chief elder was the commanding officer.

That there was plenty of institutionalized mystical libertinism in the sixteenth century has been well established. There is documentary evidence of the playing of forbidden musical instruments by dervishes, often for the benefit of large numbers of Janissaries.[35] There is also evidence of widespread consumption of wine and drugs by dervishes.[36] By the seventeenth century the Bektashis were the most disreputable of the recognized brotherhoods, accused of sexual misconduct and linked to unbelief and licentious behaviour on the part of the Janissaries (although these were now no longer recruited by levies from the Christian population). As such they were the principal object of attack from an anti-Sufi faction among the jurists.

The reign of Selim I (1512–20) had already seen some clashes between jurists and Sufis: this was natural, not only because of the threat now posed to the Ottomans by the Shiite, Sufi-led Safavids, but also because the dervishes often represented the interests of the Muslim families who had conquered eastern Europe, and were now at odds with the sultans themselves. Later in the sixteenth century remarkably few jurists appear to have been active Sufis. Faroqhi has shown that, out of the first 100 jurists mentioned by an early seventeenth-century source in a chapter devoted to the reign of Murad III (1574–95), only five are listed as members of Sufi brotherhoods, and only two had Sufi elders for fathers.[37] Moreover, it seems that most jurists came from families who specialized in this profession, and that this had always been the case (contrary to an old-fashioned view that it was an aspect of later decline). Faroqhi concludes that the two institutions appear to have stayed quite separate. The leaders of the brotherhoods, however, had to be confirmed in their positions by the chief jurist of the empire.

In the seventeenth century one faction among the scholar-jurists made a determined attack on the Sufi brotherhoods. Early in the reign of Muhammad IV (1648–87) the leader of this faction persuaded the government to suppress the dervish fraternities. There was immediate chaos: in eastern Turkey there was widespread rebellion, and the empire was almost destroyed by famine, mounting prices and the complete failure of its navy to cope with a threat from Venice. The sultan was obliged to give the post of grand vizier (chief minister) to the great administrator Muhammad Köprülü (d. 1661), whose energetic measures, including the use of the Janissaries to accomplish the suppression of the anti-Sufi faction, saved the day. He was succeeded in his position by relatives: at the end of the century we find one of these combining the function of grand vizier with membership of the brotherhood of the Whirling Dervishes, who in spite of their famous dance were seen as more academic and respectable than many of their rivals.

Sufi lodges

We can obtain some idea of life in the Sufi lodges and its relation to the empire as a whole from Faroqhi's work on the accounts which record their income and expenditure. The books of one medium-sized lodge in Konya, with twenty-four employees, covering the years 1566–1600, show how both revenue and wages consisted of money and grain. The income came from the local peasantry, according to the foundation's original endowment. (It had been set up by Ibn 'Arabi's chief disciple, Sadr al-Din of Konya, whose allegedly pro-Christian followers we encountered above.) An elder had administrators beneath him for the purpose of making the system work. Revenue paid for their salaries, and also paid employees who led the worship in the institution's mosque and gave the summons to the faithful. Six people were paid to engage in pious recitation. Others were employed to run the kitchen and look after the library and the founder's tomb. Apart from wages, expenditure was mainly upon food and maintenance. A lot of money was spent on meat and making bread. In this area 14 per cent of the dues produced by agriculture would go to pious foundations of this kind.[38]

More detailed information is available in sixteenth- and seventeenth-century documents relating to the lodge of Seyitgazi in north-western Turkey. This building has impressed art historians with its well-endowed facilities for preparing food and meetings and providing accommodation. It had a gardener, two millers, a butcher and a music master, in addition to the usual cooks. The lodge lent money at interest – a practice normally considered to be against Islamic law, though in the Ottoman period a reinterpretation allowed this to be done by religious foundations. In the late sixteenth century about 17 per cent of local householders might be in debt to the lodge, paying interest at around 13 per cent. It obtained income from the rents of shops, and from the fines imposed on criminals and owners of stray animals. In addition to the revenue from the original endowment, the government granted the lodge market dues from 1525 onwards. The principal source of income, however, was the grain produced by the local peasants. Horses and cattle would be donated by visitors to the tomb of the legendary Muslim warrior who had given his name to the lodge and its town. The estates of Sufis who died in the lodge also belonged to it: they were considered to have worldly goods in their lifetime, but not to have heirs in their families.

The Sufis who lived in the lodge were not paid salaries (as opposed to employees, such as the teachers in the college attached to the lodge, and the men who looked after the mosque and the tomb), but were given allowances in food and clothing. The amount of meat eaten was low, but cheese, cream and honey would be offered to visitors (who averaged eight a day). It is important to note that there are huge gaps in our knowledge: for example, we do not know at what point the lodge was taken over by the Bektashi brotherhood.[39]

The fortunes of the lodge of Seyitgazi declined considerably with the economic difficulties of the Ottoman Empire in the seventeenth century. These economic difficulties might perhaps be connected with the role of the craft guilds, which are in any case of interest to the student of Sufism. In the fourteenth century the empire had inherited the Irano-Islamic tradition of 'youngmanliness', and this was particularly strong in Turkey, with the military duties of war against the infidel. The Ottomans, however, could not really tolerate so dangerous an institution in their bureaucratic state, and from the fourteenth century onwards it was fragmented and channelled into the craft guilds. Thus Sufism and the ideal of 'youngmanliness' were used to subordinate the apprentices to their masters. The threefold pattern (saying–sword–drinking) encountered in early fourteenth-century Iran reappears in the sixteenth-century Ottoman Empire – but now we are told that the 'men of the sword' have the most difficult task.[40] This conforms to the greater importance of the military at this time. By the seventeenth century the ancient threefold arrangement of desire, strength and their controller is explicitly related to the work of the apprentice subject to his master's commands.[41]

Recently some economic historians have taken the view that the conservatism of the Ottoman guilds and their failure to match European developments from the second half of the sixteenth century might have constituted a reason for the empire's decline. We may also speculate that this ideology within the guilds might have helped the empire as it managed to hold itself together during its decline for such an extraordinarily long time.

The Timurid Empire in India

It is advisable to use the term 'Timurid' for the dynasty which conquered and ruled India from the early sixteenth century onwards. Normally the designation 'Mogul' (or 'Mughal') is applied. But what is important is to see the continuity and development from the Timurids of fifteenth-century Herat to those of sixteenth-century India, not only in the splendour of their painting and architecture, but in their espousal of Sufism and the extreme devotion of some Sufis to them.

The Timurid emperors in India, while having an absolute claim on all revenue produced by their territory, distributed it to a small ruling class (princes, nobles and officials), sometimes in salaries but usually in assignments of land. The emperor in person, on the advice of the chief scholar-jurist, made grants to people considered deserving or in need, mainly men of religion (jurists and Sufis). These grants represented a comparatively small share of the total revenue: about 5 per cent in 1578.[42] They would usually be continued in the family of the recipient when he died, but it is important to remember that all assignments of land were provisional and subject to the conditions imposed by the sovereign.

Knowledge of this economic background is essential to an understanding of the religious quarrels of sixteenth- and seventeenth-century India. Central to these is a tendency to use Sufism to argue that different religions have much in common or conceal a single higher truth. This tendency had already appeared in the ideas of the fifteenth-century Hindi poet Kabir: Hindu and Sufi traditions are combined in a rejection of external religion for the sake of pure devotion to God. A similar rejection of Muslim and Hindu outer forms is found in the teachings of Guru Nanak (d. 1539), seen by the Sikhs as the first founder of their religion. What will concern us, however, is the spectacular universalism of the Emperor Akbar (1556–1605).

The Emperor Akbar

Akbar grew up against an Indo-European background of court life. The members of the court were divided into three categories, carefully distinguished: the military, the religious and scholarly, and the category of pleasure (painters, musicians etc.) This last category is included by Dumézil in the lowest of his three concepts or 'functions', that of fertility, in its agricultural and erotic aspects. Akbar showed himself unable to make progress in formal studies, and remained illiterate. As emperor he demonstrated a remarkable interest in religions other than Islam, and instituted a 'house of worship', to which men of all religious traditions came to put their views.

He invited Jesuit missionaries to visit him. Some of the letters which they sent after arriving at his court have survived. At first the Jesuits were impressed by his apparent desire to become a Christian, but later they were disheartened by his being under the influence of opium, cannabis and alcohol during religious discussions. One letter, not available to earlier historians, presents Akbar as a trickster, not Christian, Hindu or Muslim.[43] Akbar managed to impose himself on the jurists of the empire as the ultimate referee in the case of their disagreement. Eventually he founded a brotherhood of his own, with himself as its elder, dedicated to the ideal of 'divine affirmation of God's Uniqueness' (*tawhid-i ilahi*). This was seen as a new religion, although Akbar obviously realized that he could not simply abolish Islam as the official religion of his empire. Needless to say, he greatly antagonized the Muslim jurists by his policy of peaceful coexistence between different faiths and concessions towards their adherents. Notably, he revived old Iranian, pre-Islamic feast days; and, since he disliked the use of the Islamic era and lunar calendar, he brought in a new era starting with the year of his own accession, together with a solar calendar, using the old Persian names for the months. Members of his brotherhood were told by him not to eat meat.

Abu 'l-Fadl

In order to understand Akbar it is necessary to look at the Sufi views of his biographer and close associate, Abu 'l-Fadl (1551–1602). Abu 'l-Fadl presents himself as Akbar's disciple: he saw the sovereign as the Perfect Man, and the elder not only of his brotherhood but of all his subjects. However, it would be more appropriate to see Abu 'l-Fadl as Akbar's instructor in Sufism. Largely through his father, he had obtained a knowledge of the later development of Islamic philosophy's 'Oriental Illumination' school in Iran. This tradition was strongly marked by its royalist elements and emphasis on Iran's pre-Islamic past. Thus Abu 'l-Fadl sees royalty as a light which comes to kings directly from God. He wrote a history of Akbar and his ancestors, which has been admirably analysed by Marshall Hodgson.[44] In it, as Hodgson observes, one finds two separate strands: the Greek philosophical tradition and the Sufism of Ibn 'Arabi. This is what we have already found in the case of Jami at the Timurid court of Herat in the fifteenth century. As in Jami's work, there is no attempt to produce a synthesis of the two traditions. Like the Sufis who looked directly to the Timurid princes of the fifteenth century, Abu 'l-Fadl concentrates on the king himself, and does not concern himself with lesser figures.

Abu 'l-Fadl's personal opinions were obviously a long way from mainline Islam. He evidently regarded the belief that mankind began with Adam 7000 years before as fit only for vulgar and ignorant fools. The world was either eternal (the philosophers' position, condemned in

Islam) or extremely ancient, as indicated by Chinese and Indian records. He felt that the Jesuit missionaries were getting the better of the argument in their disputations with Muslim scholars. The Jesuits' letters present him as their most sympathetic ally, even accepting that Jesus was God's Son (a position bitterly rejected by Islam) and defending Christian scripture. Eventually, however, the Jesuits realized that, like Akbar, he was not genuinely interested in being fully instructed in Christian teachings.

Ahmad Sirhindi

Ahmad Sirhindi (1564–1624), born in the city of Sirhind in northern India, was an extremely original and controversial Indian Sufi figure. He has been the subject of much debate among modern Muslims, and many misleading views have been put forward concerning him. These have been comprehensively rebutted in the revolutionary work of Yohanan Friedmann.

In his early years, before becoming a Sufi, Sirhindi wrote a savage attack on Shiism, declaring that the Shiites were unbelievers, who should be killed. Later, after turning to Sufism, he was to become much less hostile to Shiite views, and eventually conceded a special role to 'Ali and the rest of the Twelve Leaders in the hierarchy of God's friends. In his early life he also worked as an assistant to Abu 'l-Fadl, although he was always vehemently opposed to the Greek philosophical tradition and religions other than Islam. In 1599 or 1600 he joined the Naqshbandi brotherhood, which he extolled as superior to other brotherhoods in its rejection of dancing and listening to music. His originality lies largely in his doctrines (expressed in letters) concerning the thousandth anniversary of Islam. One thousand lunar years had now elapsed since the start of Muhammad's prophetic activity, and, Sirhindi claimed, this meant that dramatic changes would soon occur. He taught that above the 'Muhammadan Reality' (in Persian, *haqiqat-i Muhammadi*), which previous Sufis had seen as the highest of all realities beneath God, there was a 'Koranic Reality', and above that the 'Reality of the Ka'ba' (the cube-shaped shrine at Mecca). A thousand years after Muhammad's death, the Muhammadan Reality had to rise up to the place of the Reality of the Ka'ba, and acquire the new name of the Ahmadan Reality (*haqiqat-i Ahmadi*). We must observe that Ahmad was both an alternative name of the Prophet Muhammad and the name of Sirhindi himself. Sirhindi declared that Islam now required a 'Renewer' (*mujaddid*). He also declared that he was a disciple of God without any mediation. In the final stage of the Sufi journey, he said, the mystic descends from his experience with God into the world and exercises a function akin to that of the prophets. Although such a friend of God cannot be the equal of a prophet in general, he may surpass him in some aspect (as, for example, may a martyr).

With this last doctrine Sirhindi places himself in the camp of Ibn 'Arabi, although the two thinkers are often contrasted. It is frequently imagined that Sirhindi replaced Ibn 'Arabi's system with his own. Thus it is thought that Ibn 'Arabi's teaching of the 'unity of existence' (*wahdat al-wujud*) was to give way to Sirhindi's teaching of the 'unity of contemplation' (or witnessing, testimony, *wahdat al-shuhud*).

The issue is much more complicated. Sirhindi sometimes accepts Ibn 'Arabi's doctrines and sometimes rejects them. It would appear that Sirhindi, like many modern writers, wrongly believed that Ibn 'Arabi and his followers, in professing a belief in the 'unity of existence', meant that there was only one entity in existence (the position of pure monism). As Sirhindi puts it, they would see nothing but the sun, and deny the existence of the stars. Sirhindi considers them to be blinded by ecstasy, and consequently to be excused. There is a higher stage, that of the 'unity of contemplation', which means seeing God's Oneness (*yaki*) and looking at nothing else, but knowing that other things do exist (like seeing only the sun, while knowing that the stars exist). The highest stage would be like seeing both the sun and the stars.

Sirhindi, while holding extremely dubious views himself, was very stern towards others. As is common among Muslim scholars, he condemned women who sacrificed animals on the tombs of leading Sufis. He said that Hindus should be humiliated and that the killing of a Jew was always profitable to Islam. He obtained material support for his own lodge from the dignitaries of the empire, and would write letters asking for official posts to be given to his friends. For a time he was imprisoned, because of his audacious claims, by the Emperor Jahangir (1605–27), and then released, but there is little evidence to suggest, as is sometimes believed, that the emperor was eventually converted to his views. In his own time he was criticized both from a conventional Sufi standpoint, for his arrogance, and from an extremist one, for maintaining that prophethood was generally superior to 'friendship with God'. Later in the seventeenth century his doctrines were often condemned, and in 1679 the chief jurist of the empire formally prohibited the diffusion of some of them. But his followers survived, and in the twentieth century he is seen as the champion of mainline Islam.

Prince Dara Shukuh

A very different picture is afforded by the Sufi prince Dara Shukuh (1615–59), who was heir apparent to the Timurid throne. A member of the Qadiri brotherhood and a follower of Ibn 'Arabi's school, he took a keen interest in Hindu mystics, and himself translated the Upanishads into Persian. He believed that all religions taught an identical higher truth.

These tendencies were used against him in a war of succession with his brothers, which he lost. His religious opinions were then used to secure his condemnation to death. They are most clearly set out in his short treatise, *The Place Where the Two Seas Meet* (*Majma' al-bahrayn*). The two seas are Sufism and the religion of the 'unitarians of India' (*muwahhidan-i Hind*). Dara Shukuh's work is largely devoted to enumerating the parts of the universe. Here, since the Hindus on the one hand and the Muslims (as the heirs to the Greeks and ancient Iran) on the other share a common Indo-European legacy, there are naturally many points of resemblance.

In specifically religious matters Dara Shukuh is on less firm ground. He presents Hindu mystics as teaching that God is the Spirit of the world just as the world is his body. Dara Shukuh should have known that although some Sufis had composed verses to this effect such poetic exaggeration ought not to be taken as a literal expression of Sufism's teachings concerning God's self-manifestation in the universe. He also tries to find Islamic materials to justify the belief that there will be an infinite recurrence of historical cycles, with an exact reduplication of people and events. There is a saying attributed to Muhammad which supports this view, but Dara Shukuh must have realized that it was hardly typical of Sufi doctrine. Elsewhere, in his exposition of Ibn 'Arabi's theory of the 'unity of existence', Dara Shukuh seems to make the same mistake as Sirhindi, believing that it means that God is the only entity. However, instead of rejecting this idea or trying to transcend it, Dara Shukuh gives it his whole-hearted approval.[45]

Emperor Awrangzib

Dara Shukuh's brother, Awrangzib, who was responsible for his execution and now ruled as emperor, had markedly anti-Hindu policies and viewed the killing of Shiites as commendable. He was a man of great piety, who spent much time in religious reading and prayer, and stopped music and dancing at his court. He was praised as a Sufi elder, and would visit leading Sufis, while insisting on respect for their tombs. His policies cannot be linked to the influence of Sirhindi, some of whose opinions he had officially condemned. In general, his religiosity would appear to have been of a highly conventional kind, as opposed to that of Akbar and Dara Shukuh. His zeal for oppressing and humiliating the Hindus is often considered to have been a major cause of the chaos in which he left the empire at his death in 1707, although some modern Muslims deny this charge, which they see as an invention of British colonialism.

The Safavid Empire in Iran

The Safavid Empire in Iran was a most extraordinary state. It was founded by a Sufi leader, who needed a Sufi brotherhood beneath him to accomplish this remarkable feat. As time went on the Sufi character of the empire would be reduced and finally abolished. As in other Muslim states, the ruler's subjects either paid taxes or received them as military commanders and men of religion. What is striking is that at the beginning of the Safavid Empire the military commanders held their positions as the ruler's Sufi disciples.

Isma'il

The Safavid brotherhood in north-western Iran had changed in the fifteenth century, with the adoption of Shiite views and militaristic aims, and enjoyed the support of the Turkoman nomads. One leader, and then his son and successor, had been killed in battle. Now the grandson, Isma'il, was to exact a terrible revenge.

Born in 1487, he became the leader of the brotherhood at the age of seven and began his astonishing military career at the age of twelve. Contact with the tribesmen in eastern Turkey had been kept through the intermediary of 'deputies' (*khulafa'*), and they now rallied to him. Together, they conquered Iran, and Isma'il formally and brutally imposed Twelver Shiism as the official faith there. He ferociously suppressed all other Sufi brotherhoods which refused to accept Shiism. Thus the organization which had been founded in southern Iran by Kazaruni in the eleventh century was simply wiped out, with the massacre of 4000 people. It lived on outside Iran, because it had become a major international network, which offered banking facilities for merchants. Other brotherhoods were either crushed as effective forces, or left Iran, or professed Shiism. The Safavid movement was threatening to conquer the Ottoman Empire, since it possessed widespread tribal support in eastern Turkey and attracted followers by its generous distribution of booty. But the Ottomans defeated Isma'il in battle in 1514, and he was never the same again. He spent his time in the traditional royal pastimes of drinking and hunting until his death in 1524.

Leading historians still maintain that Isma'il thought he was God incarnate, and call his rule a theocracy. The word 'theocracy' is one that it is always best to avoid. It is often used to mean rule by specialists in religious affairs, while literally it means rule by a god. There is evidence that some of the Safavids' nomadic followers believed their leaders to be divine. Modern scholars have asserted that Isma'il's poems constitute claims to be an incarnation of God. If we examine the verses quoted to support this view, however, we find that there is no indication of 'incarnation', but on the contrary the usual Sufi tradition of God's self-manifestation, coupled with the Shiite theme of the mystic's becoming a Leader just beneath God. The poet identifies himself with a number of entities (legendary kings, a ring, a pearl) in a manner familiar to the reader of verses composed by Rumi in the thirteenth century. It is in this context that Isma'il says:

> The secret of 'I am the Truth (*haqq*)' is hidden in this heart of
> mine
> For I am the absolute Truth and what I say is the truth

Here the use of the word *haqq* in its literal meaning of 'verbally uttered truth' weakens the charge of self-deification, which in any case is countered by the same poem's assertion that the author is the least of slaves. In a similar composition Isma'il declares:

> I am the eye of God I am the eye of God the eye of God
> Come now and see the Truth O blind man who have lost your way
> I am that absolute doer of whom they tell
> I am the commander of the sun and moon
> My existence is the House of God know for sure
> Prostration to me is incumbent upon you in the evening and at
> daybreak[46]

Now the order to the blind man weakens the suggestion that the word for 'eye' ('*ayn*) should be taken in the sense of 'quintessence'. Similarly, the poet's self-identification with the House of God – the shrine of the Ka'ba at Mecca, in the direction of which Muslims prostrate themselves in the dawn and evening worship – leads one to question the use of the verse as evidence that Isma'il insisted on being worshipped as a god through prostration. We have seen prostration before the Sufi elder in India. It is certainly against Islamic law, since prostration is reserved for the worship of God, but it does not follow that Isma'il claimed to be divine.

Isma'il did nonetheless leave the Safavid Empire an uncomfortable revolutionary legacy. He had led his nomadic followers to believe that the messianic return of the Mahdi, the 'divinely guided one' was about to happen, whether in his own person or not. These tribesmen were now an important military elite, distinguished by their red turbans, which gave them the nickname Qizilbash (redhead). They continued to represent a radical and volatile threat to the dynasty which they had put in power, and which now tried to neutralize them. In the course of the sixteenth century the Qizilbash soldiers were transformed into special guards beneath the ruler. 'Abbas I (1587–1629) managed to reorganize the army in such a way as to produce a drastic reduction of their influence. He massacred those members of the Safavid brotherhood who represented its oldest traditions, and ensured that others would be given menial jobs. Accordingly, in the seventeenth century the Safavid Sufis became prison officers, porters and cleaners.

The philosopher Sadra

At this time there was a rich flowering of the Greek philosophical tradition in Iran. Moreover, the philosophers, under their usual royal patronage, were involved in the translation of Sanskrit works. We now encounter a thinker of great stature, Sadra of Shiraz (d. 1640), who ranks as the most impressive unifier of the ideas that were familiar to the Muslim world. As a philosopher, he tackled anew the problem of reconciling the 'wisdom of Oriental Illumination', Shiite theology and the Sufism of Ibn 'Arabi. A somewhat mechanical combination had been put forward in the fifteenth century, but it was evident that a real synthesis would demand a dramatic change of perspective. This Sadra provided, thereby making himself the founder of Islamic existentialism.

He began by declaring that existence precedes essence. God first generates what is called 'the self-unfolding existence' (*al-wujud al-munbasit*): the first self-manifestation of God to himself and the shadow of God in all things. Then he says 'Be!' and in doing so emits his Breath. This Breath is the highest intelligible substance. It generates prime matter as its shadow. So existence for Sadra corresponds to light in the 'philosophy of Oriental Illumination': there is a hierarchy without sharp dividing lines.

In this perspective provided by Sadra the universe can find its fulfilment, according to the dynamic thrust of a new and original doctrine: that of 'substantive movement' (*haraka jawhariyya*), which means that a perpetual movement affects the very substance of things, in the upward progression from prime matter to Ibn 'Arabi's Perfect Man. The whole universe is simultaneously in a position of being what it is and becoming something else, in conformity with Sadra's principle of the 'ambiguity' (*tashkik*) of existence. It is according to this principle that he, like many Shiite theologians, can declare that man is free, since freedom and determinism are the same. Such things are known to a man by intuitive experience, which can never be disproved by correct philosophical arguments. Observations of this kind have led to disagreement about whether Sadra should be seen primarily as a mystical thinker. In one major study of Sadra Fazlur Rahman tried to argue that on the contrary he should be seen as a profoundly rational figure. Subsequently, however, Rahman changed his position, maintaining that Sadra is torn between rationalism and Ibn 'Arabi's mysticism, unable to achieve a real reconciliation of the two.[47] It is noteworthy that Sadra made open attacks on libertine dervishes, lamenting their influence, not only on the masses, but on craftsmen in particular.

Clashes with jurists and libertine dervishes
In 'Abbas II (1642–66) the Sufis found a ruler who gave them extremely generous financial support. After his death they were tolerated for a time, in spite of attacks coming from jurists, which may be compared with the attacks made by Ottoman lawyers in the same period. A French traveller explained this hostility as due to the neglect of social duties produced by Sufism (the same line taken by Sadra against the libertine dervishes). He gives an account of an incident which he witnessed in the Iranian capital, Isfahan, when a preacher declared in public that the Sufis should be killed: after the sermon five or six Sufis in the audience beat him up, claiming that an advocate of violence could hardly object.[48]

In Iran the libertine dervishes were generally called Haydaris, after an Iranian seen as the first founder of their loosely knit associations, Haydar (d. 1291). Another French traveller of this time shows how they had great influence preaching to merchants and artisans in the bazaars.[49] They would be dressed only in sheepskins and goatskins. In contrast to them we find the Sufis themselves, who now, given the degeneration of the Safavid brotherhood, were usually in what was called the Ni'matullahi 'path', after its founder, Ni'mat Allah (d. 1431). This, like the Haydaris, had accepted Shiism. Its spiritual leaders were now in India. During this period the Haydaris and the Ni'matullahis were assigned to different wards of Iranian cities. They were in effect opposing factions, whose mutual hostility seems to have perpetuated older rivalries between different parts of these cities. At fixed times of the year they would engage in ritual battles, which frequently produced serious casualties. Fights of this kind, like the English village tug of war, appear to belong to an archaic heritage.

At the end of the seventeenth century the jurists were victorious in their campaign against the Sufis. This was largely the achievement of one man, Majlisi (d. 1699). He was the son of a famous scholar who had been both a jurist and a Sufi, and he himself pursued a variety of studies when young, taking an interest in philosophy and mysticism. Later, however, he abandoned these fields and devoted himself to collecting the sayings attributed to the Shiites' early Leaders. He declared that his father had not really been a Sufi at all, but had pretended to be one in order to draw the Sufis out of their errors. This peculiar manifestation of filial piety has been greeted with scepticism by modern Iranian scholars.

Majlisi became the chief jurist of the empire and, with the accession of the devout Sultan Husayn (1694–1722), obtained enormous personal power. He was able to have the Sufis expelled from the capital. Majlisi insisted on full obedience to kings and declared that, if they are tyrannical, one must hide one's true opinions. He praised his royal masters in the most fulsome terms and received considerable financial support from them. His hostility was not confined to Sufis, but was also directed towards philosophers, Christians, Jews, Mazdeans and Sunni Muslims. His intolerant zeal led him to persecute all of these, and insist that non-Shiites be made to convert. In the Sunni populations of the outlying parts of the empire he provoked a reaction that was to bring the Safavid state down. Such was the bizarre fate of a dynasty which had come to power through Sufism only to reject it in the end.

Outside the empires

A survey of Sufism in the sixteenth and seventeenth centuries would be misleading if it did not also look at Sufis outside the three great empires. The areas examined here will be the kingdom of Bijapur in south-western India, Morocco and Chinese Turkestan.

The kingdom of Bijapur

From 1490 to 1686 an independent dynasty, that of the 'Adil-Shahi sultanate, ruled over a state in south-western India with Bijapur as its capital. This state was Shiite until 1583, when it changed to mainstream Sunni Islam. Under Shiite rule conditions were not favourable for Sufism, but afterwards a number of Sufis came and settled. These have been the subject of an important study by Richard Eaton, which is marred by over-use of nineteenth-century hagiographies and a complete acceptance of Trimingham's socio-historical reconstruction of fifteenth-century developments, transposed to this period of Bijapur's history.

Eaton's work is valuable when it allows the earliest materials, notably the recorded conversations of the Sufi teachers, to speak for themselves. One notes with interest the anti-Shiite sentiments of the leading Sufi Shah Sibghat Allah (d. 1606; the title 'shah' is now common among Indian Sufi masters), who even sent his followers to attack the annual Shiite procession of mourning for 'Ali's son Husayn. The resulting violence brought about the Sufi elder's house arrest on the orders of the sultan, who wisely gave him a generous allowance for a pilgrimage to Mecca. Sibghat Allah had already been a good friend of the sultan's treasurer, and wrote letters of recommendation for people who wanted government posts.

This activity was particularly characteristic of another Sufi elder, Hashim 'Alawi (d. 1646), who, we are told by one of his deputies, would receive a large number of job hunters every day. Sometimes this was just a case of people who wanted employment as servants working for nobles. He acquired 5500 followers. Hashim had interesting remarks to make about the scholar-jurists of Islam. One of these had criticized the Sufi practice of the oath of allegiance (*bay'a*) between elder and disciple. Hashim answered by saying that jurisprudence was useful for little except the details of personal hygiene. On another occasion, however, he observed that the specialist in formal knowledge and the Sufi are complementary to one another, like the farmer and the oil presser.

One Sufi leader of sixteenth-century Bijapur, Burhan al-Din Janam (d. 1597), a member of the Chishti brotherhood, which we have already encountered in fourteenth-century India, is noteworthy for his violent hostility to Hindu ascetics, who, he says, perform their worship merely through ostentation and in order to deceive the public into giving them alms. The obtaining of money, however, is formally justified by one of Sibghat Allah's deputies, who, when his own disciples criticized his acceptance of a grant from the sultan, replied that the money could now reach the people instead of just going into the treasury. He himself used to be carried around in a litter like a noble.

Morocco

The history of Morocco from the fifteenth to the seventeenth century is marked by great political instability. There were Christian invasions and repeated collapses of central authority. From 1510 to 1630 a dynasty which claimed descent from Muhammad, the Sa'dis, held power. They persecuted some Sufis and allied themselves with others. From 1603 there was disintegration and division of power, until 1668, when another line of rulers, also claiming descent from Muhammad, and known as the 'Alawis, managed to install itself. Modern writers have put much stress on the supposed importance of this 'rise of Muhammad's descendants', but one leading specialist, Jacques Berque, has pointed out that it is hardly new, since such descent was claimed by much earlier dynasties. We may observe that the tendency of men of religion, whether Sufis or not, to claim descent from Muhammad while rising in the social scale was already widespread in the Muslim world.

This period of Moroccan history has commonly been called that of the Maraboutic Crisis, from the French word *marabout*, which French colonial sociologists used to designate a leading Muslim mystic. The word represents the Arabic *murabit*, which in North Africa has meant not only a man of religion but also a man of war. For the word *ribat* (from the same root), which means a hospice, and is one of the terms used in particular to designate a Sufi lodge, also means a fortified outpost in the war against unbelievers. The trouble, as Berque has shown, is that French colonial historians employed the adjective *maraboutique* to invent a vast ocean of mysticism, whereas the evidence for this period often indicates purely formal, academic, religious activity. Besides, there is nothing to suggest a sudden new flowering of Sufi power at this time. We may remark that 'crisis' is not a very good word to use to cover a couple of centuries. In short, the concept of Maraboutic Crisis is an illusion.

There are, nevertheless, fascinating episodes in Moroccan history in which Sufism plays a part. Such is the case of Abu Mahalli (d. 1613), often thought to be a marabout. In fact he is a student of many different disciplines, and much concerned with the political troubles of his time. He writes a scurrilous attack on one leading Sufi with whom he has been closely connected, accusing him of misconduct with married women. But for Abu Mahalli the Sufi impostor is only one type among many of those who falsely rise above other men, such as academics or rulers. Abu Mahalli's works show him tormented by the problem of his own personal intervention in politics. Eventually, he starts a revolt and becomes a king in the city of Marrakesh, but reigns only for a year before being killed in battle.

In the chaos between 1603 and 1668 much power was exercised by the lodge of Dila' in central Morocco. Its masters were not really marabouts in the French colonial sense, but academics and warrior-politicians. They served as mediators between Islamic civilization as a whole and the rustic tribesmen of the Atlas mountains. They would dispense hospitality according to class: vegetables for the poorest, chicken for those in the middle and mutton for the elite. The evidence shows that they specialized in law, grammar or poetry: if one of them was singled out to be called a *murabit*, it meant that he was different from the rest in his exceptional unworldliness.

Modern western publications call all these people 'saints', as they do the academic Sufi 'Abd al-Qadir, of the city of Fez, who died in 1680. We have a long biography of him, written by his son. The father is presented as living not off the gifts of students and princes, but through his profession as a copier of manuscripts. He is a true exponent of the path of 'blame', not in the sense of behaving scandalously in order to attract the blame of others, but rather in an ironic inner detachment from the respectable society of which he is a part. One may observe that even when a biography of this kind is written, as in this case, within five years of the subject's death, it is still really a string of edifying conventional touches.

Chinese (or East) Turkestan

In what is now part of north-west China (Xinjiang), Muslim princes who claimed descent from Chinggis Khan were still ruling in the sixteenth century. They now represented urban Muslim civilization against the surrounding nomads. The nomads were weakened for a time, and so Islam flourished. They were obliged to pay tribute, and so there was plenty of wealth to finance the construction of mosques and colleges, and to subsidize Sufis. Consequently some Sufis came from what is now Soviet Central Asia and established good relations with the local princes. In particular, one Muhammad Sharif (d. 1555) actually founded a brotherhood which embodied the celebrated Uwaysi tradition, the practice of seeking guidance from the spirit of an elder who is either physically absent or dead. To turn this into a brotherhood of living people in day-to-day contact with one another might well seem contradictory, but during the rapid expansion of Islam in sixteenth-century East Turkestan it made some sense. There was no particularly distinguished local Islamic past to which people could relate, apart from some long-dead royal martyrs. These were now conveniently integrated into an imaginary history of the Uwaysi brotherhood, compiled by a certain Ahmad Uzgani (date of death unknown). He claimed that the spirits of the previous leaders of the brotherhood had told their life stories to him. The lives were sometimes those of legendary Islamic figures whose graves had been 'discovered' – by Muhammad Sharif, it would appear – in some cases on the site of pre-Islamic shrines. Of particular interest are the lives of four obviously imaginary women mystics, who correspond to the figures of Mary the mother of Jesus on the one hand, and of the legendary converted courtesans of Christian antiquity on the other, and thereby validate our analysis of reflections of these figures in earlier Muslim hagiography.

The first woman is called Servant (in Central Asia this was believed to be the meaning of the name Mary). Her mother is called Mary. Like Mary the mother of Jesus in Islamic tradition, she is born to parents who have long awaited a child, is frightened by meeting a man and is cleared of an accusation of fornication. The second woman is called Pious. Her father forces her to marry, but she prays for deliverance and her husband dies. She makes a withered tree bear fruit (as God does for the mother of Jesus in Islamic tradition). A third woman is called Hazel-nut. She is a fine singer. Her father is a libertine dervish, who forces her to become a prostitute. After twenty years she repents. Her miraculous burial is related by a dervish (just as the miraculous burial of Mary of Egypt is related by a monk). A fourth woman is called Knowing. A singer, she is given to a tyrannical king, and prays for deliverance. The king dies. She repents of her profession, and marries an elderly and impotent mystic. While the first two biographies are reflections of Jesus' mother, and the third corresponds to the Christian legends of the penitent courtesans, the fourth combines both of the contrasting figures that we have seen above: the asexual wife and the singer-entertainer who repents.[50]

The fortunes of the nascent Uwaysi brotherhood in East Turkestan were short-lived. They disappeared as the local Naqshbandi Sufis took power in the region from their Mongol patrons. In 1570 a family of Naqshbandi leaders, known as the Khojas ('masters'), began to rule from the city of Yarkand, obtaining sovereignty thanks to tribal support. Their descendants continued to reign until the Chinese conquest in 1758, and were to rise in revolt again in the nineteenth and twentieth centuries.

4 INTO THE MODERN WORLD

THE EIGHTEENTH CENTURY

Eighteenth-century Islam has not been studied much, and its specifically religious aspects have hardly been investigated at all. This is presumably because this period has traditionally been seen as one of decline, too late for the admirer of classical Islamic culture, and too early for the champion of modernity. The lack of research obliges us to take an approach which differs from that pursued in the preceding chapters. First we shall look at the general background. Then we shall look at three leading Sufis: one from the beginning of the century, in the Arab world; one from the middle, in India; and one from the end, in Iran.

The background

The fortunes of Islam in the eighteenth century are marked by failure. The Ottoman Empire experienced both defeat and victory when fighting the Austrians, but lost the Crimea to Russia in 1774. In Iran the Safavid Empire collapsed in 1722, because of its policies of anti-Sufi and anti-Sunni persecution. Chaos and disaster followed repeatedly in the course of the century, with massacres and extreme depopulation of the cities. In India there was a resurgence of Hindu power, and then the new ruler of Iran, Nadir Shah (1736–47), sacked Delhi in 1739, effectively signalling the end of Timurid dominion. In the second half of the century the British took over on a large scale, notably following the notorious and catastrophic 'plundering of Bengal'.

It is not surprising, then, that this period has been viewed as dominated by decline. Many modern scholars have thought that whereas Europe had the Enlightenment, Islam went into regression. Against this view, some recent writers have argued that the Ottoman

Empire did not go into absolute decline, or regress in relation to its own past, but declined only in some areas where it was in competition with European progress. In trade the merchants were able to hold their own, whereas the craftsmen (for reasons which have been suggested above) went under, unable to keep up with European advances. Moreover, there was an important rise in the power of provincial urban notables, which prefigured the modern emergence of independent states such as Egypt and Syria, and could be seen as a positive development. As regards Iran, there was a significant improvement in the thought of the Shiite jurists, then largely concentrated in Iraq: they rejected the habit of simply looking for the answers to legal problems in existing compendia, and turned instead to individual initiative in deciding questions by the use of reason. Thus the jurists of Shiite Iran gave themselves power, responsibility and experience, to be exercised to dramatic effect in our own time. Islam in India produced a major thinker, Shah Wali Allah of Delhi (1703–62), who will be discussed below as a Sufi, but who is also of immense importance to contemporary South Asian Muslims for his incisive ideas in the fields of law, politics and sociology.

How did Sufism fit into all this? Given the present state of research it is impossible to say. The Muslim scholars, the *'ulama'*, whether particularly specialized in Sufism or not, could be found among the wealthiest inhabitants of the towns. They would supplement their incomes by holding Sufi meetings in private houses. Enormous allowances were paid to the leaders of the Sufi brotherhoods out of pious endowments. Whereas the rector of the Azhar, the main academic institution of Egypt, was paid 19,870 *paras* a year, and a poor worker might receive only fifteen a day, the head of the Bakri brotherhood would get 260,000, and another important Sufi leader in Cairo 148,635. Such an income could be doubled by holding another official post at the same time. Yet more revenue could be obtained by being an administrator of pious foundations, and then could be invested in land, houses and shops.[1]

A threat to this cosy existence now came from the Arabian peninsula: the reformer Muhammad ibn 'Abd al-Wahhab (1703–87) engaged in a vigorous rejection of Sufism itself, and the extreme veneration of Muhammad which accompanied it. He allied himself with the Sa'udi family which now rules in Arabia, and which launched a violent assault on the tombs of leading Muslims of the past. The Wahhabi movement which bears his name is today an important counterweight to Sufism.

A valuable picture of the dervishes of the Ottoman Empire has been left by Ignatius Mouragea d'Ohsson, in the fourth volume of his *Tableau général de l'empire ottoman*, published in 1791. One noteworthy aspect is the isolated character of the Naqshbandi brotherhood, which d'Ohsson sees as a mere religious association, as opposed to the other brotherhoods, which he calls 'orders'. This brotherhood includes members of all classes of society, who just take part in extra prayers and recitation of the Koran, gathering together for this purpose in every urban neighbourhood of the empire. Other brotherhoods have more colourful practices: for example, the Rifa'is – so called after their supposed founder who died in 1182, and known in the West as the Howling Dervishes because of their loud 'remembrance of God' – attract attention by putting heated iron instruments in their mouths. The Whirling Dervishes continue, according to d'Ohsson, to retain the special affection of the powerful. In their assemblies they pray not only for the ruling dynasty, but for the grand vizier, the military and civil administrators, and the scholar-jurists. The Bektashis alone perform their exercises behind closed doors. (However dangerous their activities may have been, Faroqhi has shown that they retained good relations with the government throughout the eighteenth century.) Married dervishes have private homes outside the lodges, but are obliged to spend the night in the lodge once or twice a week. Many dervishes, says d'Ohsson, are thoroughly immoral and habitually drunk: in this class we find of course the members of openly libertine groups.

'Abd al-Ghani al-Nabulusi (1641–1731)

Nabulusi's surname means that his home town was Naplus in Palestine. He was a prolific writer and a member of both the Qadiri and the Naqshbandi brotherhoods (membership of different brotherhoods was common at this time). He is important for his detailed descriptions of his travels, though his interests lay not so much in contemporary affairs as in recounting his own religious experiences and the legends of the past. Indeed, he is a thoroughly backward-looking figure. Many of his writings are defensive: in justification of the Whirling Dervishes, of the dancing and music of the Sufis in general, of their use of tobacco, of 'gazing at beardless boys' and so on. Not surprisingly, given his enthusiasm for defending practices often condemned, he was himself a controversial character, venerated by some, but accused of impiety by others – he was even physically attacked in a riot. When he died, at Damascus in 1731, the bazaars of the city closed for the day of his funeral. His literary activity belongs mainly to the seventeenth century with its background of conflict between Sufis and lawyers.

When we look at Nabulusi's commentary on the Wine-song of Ibn al-Farid we find, as is usual in late Sufi commentaries, an extensive application of the system of Ibn 'Arabi, dominated by the idea of the Perfect Man. At first sight one might imagine that this was a commentary out of the fifteenth century, like the ones composed by Jami, in which earlier poetic talent is submerged in a flood of theorizing. But reading on one discovers that what have been called the 'brotherhood mentality' and the extreme veneration of the personal guide, already familiar from much earlier than the fifteenth century, have now invaded the higher theoretical literature, and taken their place beside abstract metaphysical speculation. Thus when Ibn al-Farid writes

> And if they had sprinkled some of that wine on the dust of a dead
>   man's tomb
> His spirit would have returned to him and his body would have
>   come back to life

Nabulusi (who has previously explained that the wine is that of divine love) assures us that many of God's friends have brought the dead back to life, through *karama*, the miraculous grace of the 'friends', this being part of Jesus' spiritual legacy. In earlier Sufism it would have been normal to restrict the miraculous powers of the Sufis to a much less impressive range.

Referring to Ibn al-Farid's verse

> And if the wine had given its colour to the palm of a man holding it
>   in a glass
> Then he would not have gone astray in the night since he had a
>   star in his hand

Nabulusi remarks that this refers to the disciple's putting his hand into that of the perfect elder when taking the oath of initiation. The hand clasp represents God's purchase of the disciple's soul.

When the poet says

> And if an enchanter had traced the letters of the wine's name on
> The forehead of one possessed the sign would have cured him

Nabulusi sees the enchanter as the Sufi teacher, initiating the disciple with the special frock (*khirqa*). Ibn al-Farid continues:

> And if its name had been inscribed upon the banner of the army
> That inscription would have made drunk all those beneath the flag

The commentator explains that the banner is the Sufi 'path' (*tariqa*, brotherhood) indicated by a founder for its members. When the poem says

> Good health to the people of the Christian monastery How drunk
> they became with it
> Though they did not drink of it but intended to do so

Nabulusi explains that these are specific friends of God who have taken their inheritance from the spiritual station of Jesus, but are in the religion of Muhammad. They have not yet reached the final goal.

Nabulusi, with his excellent knowledge of Ibn 'Arabi's system, is in a position to insist, in its defence, that it is not an expression of pantheism: it does not teach that God is identical with created things. The theory of the 'unity of existence' teaches that a man's existence is also that of God. But the sharing of that same existence does not mean that a man's ultimate identity is the same as God's or that God's is the same as a man's. Each is distinct from the other. A man, although he obtains existence from God's Essence, does so only in a conditioned manner, with an inferior status appropriate to himself.

Shah Wali Allah of Delhi (1703–62)

Wali Allah of Delhi is not only an extremely impressive thinker, but also, when he is not being Indian, a thoroughly Islamic one. Other leading thinkers of the Muslim world have tended either to stand within the Greek philosophical tradition or at least to keep very close to it. But Wali Allah has a resolutely anti-philosophical position, firmly inside the religious sciences of Islam. He has been the subject of many modern studies. Here we shall look at his thought as analysed in the admirable recent monograph of J. M. S. Baljon.

Wali Allah was in no doubt as to his immense importance. He was initiated into the Qadiri, Chishti and Naqshbandi 'paths', but informs us that God told him that he was being entrusted with a special mission which put him far above their members. He dreamt that he was given Muhammad's pen, and had a vision in which the Prophet gave him the initiatory hand clasp of the Sufi brotherhoods. Consequently, Wali Allah saw himself not just as the usual 'pole' or chief of God's friends, and not just as the usual 'renewer' of Islam believed to come in every century, but as someone entrusted with a new articulation of Islamic law – rather in the manner of an extremist Shiite Leader, in spite of his personal disapproval of Shiism.

Wali Allah believed that God inspired him through specially privileged parts of the universe. One of these, the 'world of the image' (*'alam al-mithal*) has a place in the thought of many Muslim mystics and philosophers, but in Wali Allah's case seems to have been particularly significant. It acts as an interface between this visible world of ours and the world of spirits above it, and it also serves as the imagination of the Universal Soul. Thus God's intentions are transmitted through angels, colours and refined substances in the 'world of the image' before making their way into the visions of mystics. The most important place in the 'world of the image' is the 'enclosure of sacrosanctity' (*hazirat al-quds*), in which God manifests himself to the spirits of perfect people, who themselves merge into one divine man (*insan ilahi*). This enclosure also serves as a medium for operations conducted by an elite in a complex hierarchy of angels, as prophets and reformers are guided on their way. Moreover, the 'enclosure of sacrosanctity' represents God's 'most supreme theophany', that is to say God's greatest act of self-manifestation. This is not so much an event as an entity, the shadow of God, what Ibn 'Arabi called the Muhammadan Reality. Wali Allah lays particular stress upon a little-known idea of Ibn 'Arabi's, according to which God's acts of self-manifestation correspond to a special part of a man's heart, called the 'gem of bewilderment', because the divine rays which hit it are reflected into the mystic and consequently bewilder him.

It appears that Wali Allah, like Dara Shukuh in India a century before, believed in a succession of 'cycles', in which, after the world is brought to an end, it is created again. He himself quotes the legend of the phoenix's rebirth from its ashes to illustrate this idea, which he seems to have taken from Indian sources. However, he does not follow Dara Shukuh in misunderstanding Ibn 'Arabi's general theory of the 'unity of existence'.

Wali Allah speaks of Ibn 'Arabi with great respect, and argues that Ibn 'Arabi's opinions can be reconciled with those of Sirhindi on the 'unity of contemplation'. Thus Wali Allah maintains that the expressions 'unity of existence' and 'unity of contemplation' designate different stages of mystical experience and alternative views of the universe. In the mystical stage of the 'unity of existence' man is entirely absorbed in God as the ultimate Reality. In the higher stage of the 'unity of contemplation' he realizes that God and man are united but retain their own individualities. As a view of the universe, the theory of the 'unity of existence' teaches that the world has one substance, just as wax models are all made of wax. The theory of the 'unity of contemplation' teaches that the world is a multiplicity of reflections coming from the names of a single God. Wali Allah concludes that Ibn 'Arabi had preserved the ultimate difference between God and created things, but had been misrepresented by his successors. As for Sirhindi's occasional criticisms of Ibn 'Arabi, these rest upon misunderstandings.

Although conscious of his own intellectual superiority over Sirhindi, Wali Allah still saw him as his predecessor, and indeed belonged to his 'Renewerist' sub-brotherhood of the Naqshbandi 'path'. The influence of Sirhindi seems to be most apparent in Wali Allah's theory of the 'subtle organs' within man. There is a lower series of five of these, consisting of the lower soul, the heart, the intellect, the spirit and the 'secret'; and a higher series of five more, consisting of the 'concealed' (*khafi*), the 'light of sacrosanctity', the 'gem of bewilderment', the 'most concealed' and the 'greatest I-ness'. Wali Allah says that his father taught meditation techniques attributed to Sirhindi, and drew circles representing some of these 'subtle organs' in connection with such techniques. It does indeed appear that Sirhindi's successors taught that these 'subtle organs' were localized in man's body and head in the same places, or near to the same places, as are given by Hindu writers, in their discussions of the *cakras* (the word *cakra* can mean both one of the various 'centres' in the body and one of the various circular diagrams used for meditation). Eventually, explains Wali Allah, at the highest level of the 'greatest I-ness', the mystic can see the whole universe within himself.

The 'subtle organs' correspond to stages in Wali Allah's theory of history. Just as there is political degeneration after Muhammad's death, so too there is spiritual progress, as the 'subtle organs' successively come into play and eventually find their highest self-realization in Wali Allah himself. This theory of history is linked to an original theory of sociology, based on the distinctive concept of 'finding help [from the environment]' (*irtifaq* 'utilization'): Islamic society represents the culmination of man's progressive utilization of nature and society as he rises from primitive culture through urbanization to the city-state and the empire. So Wali Allah is a social critic who censures contemporary rulers for extravagance and high taxation.

Nur 'Ali-Shah of Isfahan (d. 1800)

In the late eighteenth century there was a revival of Sufism in Iran, with the coming of one of the leaders of the Ni'matullahi brotherhood from India, where many of its members had been based. This leader, called Ma'sum 'Ali-Shah (d. 1798), soon acquired an important following, but both he and several of his disciples were cruelly persecuted and eventually killed. These misfortunes were due largely to a leading jurist, Muhammad Baqir Bihbihani (d. 1803), who gave Shiite lawyers the opportunity to exercise the independent initiative which they use so powerfully today, and his eldest son, who was probably responsible for poisoning the new Sufi leader's most famous pupil, Nur 'Ali-Shah.

This atmosphere of persecution permeates Nur 'Ali-Shah's didactic poetry, which has been the subject of a thoughtful study by Michel de Miras. Of particular interest is Nur 'Ali-Shah's treatment of the theme of the Sufi elder, who is even shown as receiving prophetic revelation (*wahy*), in direct contradiction to the standard Muslim doctrine that this ended with Muhammad. The poet teaches that such a master practises the discipline of 'passing away' in his own elder as well as in God. The combination of Shiism with Sufism in Nur 'Ali-Shah's work results in his presenting 'Ali, the First Leader of the Shiites, as the Holy Spirit who guides Gabriel. The Holy Spirit is also identical with the secret of God (*sirr Allah*). In a way the First Leader is also identified with the hidden Twelfth Leader, who is in turn identified with the living head of the hierarchy of God's friends.

In a short symbolic story by Nur 'Ali-Shah, we find him observing a ragged elder who is being stoned by children in the street. At first Nur 'Ali-Shah does not dare introduce himself, but eventually he discovers the elder in the desert and asks how he can be guided on a journey in his own interior world. He is taught a special name, given a tablet, and told to visit a series of cities, uttering the name in order to enter each city and looking at the tablet to leave it. The disciple encounters many ignorant and evil people in these cities, until eventually he comes to the city of the heart. Here he comes to a throne of light, with four people holding on to it, and 361 in a circle round about. A handsome elder seated on the throne induces a state of unconsciousness in Nur 'Ali-Shah, who has nine heavens revealed to him. He travels in them for years, and then experiences four visions, in which he sees worlds that it would take a lifetime to describe. Then he goes on to four mystical 'states': in the first he sees his own beginning and end; in the second he sees that the world is a man of whom he is the spirit; in the third he sees that he has a spirit without a body, and something named, but without a name; the fourth is indescribable. He wakes up, and the elder on the throne sends him back on a mission to ordinary mortals, who torment him and try to kill him.[2]

THE NINETEENTH CENTURY

The nineteenth century presents obvious problems for the student of Islam and Sufism. The history of this period is usually seen as being that of European colonialism and Islamic attempts at 'reform'. Present-day interpretations often reflect prejudice and a naive belief in infallible laws of social change. There is plenty of documentary evidence, but scholars are only just beginning to study it in a serious manner. Here we shall look briefly at the historical background before considering Sufism in three areas in which good studies have been made (North Africa, Egypt and Turkey), and concluding with some very limited observations about Sufism in the rest of the Muslim world.

The historical background

Two events in the late eighteenth century were to serve as a prelude to the history of Islam in the nineteenth: the French Revolution of 1789 and Napoleon's occupation of Egypt in 1798. The dynamism of European change and the vulnerability of Muslim countries to attack were now abundantly clear. Later, the French were to take over in Algeria from 1830 and in Tunisia from 1881. The Ottoman Empire's attempts at modernization were not very successful: it lost Greece after the war of independence (1821–30); and then Egypt became autonomous, before falling under British rule from 1882. In Iran an unpopular dynasty, that of the Qajars, lost territory to Russia, which also made important gains at the expense of other Muslim rulers in Central Asia. In India the British took over completely. It was really only in Africa that the Muslims had some success, with a dynamic and expansionist spirit: military leaders (notably the famous Mahdi of the Sudan) set up new states before their followers fell beneath the inexorable advance of superior European firepower.

These events posed considerable questions for the Muslims. If the holy war against the unbeliever failed, how should one view those Muslims who found themselves under non-Muslim rule? Should modern western ideas and institutions now be adopted? The replies given by nineteenth-century Islamic thinkers have been the subject of differing judgements by later scholars. In recent years the modernizing and westernizing 'reformists' of the nineteenth century have been increasingly seen as superficial, both in their thinking and their profession of Islam, while other figures have been found to be more deeply Islamic and rooted in the past than had previously been realized.

North Africa

North Africa was to witness the rise of new brotherhoods in this period, and strikingly different responses to colonial intervention from Sufi leaders. An idea of the changing times can be obtained by examining the autobiography of one very old-fashioned Sufi master before turning to other, more active organizers.

The Darqawi brotherhood, named after its founder, Ahmad al-Darqawi (1760–1823), is now sometimes linked with the label *neo-Sufism*. But it seems highly traditional in its practices, notably in the ancient discipline of attracting 'blame' by colourful behaviour, such as carrying buckets of excrement around in public. One member of this brotherhood, Ahmad Ibn 'Ajiba (*c.* 1747–1809), has left an autobiography which gives fascinating insights into daily life and an intimate account of the author's interaction with his environment, in sharp contrast to the much-vaunted and misleading apologia composed by Muhammad Ghazali seven hundred years before.

Born near Tetouan in northern Morocco, Ibn 'Ajiba was brought up in a village, and as a child would divide his time between going to school and looking after his family's sheep on the mountainside. Then he left the village for studies in the town of Tetouan and the city of Fez, and covered the whole range of the religious sciences. At the age of thirty he began to feel a desire to abandon these for the mystical life. In particular, like many North African Sufis of this time, he concentrated on the Prophet Muhammad in his devotions, and frequently saw him in dreams. But he married and obtained various teaching posts in Tetouan, holding a very respectable position in society for many years. Then, in 1793, he met the founder of the Darqawi brotherhood and one of his assistants, whose disciple he now became. He had previously been fairly well off – with a garden and two orangeries (which belonged to a pious foundation set up by one of his ancestors), a cow, a salt pit and a large library. Now he sold his non-Sufi books and borrowed money to pay for his new master's wedding and build a house for him. In compensation, he says, God gave him three houses, one of which he demolished at his master's command. After being told to engage in more expenditure on good works, he wore a shabby robe and then the patched frock of the Sufis. His master told him to give away everything, except what was needed to feed his family for a day or two; to beg in public; to clean the market, bearing the refuse on his shoulders; and to become a water carrier, giving drinking-water to people in the street.

The pursuit of 'blame' was to bring some trouble with the authorities: Ibn 'Ajiba's brother was accused by a husband of secretly initiating his wife. All the Darqawis of Tetouan were imprisoned, and charged with 'innovation' (*bid'a*) in wearing the patched frock. They were released after giving an undertaking (not kept, it seems) to end their practices. Ibn 'Ajiba left Tetouan for the countryside, and acquired hundreds of disciples. He ended up with four wives, but lost some children in an outbreak of plague – Ibn 'Ajiba attacked the authorities for ordering the evacuation of the towns in an attempt to curb the disease, and declared that its spread had to be left to the decision of God.

A rather different fraternity was founded by one Ahmad al-Tijani, who was born in 1737 at 'Ain Madi in southern Algeria. This has been well studied by Jamil Abun-Nasr. Tijani, after joining various brotherhoods and travelling extensively, announced that the Prophet Muhammad had appeared to him in daylight and prescribed special prayers for the new organization which he was now to lead. Since he got on very badly with the Turkish rulers of Algeria, he left for Morocco, where he died in 1815. In Morocco he enjoyed the protection and patronage of the sultan, but was otherwise unpopular. However, Tijani and his followers were rich, and were able to expand their brotherhood elsewhere. One follower composed a biography of his master, which was heavily plagiarized from a biography of an earlier North African Sufi. This did not prevent Tijani from declaring that Muhammad had appeared to him again in daylight, saying that he himself had composed the book.

Tijani claimed to be the Seal of God's Friends in the historical cycle inaugurated by Muhammad. He declared that the spiritual overflowings (*fuyud*) which came from Muhammad were distributed through him over the whole span of the history of the world. He himself was immune from sin. Because he was taught directly by Muhammad, he abandoned his membership of brotherhoods other than his own, and required his followers to do likewise. He ordered them not to visit living 'friends of God' or the tombs of dead ones. Tijani explained that his followers were bound to sin all the time, but could rely on his own guarantee of salvation. This included anyone who saw him and did not become his enemy. He claimed that Muhammad had told him not to cut himself off from the world, and so lived in luxury, wearing expensive clothes, eating choice food and advising his followers to stay rich. Tijani declared that one prayer taught him by Muhammad resulted in Muhammad's physical presence. This prayer contains an appalling misuse of Arabic: the word *asqam* is used in the obvious belief that it means 'most straight', when in fact it means 'most defective'.

Tijani's successors distinguished themselves by a spectacular enthusiasm for collaboration with French colonialism. Here they clashed with the celebrated hero of Algerian Muslim resistance to the French conquest, the Amir 'Abd al-Qadir (1807–83), whose activities were identified with the Qadiri brotherhood. Tijani's elder son was killed in a rebellion against Turkish rule in 1827. The founder's younger son, however, was able to survive an armed attack on himself and his supporters by 'Abd al-Qadir in 1838. He then agreed to accept French rule. Many Algerian Muslims emigrated to avoid this. Those who remained were led by the Tijanis into a long public display of obsequiousness towards the new masters.

A sharply contrasting response to European colonialism was made by the Sanusi brotherhood in Libya. This has been the subject of a study by a famous British anthropologist, Sir Edwin Evans-Pritchard, first published in 1949. Evans-Pritchard's book is mainly historical. If we compare it with the recent work of Berque on the lodge of Dila' in seventeenth-century Morocco we find much the same picture: that of an organization of academics and warrior-politicians, purveying Islamic civilization to tribesmen.

The founder, Muhammad al-Sanusi, known as the Grand Sanusi, was born near Mostaganem in northern Algeria about 1787. After long studies he established his brotherhood near Mecca fifty years later. He encountered much hostility, and consequently moved to Libya. There he built his headquarters at an oasis, constructing a mosque and a college, with accommodation for teachers, students and guests. His library covered the whole range of the Islamic religious sciences. He was able to graft his organization on to the local tribal network of Bedouin before dying in 1859.

His elder son, Sayyid al-Mahdi (1844–1902) succeeded him. Under his leadership the brotherhood conducted missionary propaganda against French expansion in sub-Saharan Africa. By the end of his life the Sanusis were the victims of armed attacks by the French, in a prelude to twentieth-century persecution by the Italians. The Sanusis were to resist the Italians bravely, although eventually they co-operated with the British, just as in the nineteenth century they had collaborated with the Turks.

The founder of the Sanusi brotherhood in Libya met Arab tribes which had conquered the country; he also met dependent tribes, some of which claimed descent from great Sufis of the past and thus were seen as specially possessed of 'blessing' (*baraka*, life-increasing force). The Grand Sanusi belonged to a type of figure familiar to the Bedouin: the *murabit*. We have noted that this word means both a man of religion and a fighter in the holy war. Accordingly, here again, we find something different from the old-fashioned French colonial picture of the marabout as a wildly ecstatic magician, or the common image of a 'saint' engaged in heroic acts of piety. The Sanusi brotherhood was based on the tribes, not on urban centres: its lodges were distributed according to the tribes' sections, and operated in between these, being given lands by them and obtaining their assistance in the work of cultivation. These lands were pious endowments, possessed by the lodges themselves. In return the lodges operated not just as schools but also as commercial, military and legal centres. The Ottoman Empire gave the brotherhood a charter, exempting it from taxation and allowing it to collect taxes from its supporters. The Turkish authorities left the Sanusis to do the government's work for it as far as the Bedouin were concerned.

The doctrines of the Sanusis have been studied by Nicola Ziadeh. They offended Egyptian jurists by their insistence on taking independent initiative in legal matters. The Grand Sanusi accepted a classical pattern of mystical development, in which coloured lights correspond to an upward movement through hierarchies of worlds, 'states' and spiritual organs. But, like the founder of the Tijani brotherhood, he emphasized the importance of aiming at direct communication with Muhammad during one's waking hours, and not just in dreams. For this one prays to God, asking to be united with Muhammad. The Sanusis rejected the artificial production of ecstasy, music, dancing, singing and other colourful Sufi practices. They are often seen as *neo-Sufi reformists*. To be sure, they rejected luxury. But they always tolerated other Sufi brotherhoods and allowed the veneration of leading Sufis and their tombs.

Egypt

The political history of nineteenth-century Egypt is unusual and complicated. In 1801 the brief French occupation came to an end. An Ottoman commander, Muhammad-'Ali, won power in 1805. He soon confiscated the lands of the pious endowments, as part of a wider agricultural reform. After more Europeanizing changes to the economy he turned against his Ottoman overlords. After his death in 1849 his successors continued with strong westernizing tendencies, but produced financial disaster, foreign intervention and British occupation from 1882.

Fred de Jong has made a painstakingly detailed survey of the ways in which the Egyptian government used Sufi leaders as bureaucratic chiefs during the nineteenth century. It did so because its own administrative machinery was not adequate for the task of controlling the members of the brotherhoods. Accordingly, it selected for its purposes the Bakri brotherhood, so called after an aristocratic family which had transformed itself into the nucleus of a Sufi organization. The government then invested successive leaders in the family with extraordinary powers of supervision over other brotherhoods and religious institutions.

The leader of the Bakri fraternity had already obtained informal authority as an arbiter to whom members of some other brotherhoods appealed to resolve disputes. This authority was apparently won in the chaos following the French withdrawal in 1801. In 1812 the ruler of Egypt, Muhammad-'Ali, gave a new leader of the Bakri brotherhood wide official powers, not only over many other brotherhoods, but also over many Sufi lodges and tombs. This administrative innovation seems to have been linked to the land and tax reforms then being carried out. With the confiscation of the lands of the pious endowments the religious scholar-jurists of Egypt became more dependent upon the ruler, and, if they were also Sufis, as was often the case, upon his new Sufi superintendent. Thus from the middle of the century onwards a gap opened up: the Sufis became less academic, since they needed only the Bakri leader's patronage, and in reaction the academics became less inclined to Sufism.

From 1855 to 1880, with another new leader, called 'Ali al-Bakri, official power over the brotherhoods was consolidated further. This was done through recourse to a new principle, that of 'priority' (*qadam*), which meant the right, if a brotherhood could prove that it had settled in an area first, to hold on to that area for itself alone. This principle was needed to replace the right to collect taxes from a given area, which leading Sufis had often possessed, before its abolition in Muhammad-'Ali's reforms. Heads of brotherhoods were now dependent upon Bakri for legal recognition and the government stipends which went with it. This recognition was also essential for public processions, assemblies and distribution of food. Such public activity was particularly important during the celebrations which surrounded the Prophet's birthday. Then one ritual took place which was famous above all others: the leader of the Sa'di brotherhood rode a horse over a long line of his prostrate followers, without apparent injury to them. Apart from these anniversary celebrations and those held to commemorate great Sufis of the past, the brotherhoods also appeared in public for ceremonies marking the preparation and completion of the pilgrimage to Mecca. Here, in the 1870s, they took over from the craft guilds, as they did in social organization generally. Previously it was imagined that the decline of the guilds brought a decline of Sufism, as associated with them. But de Jong has argued that on the contrary the fall of the guilds produced an increase in the number of Sufi brotherhoods in the late nineteenth century.

From 1880 to 1892 a young and ineffectual leader, 'Abd al-Baqi al-Bakri, was in charge. In 1881, under pressure from the ruler of Egypt, Tawfiq (1879–92), he prohibited the brotherhoods' more colourful practices, such as the eating of live coals, snakes and glass. Music was also banned, as were distinctive and varied forms of 'remembrance' (*dhikr*), which was now limited to that of God alone. The brotherhoods reacted by dissociating themselves from the Bakri leadership, which in any case failed to enjoy the complete support of the government. Eventually 'Abd al-Baqi felt obliged to recognize new brotherhoods which had bypassed the barrier of 'priority' set up by old ones. This barrier collapsed, so that only official recognition itself now mattered, constituting the main check on the formation of splinter groups.

In 1892 'Abd al-Baqi died and his brother, Muhammad Tawfiq, became leader of the Bakri brotherhood. He immediately reasserted the authority of his family, and gained the government's support. His power was increased with the introduction of new regulations in 1895. From this time on there was an office of 'elder of the elders of the Sufi brotherhoods', with a clearly defined legal and constitutional basis.

Turkey

As we turn to the part of the Ottoman Empire which roughly corresponds to the present-day Republic of Turkey, we should briefly note the course of political history in the nineteenth century. This falls into three main periods. First, there is the reign of Mahmud II (1808–39), which is characterized by the concentration of power in the figure of the sultan himself, through the suppression of military, administrative, legal and religious counterweights to his authority. Then, from 1839 to 1876, there is the era of the 'Reorganizations' (*Tanzimat*), when new regulations tried to impose Europeanization, notably in education and civil liberties. Lastly, there is the reign of 'Abd al-Hamid (1876–1909), which is noteworthy for its absolutist and authoritarian use of Islam to justify the rejection of constitutional legality.

The first of these historical phases contains two spectacular episodes of governmental intervention, both in 1826: the massacre of the famous Janissary soldiers and the dissolution of the brotherhood to which they had traditionally been linked, that of the Bektashis. The Janissaries had been opposed to westernizing military reforms. But the reasons behind the action taken against the Bektashis are less obvious. The subject has been very well studied by Faroqhi and by John Robert Barnes. Officially, the reasons given were religious: the Bektashis were Shiite and libertine. A few were executed and others were sent to live in cities dominated by respectable scholar-jurists. Many lodges were demolished. The property of the brotherhood was confiscated. Although this was considerable, the practical difficulties involved in selling it meant that the gain to the treasury was not particularly great. The government's intervention seems to have been part of a wider strategy, similar to that employed in Egypt, aimed at imposing financial and bureaucratic control in the religious sphere.

The inventories of the Bektashis' possessions and the records of their sale provide valuable information about the brotherhood's activities before the government's action. Faroqhi has shown that the Bektashis were producing wine. One large lodge in south-western Turkey had a library of almost 150 volumes. Contrary to what has been supposed about the Bektashis, namely, that they represented an emphasis on 'popular' culture and literature, the list of the library's contents demonstrates that they were orientated towards high classical Persian and Turkish poetry. On the other hand, this predilection for poetry may be contrasted with the North African lodges' more academic interests in the Islamic religious sciences. The same large lodge was well equipped for the consumption of food and drink, but in a way which indicates comfort, not luxury, and corresponds to the central function of offering hospitality to visitors.

The process of confiscation and the government's later treatment of other brotherhoods have also been studied by Faroqhi and Barnes. Seizure of lands which constituted pious endowments was justified by the argument that they had previously belonged to the state and the

Bektashis had forfeited all claims by falling into unbelief. The government sold the lands to middle and small landowners, probably to strengthen them against the wealthiest ones.

In the following years, the state tightened its grip on the other brotherhoods and dervishes in general. It insisted that residents of the lodges should be replaced after their deaths only by men who respected Islamic law. The elders of individual lodges were obliged to give their followers permits, without which the wearing of a brotherhood's distinctive dress was prohibited. Elders were forbidden to exercise functions in more than one lodge. Dervishes were required to take part in the ritual worship. The government took over the collection of revenue from the lands of the lodges' pious endowments, and brought about a severe reduction in some Sufis' means of support. Clearly, the state was intent on making the dervishes as financially dependent upon itself as possible. It began to insist that government revenue should be granted to Sufis only when they replaced dead recipients. Moreover, the government cracked down on wandering dervishes in the capital. It registered them and recorded their movements. In general, the state was able to take advantage of the dervishes' need of funds, which in any case had often been very great already, where there had been no pious endowments for them. As Klaus Kreiser has observed, in Turkey the government preferred to use its own bureaucracy, whereas in Egypt it used the Sufis to do its administration.

The relationship between bureaucracy and Sufism takes a different form in the history of the Naqshbandi 'path'. The 'Renewerist' sub-brotherhood of this, which we have already encountered in India with the figures of Sirhindi and Wali Allah, had spread to the Ottoman Empire in the seventeenth and early eighteenth centuries before acquiring new leadership from one Khalid al-Shahrazuri (1776–1827), whose followers are called the Khalidis. This leader, like his predecessors, insisted on summoning rulers to follow Islamic law. Many nineteenth-century westernizing bureaucrats were 'Renewerist' Naqshbandis (though often the same people belonged to the Whirling Dervishes as well). A lot of them were killed in an anti-westernization revolt in 1807. However, Butrus Abu-Manneh has shown that Sultan Mahmud II, in spite of his Europeanizing aims, probably viewed the Khalidis with suspicion, and they were subjected to official persecution.

A picture of highly old-fashioned attitudes is given in the auto-biography of one Khalidi bureaucrat, Ibrahim Khalil (1828–1907?), which has been efficiently summarized by Marie Luise Bremer. The son of a Janissary soldier, he rose high in the military administration. He decided that he had found the highest 'friend of God' in his time in a Khalidi elder of Erzincan in eastern Turkey, called Mustafa Fehmi (d. 1881). The political reforms of this period seemed to him to be anti-Islamic. His anti-Russian feelings and his belief in supernatural powers were so strong that by the time of the Russo-Japanese war of 1904–5 he considered that his own spiritual intervention was giving Japan victory. Just as his Sufi mentor disapproves of learning French, Ibrahim rejects European clothes. The use of Sufi connections to obtain positions in the bureaucracy does not worry him, however – although promotions, earnestly desired in prayers, are attributed to the supernatural rather than the temporal influence of the elders.

When Ibrahim first goes to school he falls in love with another boy, and when he enters the administration he becomes enamoured of a young colleague. His mother marries him off, and he joins the Whirling Dervishes. But later he meets his Khalidi master, and the 'metaphorical love' which he had felt before is now changed to 'real love', not, as one might imagine, for God, but for his new teacher. There will be a subsequent lapse into the metaphorical level, occasioned by a handsome youth; but while Ibrahim's fellow Naqshbandis generally disapprove, his spiritual director praises him. Here, as in other instances, one may doubt whether 'neo-Sufism' or 'Sufi reformism' is an appropriate label with which to designate the Khalidi movement: modern writers have been too quick to use these expressions, failing to recognize the continuity of traditions from the medieval past. Nor would there seem to be, as is often imagined, a 'reformist' rejection of a so-called 'cult of the saints'. Ibrahim recites Naqshbandi prayers over the head of John the Baptist in Damascus, in order to ward off the plague. His adherence to the Naqshbandi brotherhood does not prevent him, as a true Whirling Dervish, from listening to the flute. And his Khalidi elder welcomes and honours a wandering dervish who had once been a rich merchant, but has given up his wealth, and now arrogantly demands money and displays his cannabis. Here we see an interplay between Sufi elder and libertine dervish (*qalandar*) that is absolutely typical of records of fourteenth-century Indian conversations. Classic too is the rapid death of an administrator who incurs the wrath of a Qadiri elder by interfering with Ibrahim's diversion of government-owned wood to his lodge.

The rest of the Muslim world

As we move eastwards from Turkey we find plenty of variety, notably in the relations between Sufis and jurists. Again, one must beware of the common notion that nineteenth-century Islam was dominated by a widespread attack from 'Muslim reformists' upon a 'cult of the saints' in Sufism.

Iran

In Iran, attention must be given to the resurgence of Sufism in the reign of Muhammad Shah (1834–48), which has been magisterially analysed by Hamid Algar. This monarch had kept the company of dervishes when young, and came under the influence of one in particular, called Hajji Mirza Aqasi. This dervish, as the Shah's spiritual mentor, obtained effective control of the state during his reign, while appearing to be quite mad. Money was spent on beautifying Sufi tombs, and Sufis were given preferential treatment in the distribution of government posts. The jurists did not like this, though they were confident in their immense influence over the population. Aqasi conducted a running fight with them, but he and his fellow Sufis were obliged to live in fear, and soldiers who tried to intimidate the Sufis' enemies were soundly thrashed. This episode forms part of a long war between the Iranian monarchy and the jurists, which in the twentieth century was to end with the overthrow of the shah.

Central Asia

Iran, in 1863, served as a base for the Central Asian travels of the Hungarian orientalist Ármin Vámbéry, who disguised himself as a dervish and was thus able to acquire much first-hand information. He paints a disillusioning picture of the parts of Central Asia beginning to fall under Russian domination. This area was the laughing-stock of the Muslim world for its exaggerated bigotry. Sufism served as an excuse for vast numbers of impostors, who persuaded a gullible population to part with its money. In the towns of what is now the Soviet Republic of Uzbekistan a good third of the inhabitants were assiduously trying to obtain the honorific titles associated with advancement on the Sufi Path. Outside the towns one encounters the usual pattern of inherited devotion, among the tribes, to families of Sufi leaders. Thus Vámbéry found affiliation to Sufi brotherhoods to be far greater in this region than in Turkey and Iran. Moreover, he thought that they exercised such immense power that the scholar-jurists, while hating them as representing a rival influence, were obliged to belong to them in order to satisfy the population. But he did not believe that the brotherhoods were chasing after social or political goals in the manner of Masonic lodges. On the contrary their members appeared to be lazy and preoccupied largely by the consumption of opium and cannabis.

India

It is in India above all that modern writers have imagined that there was a massive onslaught from 'Islamic reformism' upon Sufism, with a 'fundamentalist' attack on a 'cult of the saints'. Originally it was thought that there had been an anti-Sufi movement, inspired by the Wahhabis of Arabia, under the leadership of Sayyid Ahmad of Bareilly in northern India (1786–1831). In fact he was a member of Sufi brotherhoods, and went on to see his own 'path' as that of Muhammad, rather in the manner of the founders of the Tijanis and Sanusis in North Africa. His military activity and attempt to lead a state of his own ended in his being killed.

The followers of Sayyid Ahmad maintained that it was perfectly permissible to mention the names of dead Sufi elders in prayers to God, provided that God was seen as the only possible benefactor. As for the popular use of picturesque offerings to Sufis of the past, to attack this was nothing new. The more studies that are done, the more Sufism is discerned among the 'reformists' themselves. Sufism is particularly evident in the revivalist centre at Deoband in northern India, as has been shown by Barbara Metcalf. Here the academics, who were also Sufis themselves, did not usually object to visiting the tombs of elders, although they condemned certain practices there. Their feelings were highly ambiguous when it came to listening to poetry, or asking a dead Sufi to intercede for oneself. They themselves tried to concentrate their attention in such a way as to have supernatural and telepathic influence on their disciples' behaviour. Indeed, the academic Sufis of Deoband taught the practice of conceiving a mental image of one's elder, and even 'passing away' within him. Some actually taught the use of amulets. Nor is Sufi influence among 'reformists' confined to Deoband. As Marc Gaborieau has observed, it is only from the time of the second world war that one encounters new forms of ideology and organization which owe nothing to the brotherhoods (but are inspired by European totalitarian political parties). The brotherhoods themselves, though supported by the British, were eventually to work for independence in the twentieth century.

Africa

If we now return to Africa, and look south of the Sahara, we find the spread of the brotherhood founded by the colourful Ahmad al-Tijani to the north. In West Africa, however, in contrast to its northern collaboration, this brotherhood came into violent conflict with French colonialism. It had one important military leader, 'Umar Tal (d. 1864), who was born in Futa Toro in the Senegal River valley and was to launch a remarkable holy war, imposing Muslim rule on areas of traditional African religion and establishing a state of his own. This brought him into clashes with the French, in spite of his early expression of friendly feelings towards them.

It is difficult to make judgements about 'Umar Tal, given the legendary character of the materials and the uncritical acceptance of late oral tradition by present-day writers in English. Modern British and American studies of Islam in West Africa are usually of questionable quality: the authors call Sufi elders 'clerics' or 'saints', in opposition to other figures, whom they label 'chiefs' or 'politicians', and thereby create much confusion. Useful criticisms have come from French specialists, notably concerning the tendency to see an enormous difference between the Tijanis and the Qadiris. This tendency seems to be due to the illusion of 'neo-Sufism', the supposed characteristics of which are evident in much earlier Islamic history.

THE TWENTIETH CENTURY

The study of twentieth-century Sufism is fraught with problems often encountered in the social sciences. Generally speaking, the main difficulty resides in the fact that the concepts most frequently used in sociology and anthropology stem from the political context of western Europe at the start of the century with its atmosphere of strained church–state relations and criticism of Roman Catholicism. Accordingly the opposition *clerical–lay* has been applied to Islam, where it has no place. Moreover, many social scientists have come to believe that their abstract concepts have a universal validity, so that, for example, the ideas of 'the sacred' and 'the profane' are seen as having an independent reality of their own, a view which the Islamic evidence does not substantiate.

Nonetheless, fieldwork conducted in the first half of the century was often very fine, showing long years of familiarity with the people studied and a good knowledge of their language and cultural inheritance. Unfortunately, from the 1950s onward such qualifications were renounced in favour of a new exaltation of methodology, which in Britain and North America is still dominant. In the 1980s, however, there has been an encouraging reaction against theory on the continent of Europe, and a new generation of social scientists there is now digging out the evidence in collaboration with specialists in literary and historical studies.

The results in the field of Islamic mysticism are embarrassing in the extreme for older western social scientists, who had portrayed Sufism as disappearing in the course of the twentieth century, submerged beneath the victorious progress of Islamic Protestantism, as was demanded by a general law of social development. Recent scholarship has revealed that on the contrary Sufism is not only surviving but in many areas flourishes.

The historical background

The history of the Muslim world in the twentieth century falls into two main phases: first, that of continuing European colonial rule; and second, that of ensuing decolonization and the mixture of political environments which have resulted. The century's development was foreshadowed by Japan's defeat of Russia in 1904–5, which showed that the East was not necessarily inferior to the West; and – before the recent prominence given to Islam itself – was dominated by two ideologies: nationalism and socialism.

To begin with, European supremacy increased. France established a protectorate in Morocco in 1912, and Italy took over in Libya from 1911. The destruction of the Ottoman Empire during the first world war brought, not the fulfilment of Arab nationalist hopes, but the extension of British and French 'protection' to the Fertile Crescent. Between the two world wars – nearly everywhere – independence was to remain a long-delayed future goal, while the autonomous states of Turkey and Iran were governed by westernizing champions of racial purity, and the Muslims of Russian-dominated Central Asia came under Soviet rule.

After the second world war there was a massive retreat by the western powers. However, some of the newly independent countries became so closely connected with the United States, notably in military matters, as to raise doubts about their real autonomy. Large oil revenues were to produce little genuine progress. Islam came to be used as a cover for a wide variety of political ideologies and systems, leading western observers to use the catch-all label of *fundamentalism*.

There has been much anti-Sufi propaganda, sometimes from the small Wahhabi sect, supported by the tribal rulers of Saudi Arabia, sometimes from organizations which have taken their inspiration from European totalitarianism. Here, in order to try to avoid premature judgements and over-generalization, we shall concentrate on areas of Sufi activity which have been studied in depth, and not endeavour to cover the whole of the Muslim world in the twentieth century. We shall devote particular attention to Africa, looking both north and south of the Sahara, and also make some amends for our previous neglect of Southeast Asia, while considering the new problems posed by the position of Sufism in the Soviet Union.

Morocco

Islam in Morocco has been the subject of an enormous study by the great Edward Westermarck, published in 1926. He began by emphasizing the widespread belief in the prevalence of *baraka*, 'blessing', as a virtually all-pervasive force. All men have 'blessing', but to a greater or lesser extent; Westermarck thought that if a man has a lot of it, then he is a 'saint'.

But Westermarck's own analysis of the terms used shows that there can be no cut-off point at which this is the case. He says that the usual terms for a saint are *sayyid* (lord), *salih* (pious man) and *wali Allah* (friend of God). But he goes on to say that someone who is not actually regarded as a saint is called *sayyid* if he is descended from Muhammad. After finding that 'blessing', perceived as a bounty from God, is encountered in varying degrees in practically everything that is not ritually impure, he is led to reject the famous opinion of Émile Durkheim, still enormously influential, that there is an impassable gulf between the holy or sacred and the profane.[3] Durkheim and Westermarck were both confusing the idea of the sacrosanct, that which is completely cut off from everything else, with the idea of life-increasing force, which is often represented by words such as 'holy', and which in Islam is 'blessing' from God.

After Westermarck, excellent fieldwork was conducted by René Brunel. In 1955 he published the results of his long researches on the Haddawa, a colourful brotherhood whose founder, Sidi Haddi, although he died as late as 1805, is almost entirely a legendary figure. This brotherhood has the usual characteristics of groupings of wandering dervishes throughout Islamic history. It emphasizes the importance of celibacy: women and female animals have been banned (as in the celebrated Christian centre of Mount Athos) from the brotherhood's lodge, which serves as the rallying point for its wanderers in northern Morocco. Although celibacy is the ideal, practised by the real members, there are some married adherents as well.

In principle the brotherhood has recruited from all classes of society in its renunciation of the world, but in practice its associate members have been observed to be fishermen or artisans. Brunel noted that their numbers in the towns had declined, as they had moved away from the control of the government's agents in order to avoid being deloused. Previously they had enjoyed close relations with the soldiery. Both men and women are recruited, but the prevailing rejection of marriage is accompanied by the tendency to pederasty usually associated with wandering dervishes. Also typical is the consumption of cannabis, which is used in the 'remembrance' ceremonies of the lodge. Under the influence of cannabis the Haddawa utter prophecies and bitter comments on the human race. They spend the night wherever sleep overtakes them: their lodge has neither dormitories nor cells. The Haddawa are also noteworthy for their extreme devotion to cats. Here Islam itself has adopted, in a much modified form, the veneration of the cat in the ancient Near East. In the case of the Haddawa, however, this devotion has been accompanied by the ritual eating of cats, and Brunel's informants told him that originally the participants in the meal would mimic cats and wear cats' skins. Obviously a local pre-Islamic cult has been adapted to the requirements of Islam. The Haddawa (like the wandering dervishes of the Muslim East) have a peculiar slang of their own. In the past they have operated as spies in the service of various masters. Brunel did well to point out the similarities with wandering Christian monks, both before and after the appearance of Islam.

An extremely influential picture of Islam in Morocco, and the role of Sufism therein, has been given by Clifford Geertz in his well-known *Islam Observed*, first published in 1968. His views are based largely on the idea of the supposed 'Maraboutic Crisis' of the sixteenth and seventeenth centuries, which he perceived to be 'the greatest spiritual dislocation' of Morocco, and which, as we have seen above, is an illusion.[4] Moreover, his conception of a 'marabout' as the very opposite of a scholar (whom Geertz would call a 'scripturalist', as if other Muslims would fail to express a regard for scripture) has been discredited by the recent work of Berque on the seventeenth-century evidence. Berque makes nonsense of Geertz's assertion that the Moroccan scholarly tradition 'was always a confined and specialized thing, a matter of a few withdrawn pedants'.[5] On the contrary, the Moroccan scholars were highly effective purveyors of Islamic culture to tribesmen, to a degree which western academics would be unlikely (and probably unable) to emulate.

Considerable attention has also been given to a work by Ernest Gellner, *Saints of the Atlas*, published in 1969. This, in spite of its title, really refers to a kinship group called the Ihansalen, in the central High Atlas mountains. Gellner's study is a transposition of Evans-Pritchard's analysis of the role of the Sanusi brotherhood in Libya, noted above with reference to the nineteenth century: sections of tribes are observed to have, in between one another, the adjudicating presence of people with religious and legal functions. In this case they are the descendants of someone credited with the founding of a Sufi brotherhood. Gellner's description of them as 'saints' is indefensible. He himself admits that they maintain that only God can dispense 'blessing'. Gellner thinks that there is something called 'Koranic law' in the towns, as opposed to the Ihansalen's practical judicial interventions. In fact Islamic and customary law have always been mixed in Muslim cities, in deference to political necessity, while in the countryside illiterate peasants have had to act as Islamic judges for want of qualified personnel. Gellner tries to present the Ihansalen as entirely cut off from the Moroccan academic tradition. But there exists a seventeenth-century treaty, drawn up by two literate Ihansalen, allying them with the academics of Dila'.[6] When Gellner speaks of 'laicized saints', 'effective saints' and 'semi-saints' one's doubts increase. He takes the view that it would be pointless to ask these tribesmen questions like 'Are the signs of "blessing" signs rather than causes of God's choosing?' The idea of an 'effective saint', he says, is ambiguous, represented by the Berber word *agurram*. It appears that this term, like a form of the Arabic *murabit*, can mean both (a) some exceptionally blessed man and (b) a descendant thereof. It might be best translated 'noble'. Thus Gellner says that sometimes the saints are not saints, and that some non-saintly families would in some contexts be classed as *agurrams*, while in other contexts all the Ihansalen are so called.[7]

Vincent Crapanzano has made a useful study of the socially despised brotherhood of the Hamadsha and their practices in and around the city of Meknes in northern Morocco. The Hamadsha are named after their supposed founder, 'Ali ibn Hamdush (d. *c.* 1720?), who is reputed to have died childless, although there are alleged descendants who claim to have inherited his 'blessing'. Some of these alleged descendants fall into trances and slash their heads in the manner for which the Hamadsha are noted, but they themselves and their followers deny that this happens – such behaviour would be thought unsuitable for the founder's progeny. The lodges of the brotherhood in the old city have both full and associate members, and also professional musicians. The members come from the lower classes of the city, without being linked to any one occupation. Associate members are characterized by variable attendance, which corresponds to psychological disturbance and its alleviation by entering into trance and head slashing. The trances are produced, in the case of a given individual, by a special musical phrase. This tune is connected with a particular member of the *jinn* (the race of spirits parallel to mankind), and also with a particular colour. The shanty towns outside the city, which are exceptionally sordid and demoralized, also have teams of Hamadsha performers, who are more concerned with the *jinn* and illness than attachment to the founder's memory, and are also more violent. These shanty-town teams appeal to unskilled labourers with a peasant background.

Crapanzano gives a striking description of a Hamadsha performance. Both men and women dance to musical accompaniment, and go into trance. Then one effeminately dressed man, who is designated by an onlooker as a passive homosexual, enters the arena and dances on his own, beating his head with knives, so that the blood runs down his back. Women lick the blood and smear it on a baby. The dance calms down and the crowd disperses, while several women ask the head slasher for his blessing.

The Hamadsha's activities are explained by Crapanzano in terms of western psychiatry. To describe conditions which might be called hysterical or psychosomatic, they themselves use expressions indicating the intervention of the *jinn*, and notably a female spirit called 'Ayisha Qandisha, who is extremely libidinous. Now Westermarck argued that this spirit's surname represents the ancient Near Eastern figure of the *qedesha* or religious prostitute, while her husband, Hammu Qiya, would correspond to the Baal Hammon of the ancient Phoenician colony of Carthage. This would be a survival of the ancient cult of the goddess Astarte, brought from the Near East by Carthaginian colonization of the Moroccan coast (the geographical concentration of which corresponds to the use of 'Ayisha Qandisha's name). We may add that the elements of dancing, head slashing, effeminate dress and homosexuality are all characteristic of ancient Syrian goddess worship. Although Crapanzano suggests that the attributes of 'Ayisha Qandisha are paralleled throughout the mediterranean and sub-Saharan Africa, the articulation of the evidence is strongly in favour of historical continuity from the classical Near East.

Egypt

Much notice has been given to a book by Michael Gilsenan, entitled *Saint and Sufi in Modern Egypt: an Essay in the Sociology of Religion*, published in 1973, and based on fieldwork conducted in 1964–6. This has been subjected to a detailed critique by de Jong, who has extensive eyewitness experience of Sufism in Egypt and a remarkable knowledge of the relevant documents.

Gilsenan concentrated his attention on one sub-brotherhood of the Shadhilis, who are named after Abu 'l-Hasan Shadhili (d. 1258) and are particularly strong in Egypt and North Africa, where their emphasis on sobriety has earned them the label 'the Protestants of Islam'. This sub-brotherhood was founded by a civil servant called Salama Hasan al-Radi (1867–1939). Gilsenan estimated its strength at 12,000 to 16,000 members. De Jong quotes a newspaper article of 1971 which puts its membership at 100,000. He observes that the Egyptian authorities have used this sub-brotherhood as a show-case model, taking all western students to it. Its successful growth would appear to have been due to governmental assistance, rather than, as Gilsenan thought, its detailed regulations. Other brotherhoods have also expanded, while all are subject to official rules. Gilsenan took the view that Salama had originally aimed at setting up an elitist group during a period of calm and peace. De Jong has pointed out that this opinion was based on one reverential biography: Salama's early writings were directed at winning over the general public during a phase in which he clashed with the authorities.

Gilsenan's work is most interesting when describing Sufi practice. He says that at the meetings of Salama's sub-brotherhood the members form an inward-facing square. This he interprets as symbolic of separation from the outside world, whose inhabitants cannot violate the 'Order'. De Jong says that it is more common for the members to form a circle, or two sets of parallel rows, with officers standing at the fringes and guiding people in. Gilsenan gives a detailed description of the ritual itself. First there is a quiet recitation of the attestation that God is Unique, as the seated brothers rock back and forth. Then they rise to chant 'Allah', first with violent expressions of breath, and then in a low tone, as a hymn is sung by specialist singers. After this a soft-breathed repetition of 'Allah' becomes increasingly louder, while the chief singer chants a supplication to the 'friends of God'. Then other names of God are chanted, with speed increasing to repeated climaxes, at the same time as more hymns are sung. Finally, there is a seated recitation of parts of the Koran. (De Jong says that either Gilsenan's description is incomplete or the practice is at variance with the official rules.)

A fascinating account is given by Gilsenan, for comparative purposes, of a meeting held by a section of another sub-brotherhood, in Aswan. Gilsenan took this section to be 'a small Order founded by a local holy figure'. De Jong pointed out that it was part of a sub-brotherhood of the Shadhilis, founded by Ahmad ibn Idris (1760–1837), generally seen as a great 'reformer' of Sufism, and having 10,000 members in Egypt. This supposedly 'reformist' pedigree contrasts oddly with its members' colourful behaviour (which Gilsenan opposes to the sedate conduct of the sub-brotherhood founded by the 'reformer' Salama). Their lodge was on the edge of the worst slum area, and the eighteen men whom Gilsenan saw gather there were said to be unemployed. They formed two lines facing inwards and built up their 'remembrance of God' to deafening shouts, thrusting their bodies back and forth. One man hopped around in a daze, while another, to howls of 'Allah!', hurled himself against the walls. After one and a half hours of jumping up and down the men suddenly stopped, and did not seem in the least tired.

More recently, de Jong has noted the numerical strength of the brotherhoods in Egypt, with some six million adherents in 1982, representing more than a third of the male population. In 1976 and 1978 new regulations greatly increased the powers of the brotherhoods' Supreme Council, which has the right to supervise all Sufi activity, public or private, and has legislative, judicial and executive functions. Thus the large number of Sufis does not mean that the leaders of the brotherhoods are particularly powerful: in practice greater control has passed into the hands of the state, exceeding nineteenth-century developments.

Turkey

In 1925 the new Republic of Turkey officially closed all Sufi lodges, banned all Sufi titles and prohibited all activity on the part of the brotherhoods. In practice, some Sufi activity has continued up to the present time, in spite of being illegal, but this illegality has made research extremely difficult. In recent years Sufi meetings have been held in public, without intervention from the authorities. Members of the government and other politicians are known to have been closely connected with the Naqshbandi brotherhood.

Although not many studies have been made of Sufism in twentieth-century Turkey, there is one classic work, *The Bektashi Order of Dervishes*, by J. K. Birge. This incorporated observations made in Turkey and Albania from 1913 onwards, and was published in 1937. Recently more research has been done on the Bektashis, notably on the brotherhood's survival in Albania (where it was finally banned in 1967) and Yugoslavia. However, Birge's study is so rich in detailed descriptions and general conclusions that I shall confine myself to summarizing it alone.

Birge found that the Bektashis held a wide variety of beliefs, from atheism to solipsism, and that the less intellectual members thought that after death men's souls were reincarnated in animals. Some believed in a trinity of God, Muhammad and 'Ali (identified with one another), and incorporated the teachings of Shiism and Hurufism (the doctrine based on the letters of the alphabet, noted above in our survey of the fourteenth and fifteenth centuries). Moreover, they were famous for having a great secret, which Birge thought to have various aspects: theological, in the identification of God with man; political, in their Shiism; social, in their allowing unveiled women to share in their rites; and symbolic, in their use of wine.

The Bektashis were found by Birge to be divided into sympathizers, initiates, full dervishes, members of a celibate branch, elders and deputies, all beneath a supreme leader. They had Shiite prayers for special group worship, and an annual service of repentance and expiation of sins, which is obviously inherited from the eastern Christian practice of collective confession. They had taboos, evidently continued from the shamanistic religion of the Central Asian Turks, which required them to avoid the hare and show reverence to the threshold of a door.

What was most impressive was their initiation ceremony. This was performed in the hall of the lodge, at one end of which there was a throne, holding candles. Around the room there were sheepskins, on which the brothers sat. Before the ceremony a ram had been slaughtered. The candidate was brought to the elder, who warned him of the dangers of the Bektashi 'path' and told the candle officer to light the candles. This was then done, to the accompaniment of expressions of devotion to Muhammad's family. The candidate was then introduced to the ritual belt of the brotherhood and given the brothers' approval of his admission. He was instructed in the Bektashi profession of faith and had the brotherhood's distinctive twelve-panel headpiece put on his head. The elder tied three knots in the belt, symbolizing the rejection of lying, stealing and fornication, and bound it round the candidate's waist. He gave him the initiatory handshake, and the candidate was introduced to the various symbolic articles in the hall. A drink was then consumed, alcoholic according to one informant, non-alcoholic according to another, before a concluding prayer. It is not disputed that after this formal ceremony alcohol was consumed, and men and women danced together.

Birge, following the great Turkish scholar Fuad Köprülü, listed various elements of Bektashi practice as resembling Central Asian Turkic shamanism, in particular the involvement of women and the sacrifice of the ram before the initiation ceremony. He also saw parallels with Christian sacraments, notably in the ablutions which were performed before the actual initiation, in the use of wine, and in admission to the brotherhood's celibate branch. We may observe that the threefold tying of the belt corresponds to the Indo-European triad of religious knowledge, force and fertility, which would be seen as dishonoured by the sins mentioned: the putting on of the belt presumably comes from the Iranian 'youngmanliness' tradition, not from the Turks of Central Asia, since among the latter initiation is performed by *undoing* a belt.[8]

The Soviet Union

We have seen above how Vámbéry, in the nineteenth century, portrayed Sufism in what is today Soviet Central Asia: an excuse for an army of crooks to delude a gullible population, in an atmosphere of mindless bigotry. He discovered that the brotherhoods had an enormous membership, including many jurists, whose own profession had little influence. In 1908–9 another observer, a Tsarist inspector called K. K. Pahlen, found a similar picture of intellectual backwardness and Sufi power. He thought that in an assembly of seventy jurists between ten and twenty at least were Sufi leaders.[9] Such evidence contradicts the recently expressed opinion that Islam in the USSR has become Sufi-dominated in a reaction to Soviet rule. This was the view of Alexandre Bennigsen, the main specialist in this field in western Europe, who provided the perspectives for several other scholars. He thought that there was an 'official' and an 'unofficial' or 'alternative' Islam, the latter being Sufism.

Bennigsen took this idea from Lucian Klimovich, the principal Soviet anti-Islamic propagandist of the Stalin and Krushchev eras. Other researchers have certainly acted unwisely in transposing it to the rest of the Muslim world. For one thing, it is very difficult to acquire information about Sufism in the USSR. Besides, Bennigsen himself thought that Sufism under Soviet rule was very different from Sufism elsewhere. Moreover, when one speaks of 'official Islam' in the USSR one is also speaking of a special case: the temporal authorities have given official registration to a small number of Muslim jurists (some of whom have been Sufis), while the Sufi brotherhoods have been illegal. Predictably, Soviet writers have depicted registered religious leaders as respectable and acceptable, and unregistered ones as mystical and superstitious. To make things more confusing, Bennigsen, when using Soviet writings, repeatedly spoke of 'clerics'. This produces chaos, since it is impossible to judge how many of these supposed 'clerics' are jurists, Sufis, or both.

Bennigsen, together with S. Enders Wimbush, wrote one book devoted entirely to Sufism in the USSR, *Mystics and Commissars*, published in 1985. This was based on the work of Soviet sociologists who, like sociologists elsewhere, expressed strong reservations about the value of questionnaires while depending heavily upon them. One wonders what significance can be attached to the replies elicited by the direct questioning of Soviet Muslims, given the eastern Islamic peoples' long tradition of lying to officials. It is also necessary to bear in mind that in the northern Caucasus, where much of the Soviet fieldwork has been done, there exists a very intense anti-Russian feeling, largely due to the brutal persecution (later denounced by Soviet writers) inflicted upon the population. Here the sociologists have found that a very high proportion of the Chechens are Sufis. But one must allow for the usual phenomenon of inherited allegiance to a family of Sufi masters, which is very different from the pursuit of the Sufi Path itself.

For their study of Soviet Central Asia, Bennigsen and Wimbush made extensive use of a survey of Islam in Karakalpakistan, by Zhumanazar Bazarbaev, published in 1973. In this they found that 11.4 per cent of the adult population were 'convinced believers'. Then they projected this on to the rest of the region, in order to produce an estimate of the strength of Sufism, but were uncertain whether to judge the Sufi proportion of the 'convinced believers' to be nearer one-half or one-sixth. Moreover, they maintained that the age distribution of Sufis was difficult to ascertain. Bazarbaev noted the predominance of retired people, but Bennigsen and Wimbush claimed that Sufism attracted the young. As in the rest of their work, Bennigsen and Wimbush follow the principle that since Soviet writers would usually represent religion as dying out, any admission to the contrary should be accepted. But Bazarbaev's figures showed that out of 234 'convinced believers' none were under forty-two, and 199 were over fifty-four.[10] This corresponds to other Soviet evidence: a survey in Tashkent found that most lower-class people aged fifty-five and over were believers, and that unbelievers or people indifferent to religion returned to it at the age of fifty-five.[11] The same is true for mainstream Christianity in the USSR: children acquire religion from baby-sitting grandmothers, before giving it up or concealing it (presumably to avoid the administrative sanctions, notably expulsion from higher education, which have been directed principally against young believers) and becoming openly religious again in late middle age. One feels that, given such conditions, little can be learnt.

South-east Asia

There are about 150 million Muslims in the area which stretches from Thailand to the Philippines and includes Malaysia and Indonesia. Islam came to this area from the thirteenth century onwards. A rich Indian culture had already been firmly established there. The sources for the study of the early Islamization of the region are late and hagiographical: inevitably, some modern writers have concluded that the Sufis were responsible for widespread conversions to Islam, but one is bound to recall the discrediting of similar 'evidence' for the Sufi conversion of Indians. In the nineteenth century Dutch and British colonial domination came to what is now Indonesia and Malaysia (after a long history of commercial relations).

The course taken by Sufism in South-east Asia remains unclear. There is one famous writer, Hamza Fansuri of Barus in North Sumatra (fl. 1600), but his work looks just like a straightforward exposition of Ibn 'Arabi's doctrine. Various brotherhoods installed themselves, and of particular interest is the coming of the Khalidi branch of the Naqshbandis' 'Renewerist' sub-brotherhood in the nineteenth century. The Khalidis, with their strict legalistic orientation, have been seen as preparing the ground for 'modern' anti-Sufi activity in our own time. In the twentieth century the Tijanis came from North Africa, and achieved some success, even obtaining the approval of the Muslim jurists, in spite of increasing anti-Sufi propaganda. The anti-Sufi forces found, in South-east Asian Sufism in general, the usual targets, such as the veneration of leading mystics and the ambiguous role of handsome boys in dancing. Western writers have tended to imagine that such aspects must belong to the native milieu, whereas, as we have seen, they are anticipated in many classical Middle Eastern practices. Some specialists in the study of Islam in South-east Asia have acquired an extreme intellectual hostility towards their colleagues in Middle Eastern studies, and consequently have often failed to observe how Islam's relationship to its environment has been largely determined by earlier developments.

In fieldwork done after the second world war – when Indonesia and Malaysia emerged as independent states – the variation in approaches and results follows a familiar pattern. Geertz's book *The Religion of Java*, published in 1960, contained second-hand reports of Sufis as insignificant old men on the brink of extinction. The brotherhoods were presented as spent forces, submerged beneath the rising tide of 'modernism'. By contrast, an extremely nuanced picture is given in the admirable summary of recent research compiled by Denys Lombard and published in 1986. On the one hand, the spectacular practice of hurting the body with iron spikes has virtually died out. A few members of the Qadiri brotherhood in West Java have engaged in this practice in recent years. They are poor peasants, who gather in groups of at most eight, and begin with prayers, in which the elder asks for the help of the brotherhood's supposed founder, 'Abd al-Qadir. The elder may use some incense or coconut oil to 'soften' the points of the spikes. Then they sing the praises of the founder, to the accompaniment of drums. After this they take the spikes (about fifty centimetres long, fixed in large wooden cylinders) and stick them into their stomachs and chests. Recently this practice has degenerated into an officially organized entertainment for tourists. On the other hand, Sufism is flourishing in West Sumatra, where in 1974 the authorities estimated that over 113,000 people out of a population of almost three million Muslims belonged to a brotherhood. Huge crowds come to the annual celebrations at the tomb of Shaykh Burhan al-Din (d. 1699) at Ulakan. Seventy-eight specially constructed hostels correspond to the various villages whose inhabitants come to stay.

A more detailed evaluation of Sufi allegiance has been made after investigations at the Naqshbandi village of Babussalam in North Sumatra. This village was founded in 1883, by one 'Abd al-Wahhab, who took the surname al-Khalidi, which designates adherence to the Khalidi branch of the 'Renewerists', and died in 1925. He intended it to be self-sufficient and autonomous. It has 1300 inhabitants, mainly poor fishermen and workers on the old rubber plantations, all of whom have to join the brotherhood. Two special houses, for men and women respectively, are set aside for retreats, with fasting and praying in cells. But by 1976 the number of people choosing to take part in these retreats was dropping, and attendance at Sufi meetings had fallen from several dozen to seven or less, all middle-aged.

Yet another impression is given by the college of Rejoso in East Java, where one finds a flourishing development of Sufism in combination with academic studies. The director is said to have 150,000 disciples elsewhere, while on the spot hundreds of villagers, women outnumbering men, attend weekly meetings. The college is noted for its docile collaboration with the government. In 1975 its director became the president of the Indonesian association of Sufi brotherhoods, with responsibility for controlling those recognized as legitimate. He has been much criticized for his electoral campaigning on behalf of the ruling party.

Senegal

Finally, we return to West Africa, to review the large amount of recent work devoted to an offshoot of the Qadiris in Senegal, the members of which are called the Mourides (from the Arabic *murid*, the usual word for a Sufi disciple).

Donal B. Cruise O'Brien has written an extended study, published in 1971, of this brotherhood, which is independent of the other Qadiris and began in the late nineteenth century among the Wolof people of north-western Senegal. It is noted for the luxurious life-style of its leaders, who have spent their wealth on expensive American cars and French perfumes. The early life of its founder, Amadu Bamba (*c.* 1850–1927), coincides with the period of the French conquest of the region. According to O'Brien he was not an exceptionally striking personality. He promised salvation to his disciples, and insisted in particular on the importance of working in the service of one's elder. This has become the most significant feature of the Mourides, and has led rival brotherhoods to follow suit. The Mourides are well known for their skilled artisans, who are especially numerous in the villages which owe them allegiance. Some of their elders have been fond of alcohol, but here, as in North Africa, disciples have put forward the explanation that their 'blessing' transforms it into milk.

The devotion of the disciples has been sustained by promises of paradise. On one occasion, at the funeral of an employee of the brotherhood's main mosque, those who attended were told that all their past sins would be forgiven. But the reasons for devotion to an elder are not always clear. In one zone the local elder is often the village chief. Moreover, the Franco-Arabic word *marabout*, so confusing in North Africa where the French have used it to mean a leading mystic (while the Arabic *murabit* has meant a man of religion as well as a man of the holy war), is also employed in a very confusing way in Senegal: it is applied not only to the elder (*shaykh*), but also to a wide range of other people, such as all those who perform Muslim religious functions or are believed to possess a significant knowledge of Islam, and a vast number of healers, vagabonds and lunatics. One must note in particular a branch of the Mourides called the Bay Fall, the members of which do not worship or fast, but are famous for self-flagellation and (alcohol-induced) drunkenness. Their eccentric founder, Ibra Fall (*c.* 1858–1930), played an important part in the rise of the Mourides, and created its distinctive institution of the *dara*, the group of young men working to serve an elder.

The Mourides, O'Brien found, were bad cultivators, partly because of the Senegalese concentration on peanut farming as the mainstay of the economy. Since this brought quick cash returns for the elders, they promoted its rapid extension in an ecologically ruinous pursuit of wealth, which was spent on expensive clothes and food, and on the acquisition of beautiful young concubines. The Mourides had tried to adjust to urban life, and since 1945 had in fact made their main efforts to expand in the capital city of Dakar. Here they recruited a large proportion of the artisans. At the same time their leaders became more visibly involved in politics, since they were able to deliver huge quantities of votes to westernized politicians, as Senegal moved towards independence in 1960. They also had vast influence with the government as suppliers of amulets to political leaders and senior civil servants. O'Brien concluded that the Mouride movement was a response to French colonialism: the victims of imperialism were finding a solution to their predicament. Against this view, given the evidence presented, we might feel that the disciples were the victims of a simultaneous colonization by their elders.

In 1975 O'Brien published what looked like a disavowal of his earlier, disturbing picture, under the title *Saints and Politicians*. Now he said that what appeared to be a confidence trick was not. His eyewitness observations were sacrificed to make way for the anthropological dogma of 'reciprocity'. The disciples were not being deluded into working to make others rich. There was a 'functional' explanation: they were being given land of their own, and the elders were collecting a sort of estate agent's fee for their services. O'Brien's attempt at self-criticism seems to break down when he admits that 'in practice the Mouride welfare state acts perhaps less to serve the old, the sick, the hungry (although these can and do benefit from saintly handouts) than to line the pockets of the holy man's entourage.'[12]

Much research on the Mourides has been conducted by French sociologists, and their results have been summarized by Jean Copans, with interpretations of his own, in the 1970s and 1980s. Exhaustive investigations have proved that Mouride villagers do not work exceptionally hard. It would be absurd to speak of their having a 'Protestant work ethic'. Indeed, the Mouride peasant works no harder than his non-Mouride counterpart, and the level of his efforts is determined in the first place by climatic factors. Moreover, the relationship between the elder and his disciple is only one part of the villager's life: aspects such as the organization of work and mutual assistance among villagers are in fact independent of interference from the elder.

Another French contribution to Mouride studies, published in 1981, has been made by Christian Coulon, whose approach is unusual, being that of a political scientist. His work is valuable in the account that it gives of changes in Senegal in the 1970s: there has been an Islamic revival, with an insistence on an outward display of conventional piety, and a contribution made by 'reformists', often with an anti-Sufi ideology coming from Saudi Arabia. These 'reformists', characterized by their study of Arabic, have, ironically, been employed by the Sufi brotherhoods in their own schools. The Mouride leadership has found it advisable to distance itself from the government, whereas previously it collaborated with the ruling party in the most public fashion.

Coulon, along with Copans, has been much concerned to apply the idea of 'ideological state apparatuses', an expression much used in France in the 1970s, and taken from an article by the Marxist philosopher Louis Althusser, which represents the embryo of a projected theory.[13] In it Althusser argued that private institutions can function as 'ideological state apparatuses', the end result of which being to perpetuate given processes of economic production and exploitation. Copans and Coulon took the view that previously the Mourides had functioned as an apparatus of this kind, without actually transmitting the ideology of the French or Senegalese state, but that the Senegalese state would now develop its own institutions instead.

In contrast, Jean Schmitz, writing in 1983, has given the view of an anthropologist. The Mouride brotherhood had indeed worked as a tool of French colonialism, but Senegalese politics operate essentially as a reflection of kinship structures, which produce inherited friendship and hostility. Schmitz sees in Islam's revival in Senegal an indication of the state's weakness and inability to develop strong institutions of its own. The relationship between elder and disciple is not just one between two people, in a setting of economic production, but is part of complicated relationships of instruction and marriage. It is necessary to go beyond the simple and straightforward opposition between 'saint' and 'politician' or 'chief' and 'cleric' found in British and American studies, and see how members of kinship groups are 'aristocrats' in one place and 'marabouts' in another. Thus Schmitz points out that the Wolof expression which Coulon translated as *faire la politique* in fact means 'to follow a leader', and that in Senegal a disciple can abandon his elder, but only for another elder in the same family.

CONCLUSIONS

Up to this point a strictly historical, linear perspective has been taken. Now a few themes will be explored, without entirely abandoning that perspective, but with reference to the phenomenon of Sufism as a whole. The aim will be to place Sufism in the wider context of Islam itself, which, as was noted at the outset, is not just a religion, but a civilization, and has given rise to societies whose institutions are specifically Islamic.

We shall try to see how Sufism is connected to the social and political divisions of the Muslim world, and how it is related to music and the visual arts. Looking to the future, and the problem of whether any future Islamic society can dispense with Sufism, we shall tackle the subject of interreaction between the Sufis and the Muslim scholar-jurists. This topic is closely bound up with the question which is bound to trouble future Muslim politicians: to what extent may Sufism have acted as a reactionary force? In endeavouring to provide answers, particular attention will be given to the thirteenth century, as the period in which the Sufi brotherhoods arose and Sufi theory was systematized, and also the period in which, as is exemplified by the case of Rumi, leading Sufis became extremely powerful as the collaborators of temporal rulers, and saw themselves as the 'deputies of God' after the fall of the caliphs of Baghdad.

Sufism: a form of monasticism?

Before coming to these specific problems, however, one needs to ask how Sufism's general relationship to the world can be defined. The question must be asked, 'Is this monasticism?' The answer, probably, is both yes and no, since Islam both is and is not Christianity. Some reputable specialists use the words 'monastery' or 'convent' to designate a Sufi lodge, while others would reject them with horror. To be sure, a modern Bektashi lodge in the Balkans, if belonging to the brotherhood's celibate branch, is hardly distinguishable from a Christian monastery, but then the Bektashis represent an extremist Christianizing wing of Sufism, with a background of conversion from Christianity and implantation on Christian soil. Indeed, one might feel that the Bektashis' beliefs and practices put them outside both Sufism and Islam. It would be absurd to apply the word 'monastery' to contemporary Sufi meeting places when they consist of little more than assembly rooms and the elder's home.

But might one not see, in the history of Sufism, a development from a medieval equivalent of monasticism to a modern freemasonry? The thirteenth-century division, described by Daya of Rayy, between those inhabitants of the lodge who work and those who pray is all too reminiscent of the European abbeys. In the seventeenth century one French visitor to Iran declared that the dervishes were not monks: they took no vows, and could return from begging to a normal life.[1] In the nineteenth century Vámbéry took a similar view, observing that many dervishes would later set themselves up in trade.[2] But in the eighteenth century d'Ohsson found that this rarely happened. The relative absence of celibacy in Sufism is of course a distinguishing feature, as is the preponderance of Sufis who have not 'abandoned the world'. Some Sufi writers declared that the 'true monasticism' (as opposed to its Christian equivalent) was their ideal: the fourteenth-century treatise on Sufism attributed to Ibn Khaldun openly advocates monasticism, explaining that the Koran blamed the Christians for practising it because they did not have the necessary strength.[3] We may feel that the 'true monasticism' was intended by the line in Ibn al-Farid's Wine-song:

> Good health to the people of the Christian monastery How drunk
>   they became with it
> Though they did not drink of it but intended to do so

The term 'world renouncing' has been much used, both correctly, to render an Islamic idea, and misleadingly, in wider theorizing. Certainly, van Ess is right to insist that *zuhd* (often translated as 'asceticism') means 'renunciation of the world': the explanations in classical Sufi texts leave no doubt about that. But Sufism presents itself as both incorporating and transcending *zuhd*: it is one of the 'stations' of the Path, but the dry and uninspiring 'world renouncers' are much mocked in Sufi poetry. One feels, if the pun may be excused, that here there is a *sophi*sticated example of dialectical thinking: the negation of the world is itself negated. An external observer has little chance of deciding whether a rich Sufi is engaging in an inner 'rejecting of the world' or some ironic pursuit of others' 'blame'. There must be grave doubts about the usefulness of applying expressions such as 'world affirming' or 'world rejecting' from the outside, as British and American sociologists commonly do. When the world is viewed differently from different positions in an elaborate system of religious belief, so that it is renounced on one level and admired or embraced on another, to give thinkers labels of this kind does not seem helpful.

Political power

Daya's description of the Sufi lodge, as containing workers on the one hand and worshippers on the other, comes in the context of his call, at the time of the Mongol invasions, for society to be divided in the same way. He is not the only Sufi of his time to be asking for this: Rumi's father was also advocating the subordination of mankind to the 'friends of God'. The Sufis were also opposing the introduction of a philosophical basis for theology. Against this, Ibn 'Arabi's system would prevail, with its incorporation of philosophy and theology into Sufism as the dominating member of the triad. The Sufis were also successful in convincing temporal rulers of the need to give them a leading social role. Now they, in place of the scholar-jurists, became the most respected leaders of the population, which would pay and work for them. When one looks at the way in which the Sufis took advantage of the Mongol invasions to gain influence for themselves, joining in the process of collaboration with the conquerors and preaching an organization of society in which others would labour conscientiously beneath the 'friends of God', one may be led to make comparisons with an exceptionally distasteful modern parallel: the attempt by certain members of the French Right to bring about a reactionary revolution in 1940, against the background of the Nazi conquest of their country. These Frenchmen, along with their exaltation of religion, were particularly fond of the figure of the traditional artisan, who took pride in his craftsmanship and would not dream of striking: they wanted workers to participate in paternalistic 'corporations' or guilds, which would establish a happy harmony between them and their employers.

The artisan

Now Sufism, as we have seen throughout our survey, has also shown a special enthusiasm for recruiting the artisan. This may be connected with the Indo-European heritage. It was noted above that the Islamic evidence supported Dumézil's view of the ideology shared by the various Indo-European peoples – they had a pattern of three leading concepts: religion, war and fertility. But recent research has pointed to the existence of an obscure fourth concept, the nature of which cannot be exactly defined, though it has been thought to contain the elements of danger and foreignness, and its position would certainly be beneath the other three. It appears likely that as the Indo-European peoples developed their social structures this fourth concept was transformed into the artisan class, beneath those of the priesthood, the warriors and the cultivators. Evidence from various early Indo-European societies shows that they were divided in this fourfold way. Perhaps, then, further study of the Indo-European heritage can provide the answer to the famous problem of accounting for the extremely lowly position of the artisan in archaic Greece: specialists in ancient history have often wondered why he was ranked so very low, compared to his place elsewhere in the world, and have put forward economic theories to try to explain this, though none of these theories have been found convincing. Pre-Islamic Iran also had the artisan in fourth place, and he is put beneath the ancient triad in Sana'i's poetry, as we have seen. But in Islam, if the artisan is subordinated, there is also every effort made to win him over, whether to the Sufis, to the Shiites or to the libertine dervishes. From the fourteenth century, in circumstances that are still unclear, the artisan is brought into craft guilds, the dominant ideology of which is the 'youngmanliness' tradition, strongly influenced by Sufism and now bound up with it.

How much can be known about this fourteenth-century transition? One cannot say exactly how the Ottoman Empire succeeded in channelling the institution of 'youngmanliness' into the guilds. But we have seen that in the craft guilds the artisan has Dumézil's triad re-created and internalized in his activity, in his apprenticeship to his master, as desire and angry force are brought beneath the command of wisely directing knowledge. From the thirteenth century onward, the evidence shows that, as Daya had urged, work is done to the accompaniment of the incessant repetition of God's names: the apprentice is taught to recite specially selected verses of the Koran and formulas of 'remembrance of God' appropriate for every action (stretching cloth out on the ground, picking it up, cutting it, rinsing it and so on).[4] Sufism, moreover, enables the artisan to rise above his lowly rank and progress in the spiritual hierarchy of God's friends. Thus it is in the products of the craftsman that one sees the visual beauties of Islam, as opposed to the work of the creative artist in western painting and sculpture.

Sufism and the arts

Inevitably, a certain type of modern literature insists on seeing a deep Sufi and mystical meaning in the whole of Islamic art and architecture. Such literature, however, usually appeals not so much to Sufi sources as to the Greek philosophical tradition in Islam, and predictably insists on respect for *Order* as the natural principle of all things. Thus Order is perceived as the expression of 'unity', the word used in this literature to translate *tawhid* (the attestation of God's Uniqueness). Consequently the reader is lectured on cosmic symbolism and correspondences with Hindu temples. Alchemy and astronomy (themselves disciplines which were part of the Hellenized philosophers' preserve) are combined with the neo-Platonist aspects of Ibn 'Arabi's synthesis.

Another type of modern literature introduces western sentiments into the study of miniature painting in the Muslim world. Some well-known specialists, in a joint publication, have argued that since the paintings usually illustrate poems, and the poems are often mystical in inspiration, then so too are the pictures. They give as an example an alleged depiction of 'mystics sitting in a garden', and a quotation from Thomas Traherne about feelings of oneness with nature.[5] But the text illustrated is not about mystics, but about poets, and Sufism is not really concerned with the subjective impressions of nature-mysticism, as far as its own literature tells us. If a miniature does explicitly present the Sufi practice of 'gazing at beardless boys' in order to perceive universal Beauty, the same specialists simply label it as 'a scene of parting'.[6] When Islamic miniatures portray aspects of Sufism, or illustrate poetry with some Sufi content, it is frequently to show mystics as distraught or agitated, most often when dancing with youths. The pictorial evidence provides the very opposite of the state of inner calm and integration of the mystic in the structure of the universe.

This testimony from miniature painting entirely agrees with the literary sources' description of the effects of music and poetry upon Sufis: the listeners are brought into automatic motion, weep, tear their clothes and collapse. As we have seen, the practice of 'listening' is viewed as particularly dangerous. The effects produced are those of disturbance, and it is necessary for the elder to intervene to re-establish peace. Initially, the sounds bring the Sufi into an agitated condition, and he is supposed to 'relate' what he hears to God's attributes or to aspects of his teacher. Musical theory as an academic discipline in Islam was yet another importation from the Greek philosophical tradition, and as such was regarded as alien by the Sufis themselves. The records of fourteenth-century conversations between

Sufi elders and their disciples show a naive ignorance of this discipline, as one would expect.[7] The philosophers' view of music as reflecting the rational harmony of the cosmos is fundamentally different from the Sufis' own view of correspondences between sounds, movements, lights and ecstatic 'states'.

Sufism and the scholar-jurists

On the question of Sufism's relationship with the Muslim scholar-jurists our survey and conclusions agree with those of a number of continental European social scientists, recently summarized by Gilles Veinstein: there is no uniform pattern of hostility between Sufism and the lawyers, nor indeed any discernible logic in the history of their contacts throughout the world. From the beginning there was suspicion of Sufism's possible infringements of Islamic law, but there were also respectable Sufis on good terms with the jurists.

In the first half of the thirteenth century, to be sure, Ibn 'Arabi and Rumi's wildly ecstatic teacher, Shams al-Din of Tabriz, made violent attacks on allegedly anti-mystical lawyers, but these lawyers seem to have been against Greek philosophical ideas and apparent expressions of monism rather than Sufism itself. For a thirteenth-century jurist to reject the Sufi Path entirely was evidently unusual. One chief architect of the expansion of Sufi power, 'Umar Suhrawardi, was using his own 'lodge' to house students to whom he taught jurisprudence. Afterwards it would be normal for a lawyer to belong to a brotherhood. The seventeenth century yielded outbreaks of fighting between the Sufis and some jurists in the Ottoman Empire and Iran, but it was only in Iran, with the presence of Shiism, that the break was to become definitive. In the eighteenth and nineteenth centuries critics who spoke out against Sufism in Egypt found themselves opposed by jurists who knew where their own financial interests lay. Twentieth-century Muslims have repeated the old variety of patterns: condemnation of Sufism; whole-hearted support for it; condemnation accompanied by collaboration; and nuanced acceptance of its more sober manifestations.

Islam without Sufism?

The question remains whether, in the future, Islam (as both religion and civilization) could exist without Sufism. The historical evidence suggests that it could not. For the religious core of Islam seems, from very early on, to have been a blend of Jewish law and Christian devotionalism, with a Gnostic element already present. If the Christian part were to be suppressed, what would remain would be a Judaism without Jews, a national religion without ethnic identity.

The seventeenth-century attempt to rid the Ottoman Empire of Sufism brought near-disaster, and only with the immediate reversal of this policy was the empire saved. In Iran, shortly afterwards, the success of the anti-Sufi jurists produced the complete collapse of society. In the twentieth century, it may be observed that the Turkish Republic's efforts to destroy Sufism went together with its rejection of Islam itself, and that in practice both Sufism and Islam have managed to reassert themselves in close combination. The abolition of Sufism in Saudi Arabia has strengthened the accusation that Saudi rule is not Islamic but tribal.

If one accepts that Sufism has represented an integral and essential part of Islam, then it is difficult to evaluate arguments that Sufism has acted as a politically or culturally reactionary force. (It is necessary to observe that although we have seen close parallels between the actions of Sufi leaders in the thirteenth century and those of right-wing Frenchmen in 1940, the former cannot be designated as 'reactionary' with as much confidence as the latter, who were openly reacting against modern industrial society and trying to take it back into the Middle Ages, by turning factory workers into artisans and peasants.) Certainly, the evidence portrays the ninth-century Sufi masters as loyal supporters of whatever rulers might hold power, however unjust. But it also shows that Sufi ideas could lead people into views which threatened the state. The position of Sufism with regard to the cultural renaissance in the late tenth century is ambiguous. Recently some historians have formed the opinion that this renaissance was shared by western Europe and the Byzantine Empire at the same time, but that, whereas the Europeans continued to make progress almost without interruption up to our own time, Islam suffered a set-back in the eleventh century from which it never really recovered.

How far was Sufism to blame? Daylami, the Sufi pupil of the austere Ibn Khafif, was closely connected with the revival of philosophy around 1000. Afterwards Sufism is indistinguishable from the Sunni backlash which ended Shiite domination and its fostering of the sciences. The triumph of Sufism in the thirteenth century undoubtedly looks like a defeat for the Greek spirit of inquiry, but then a similar victory for mysticism has been detected in western Christianity during the same period, and has been alleged to have long delayed the coming of the Renaissance.

In the fourteenth and fifteenth centuries Sufism was associated with

Shiite, messianic aspirations to overthrow the existing governments. Ibn Khaldun pointed out the need to obtain group solidarity (*'asabiyya*) in order to make an attempt at revolution successful. This the Safavids were to find in the tribes, thus showing a perpetual source of possible Sufi-inspired revolt. In the eighteenth and nineteenth centuries it is difficult to disentangle mysticism from 'Renewerist' (*Mujaddidi*) or supposedly 'reformist' currents. The twentieth century has often found Sufi leaders in alliance with colonialism and pro-American governments. But in order to decide whether Sufism must necessarily contribute to consolidating the position of the rich and powerful one is obliged to ask how Sufism actually works. That is a question of huge scope, put in a context of general ignorance, but it is difficult to avoid.

It is perhaps best to try to give an answer in the terms of one post-structuralist perspective, that of Gilles Deleuze and Félix Guattari.[8] Sufism works as a machine in the middle of an arrangement of other machines. Man is caught between sounds and images on the one hand and the imposing figures of God and his Prophet on the other. Around him function the machines of the state, of Islamic law, of armies and guilds, of the philosophers with their astronomy and medicine. But between God and the sensations of the outside world the Sufi chooses a friend who will direct him from the one to the other in measured alternation. Often the effect will be one of subjugation and submission, not only to the elder but also to the prince. Yet the very principle of attraction must also permit a liberating impetus towards a free flight into the undetermined pluralities of the unknown.

Beside God and his Prophet, then, there stands a third figure, the friend who completes the triad. This triad is also that of the Shiites: a dominant pattern in Islam, often more important in practice than the five pillars of attestation of belief, worship, almsgiving, fasting and pilgrimage. But how is one to recognize the friend of God? In the records of Rumi's conversations a questioner objects that there is no evidence by which God's friend can be distinguished. Rumi gets him to admit that he has faith in someone, and consequently has a self-contradictory position. We, however, may feel that the difficulty remains.[9]

How then shall we reply to the classic question 'What is Sufism?' Perhaps the answer of Ibn Khafif (noted above in our survey of tenth-century developments) is not inappropriate. He says that Sufism is not a science (which was true enough in his time, although it was later to become a systematized discipline among the other religious sciences of Islam), and not a practice (this is doubtless to be taken as meaning that although Sufism has a practical side it is also more than that). By contrast, he declares – in language apt enough in his own day, but which is difficult for the modern reader to understand – Sufism is an attribute, that is to say a quality or aspect of the Sufi. Through the medium of this attribute, says Ibn Khafif, the Sufi's essence displays itself: the innermost centre of his individual personality reveals itself and shines forth. Here Ibn Khafif uses the concept of self-manifestation (*tajalli*, theophany), which is usually employed to designate God's own action in making himself appear to the world.

One is led to turn back from the question of what Sufism is and look at the mystics themselves. And if our survey of Sufism has often provided a disillusioning picture, perhaps one should allow the Sufis the last word: they say that God's friends are mirrors in which others see their own faults reflected.

NOTES

Only the barest minimum of notes is provided here. They are usually references for quotations from Sufi poetry, details of social and economic history, pieces of evidence found only in manuscripts, summaries of technical academic discussions and remarks concerning schools of thought outside Sufism (most often in the Greek philosophical tradition in the Muslim world). For further information the reader can consult the relevant sections of the bibliography, which is arranged according to the order of subjects treated in the text.

INTRODUCTION

1　R. M. Rilke, *Briefe aus Muzot 1921 bis 1926* (Leipzig: Insel, 1937), p. 376.
2　P. Antes, *Zur Theologie der Schi'a* (Freiburg: Klaus Schwarz, 1971; S. A. Arjomand, *The Shadow of God and the Hidden Imam* (Chicago: Chicago University Press, 1984).
3　E. Benveniste, '*Profanus* et *profanare*', in *Hommages à Georges Dumézil* (Brussels: Latomus, 1960), pp. 46–53.

1　SUFISM'S BEGINNINGS

1　Cf. P. Crone, *Roman, provincial and Islamic law* (Cambridge: Cambridge University Press, 1987).
2　Isaac of Nineveh, *Mystic Treatises*, tr. A. J. Wensinck (Amsterdam: Koninlijke Akademie van Wetenschappen, 1923), pp. 246–7.
3　'Alī Ḥarrālī (d. 1240), quoted by P. Nwyia, *Ibn 'Aṭā' Allāh et la naissance de la confrérie šādilite* (Beirut: Dar el-Machreq, 1972), p. 62.
4　G. Scholem, *Origins of the Kabbalah* (Princeton, NJ: The Jewish Publication Society, 1987), p. 12.
5　M. Tardieu, 'Ṣābiens coraniques et "Ṣābiens de Ḥarrān"', *Journal asiatique* 274/1–2 (1986) 1–44.
6　C. Schedl, *Muhammad und Jesus* (Vienna: Herder, 1978), pp. 477–80.

7   L. Massignon, *Essai sur les origines du lexique technique de la mystique musulmane*, second edition (Paris: Vrin, 1954), p. 104.

8   A. J. Arberry, 'Bistamiana', *Bulletin of the School of Oriental and African Studies* 25/1 (1962) 28–37.

9   Massignon, *Essai sur les origines*, pp. 279–81.

10 M. Molé, *Les Mystiques musulmans* (Paris: Presses Universitaires de France, 1965), pp. 53–7.

11 L. Kolakowski, *Chrétiens sans Église* (Paris: Gallimard, 1969), pp. 582–609, and *Main Currents of Marxism* (Oxford: Oxford University Press, 1981), vol. 1, pp. 9–80.

2   FROM CONSTRUCTION TO SYSTEMATIZATION (*c.* 922–*c.* 1240)

1   E. Ashtor, *Histoire des prix et des salaires dans l'Orient médiéval* (Paris: SEVPEN, 1969), p. 37.

✓ 2   Cf. S. M. Afnan, *Avicenna: His Life and Works* (London: Allen & Unwin, 1958), pp. 187–97.

3   Cf. H. Corbin, *Avicenna and the Visionary Recital* (New York: Pantheon Books, 1960); and M. Fakhry, *A History of Islamic Philosophy*, second edition (London: Longman, 1983), pp. 132–3 and 157–60.

4   E. C. Sachau (tr.), *Alberuni's India* (London: Kegan Paul, 1910), vol. 1, pp. 33–88.

✓ 5   Cf. H. Laoust, *La Politique de Ġazālī* (Paris: Paul Geuthner, 1970).

6   Aḥmad Ghazālī, *Sawāniḥ*, ed. N. Pūrjawādī (Tehran: Bunyād-i Farhang-i Īrān, 1359/1980), p. 9.

7   Sanāʾī, *Dīwān*, ed. M. Riḍawī (Tehran: Kitābkhāna-yi Sanāʾī, 1355/1976), p. 26.

8   Ibn Ṭufayl, *The Journey of the Soul*, tr. R. Kocache (London: Octagon Press, 1982).

✓ 9   Cf. T. F. Glick, *Islamic and Christian Spain in the Early Middle Ages* (Princeton, NJ: Princeton University Press, 1979), pp. 151–2.

10 Cf. Yaḥyā Suhrawardī, *L'Archange empourpré*, tr. H. Corbin (Paris: Fayard, 1976); and Fakhry, *A History*, pp. 293–304.

11 Cf. D. Knowles, *The Monastic Order in England: a history of its development from the times of St Dunstan to the Fourth Lateran Council, 940–1216*, second edition (Cambridge: Cambridge University Press, 1963), pp. 28 and 194.

12 Ḥasan Dihlawī, *Fawāʾid al-fuʾād*, ed. M. L. Malik (Lahore: M. Sirāj al-Dīn, 1386/1966), pp. 152–3.

13 R. Gramlich, *Die schiitischen Derwischorden Persiens*, vol. 2 (Wiesbaden: Franz Steiner, 1976), pp. 171–5.

14 R. Basset (ed. and tr.), *Le Tableau de Cébès: version arabe* (Algiers: Imprimerie Orientale, 1898).

15 'Aṭṭār, *Dīwān*, ed. T. Tafaḍḍulī (Tehran: Bungāh-i Tarjuma wa Nashr-i Kitāb, 1967), pp. 817–20.
16 Ibn al-Fāriḍ, *The Mystical Poems*, ed. A. J. Arberry (London: Emery Walker, 1952), pp. 80, 84 and 111–2.
17 Ibid., pp. 39–40.

3 ELDERS AND EMPIRES (*c*. 1240–*c*. 1700)

1 G. Scholem, *Major Trends in Jewish Mysticism* (Jerusalem: Schocken, 1941), pp. 121–52.
2 D. Urvoy, 'Les Emprunts mystiques entre Islam et Christianisme et la véritable portée du *Libre d'Amic*', *Estudios Lulíanos* 23 (1979) 37–44 and *Penser l'Islam* (Paris: Vrin, 1980); R. Bonner and C. Lohr, article 'Raymond Lulle', in M. Viller et al. (eds), *Dictionnaire de Spiritualité* (Paris: Beauchesne, 1932–).
3 Barhebraeus, *Book of the Dove*, tr. A. J. Wensinck (Leiden: E. J. Brill, 1919), pp. 118–33.
4 P. Adnes, article 'Jésus (Prière à)', in *Dictionnaire de Spiritualité*.
5 Rūmī, *Kulliyyāt-i Shams*, ed. B. Furūzānfar, vol. 2 (Tehran: Tehran University, 1958), pp. 65–6.
6 Rūmī, *The Mathnawī*, ed. R. A. Nicholson, vol. 3 (London: Luzac, 1929), p. 321 (Book Four, line 733).
7 Rūmī, *Kulliyyāt*, vol. 2, p. 51.
8 Cf. M. Molé, *Culte, mythe et cosmologie dans l'Iran ancien* (Paris: Presses Universitaires de France, 1963), pp. 453–4.
9 Herodotus IV 5–7; Quintus Curtius VII 8, 17–19; Plutarch, *Artaxerxes*, 3.2.
10 Cf. M. Chodkiewicz, *Le Sceau des saints* (Paris: Gallimard, 1986), pp. 105–6.
11 L. Massignon, *Opera Minora*, vol. 2 (Paris: Presses Universitaires de France, 1969), p. 563.
12 Cf. S. Gupta et al., *Hindu Tantrism* (Leiden: E. J. Brill, 1979), pp. 184–5.
13 Faḍl Allāh Mājawī, *Fatāwā 'l-ṣūfiyya*, MS Oxford, Bodleian Uri 321, fo. 22^r.
14 Ibid., fos 91^v–2^r.
15 Ibid., fos 11^{r-v}, 36^v, 62^v, 69^r, 91^v–2^r, 114^v–17^v, 180^v, 206^v, 212^v–13^r and 226^r.
16 H. A. R. Gibb (tr.), *The Travels of Ibn Baṭṭūṭa*, vol. 3 (Cambridge: Cambridge University Press, 1971), pp. 655 and 702–4.
17 Dihlawī, *Fawā'id*, pp. 44, 101, 106–7, 208, 271 and 315.
18 Ibid., pp. 269–70, 364 and 391.
19 Ibid., pp. 96, 99, 207–8, 319 and 363.
20 Mājawī, *Fatāwā*. fo. 20^r.
21 Ibid., fos 212^v–213^r.

22   Dihlawī, *Fawā'id*, pp. 228–9, 290–1 and 378.

23   Ḥamīd Qalandar, *Khayr al-majālis*, ed. K. A. Nizami (Aligarh: Muslim University, 1959), pp. 69, 129–32, 184–5 and 286.

24   Dihlawī, *Fawā'id*, pp. 218–19.

25   Ibid., pp. 166–7 and 196.

26   Qalandar, *Khayr*, pp. 43, 45 and 240.

27   A. Hartmann, 'Eine orthodoxe Polemik gegen Philosophen und Freidenker', *Der Islam* 56/2 (1979) 274–93.

28   J. Rypka, *History of Iranian Literature* (Dordrecht: D. Reidel, 1968), pp. 276–7.

29   Ḥāfiẓ, *Dīwān*, ed. P. N. Khānlarī, second edition, vol. 1 (Tehran: Intishārāt-i Khwārazmī, 1362/1983), p. 98.

30   Ibid., p. 428.

31   K. R. F. Burrill, *The Quatrains of Nesimî* (The Hague: Mouton, 1972), p. 136.

32   Ibid., p. 198.

33   Jāmī, *Khirad-nāma-yi Iskandarī*, ed. (with his *Tuḥfat al-aḥrār* and *Subḥat al-abrār*) H. A. Tarbiyat (Moscow: Nauka, 1984), p. 325.

34   Jāmī, *Haft awrang*, ed. M. Gīlānī (Tehran: Kitābfurūshī-yi Sa'dī, 1958), pp. 265–6.

35   S. Faroqhi, 'Seyyid Gazi revisited', *Turcica* 13 (1981) 96.

36   I. Beldiceanu-Steinherr, 'Le Règne de Selīm Ier', *Turcica* 6 (1975) 34–48.

37   S. Faroqhi, 'Social mobility among the Ottoman 'ulemâ in the late sixteenth century', *International Journal of Middle East Studies* 4/2 (1973) 204–18.

38   S. Faroqhi, '*Vakıf* administration in sixteenth-century Konya', *Journal of the Economic and Social History of the Orient* 17/2 (May 1974) 145–72.

39   Faroqhi, 'Seyyid Gazi', pp. 90–122.

40   F. Taeschner, *Zünfte und Brüderschaften im Islam* (Zürich: Artemis, 1979), p. 450.

41   H. Thorning, *Beiträge zur Kenntnis des islamischen Vereinswesens* (Berlin: Mayer & Muller, 1913), p. 232.

42   S. Moosvi, 'Suyūrghāl statistics in the *Ā'īn-i Akbarī*', *Indian Historical Review* 2/2 (January 1976) 286.

43   J. Correia-Afonso (ed.), *Letters from the Mughal Court* (Anand: Gujarat Sahitya Prakash, 1980), pp. 95–6.

44   M. G. S. Hodgson, *The Venture of Islam*, vol. 3 (Chicago, Ill.: University of Chicago Press, 1974), pp. 73–80.

45   Dārā Shukūh, *Muntakhabāt-i āthār*, ed. S. M. B. Jalālī-Nā'īnī (Tehran: Tābān 1335/1956), pp. 17–20.

46   Shāh Ismā'īl I, *Divan*, ed. T. Gandjei (Naples: Istituto Universitario Orientale, 1959), pp. 125 and 129.

47   F. Rahman, article 'Mullā Sadrā' in M. Eliade (ed.), *The Encyclopedia of Religion* (New York: Macmillan, 1987).

48   J. Chardin, *Voyages en Perse*, ed. C. Gaudon (Paris: Union Générale d'Éditions, 1965), pp. 242–5.

49 J. B. Tavernier, *Les Six Voyages*, vol. 1 (Paris, 1679), pp. 453–4.
50 Aḥmad Uzganī, *Tadhkira-yi Uwaysiyya*, MS Oxford, Bodleian Ind. Inst. Pers. 54, fos 320ʳ–9ᵛ, 338ʳ–41ᵛ and 344ᵛ–5ᵛ.

4 INTO THE MODERN WORLD

1 A. L. S. Marsot, 'The wealth of the ulama in late eighteenth-century Cairo', in T. Naff and R. Owen (eds), *Studies in Eighteenth Century Islamic History* (Carbondale, Ill.: Southern Illinois University Press, 1977), pp. 210–13.
2 Nūr 'Alī-Shāh Iṣfahānī, *Majmū'a-ī az āthār*, ed. J. Nūrbakhsh (Tehran: Khānaqāh-i Ni'matullāhī, 1350/1971), pp. 60–6.
3 E. Westermarck, *Ritual and Belief in Morocco*, vol. 1 (London: Macmillan, 1926), pp. 35–6 and 146–7.
4 C. Geertz, *Islam Observed* (Chicago, Ill.: University of Chicago Press, 1971), p. 8.
5 Ibid., pp. 70–1.
6 M. Morsy, *Les Ahansala* (Paris: Mouton, 1972), pp. 33–4.
7 E. A. Gellner, *Saints of the Atlas* (London: Weidenfeld & Nicolson, 1969), pp. 111, 130–1, 149–51, 157, 182, 209–10 and 216.
8 J.-P. Roux, *Les Traditions des nomades de la Turquie meridionale* (Paris: Adrien-Maisonneuve, 1970), p. 102.
9 K. K. Pahlen, *Mission to Turkestan* (London: Oxford University Press, 1964), p. 83.
10 Z. Bazarbaev, *Sekuliarizatsiia naseleniia sotsialisticheskoi Karakalpakii* (Nukus: Karakalpakstan, 1973), p. 53.
11 A Bennigsen and C. Lemercier-Quelquejay, *Islam in the Soviet Union* (London: Pall Mall Press, 1967), p. 182.
12 D. B. Cruise O'Brien, *Saints and Politicians* (Cambridge: Cambridge University Press, 1975), pp. 75–6.
13 L. Althusser, 'Ideology and Ideological State Apparatuses', in *Essays on Ideology* (London: Verso, 1984), pp. 1–60.

CONCLUSIONS

1 Chardin, *Voyages*, p. 239.
2 A. Vámbéry, *Sketches of Central Asia* (London: Wm H. Allen, 1868), p. 7.
3 Cf. P. Nwyia, *Ibn 'Abbād de Ronda* (Beirut: Imprimerie Catholique, 1961), pp. lii–liii.
4 M. Ṣarrāf (ed.), *Traités des compagnons-chevaliers* (Paris: Adrien-Maisonneuve, 1973), pp. 225–39.

5 L. Binyon et al., *Persian Miniature Painting* (London: Oxford University Press, 1933), p. 8.
6 Ibid., p. 96.
7 Dihlawī, *Fawā'id*, pp. 283–4.
8 G. Deleuze and F. Guattari, *A Thousand Plateaus* (London: Athlone Press, 1988).
9 Rūmī, *Fīhi mā fīhi*, ed. B. Furūzānfar (Tehran: Tehran University, 1330/1951), p. 189.

BIBLIOGRAPHY

The bibliography is closely linked to the text. For an excellent bibliography of Sufism in alphabetical order of author, see Annemarie Schimmel, *Mystical Dimensions of Islam* (Chapel Hill, NC: University of North Carolina Press, 1975), pp. 437–67. Here it is assumed that the reader's native tongue is English, but works in other European languages are also included; only rarely have I mentioned publications in oriental languages. Except for general books, works are given in the order in which they appear in each chapter.

INTRODUCTORY AND GENERAL

'Afīfī, Abu 'l-'Alā', *al-Malāmatiyya wa 'l-ṣūfiyya wa ahl al-futuwwa* (Cairo: Dār Iḥyā' al-Kutub al-'Arabiyya, 1364/1945).

Caspar, R., 'Muslim mysticism: tendencies in modern research', in M. L. Swartz (ed. and tr.), *Studies in Islam* (New York: Oxford University Press, 1988), pp. 164–84.

Gramlich, R., *Die schiitischen Derwischorden Persiens* (Wiesbaden: Franz Steiner, 1965–81).

Meier, F., 'The mystic path', in B. Lewis (ed.), *The World of Islam* (London: Thames & Hudson, 1976), pp. 117–40.

Molé, M., *Les Mystiques musulmans* (Paris: Presses Universitaires de France, 1965).

Popovic, A., and Veinstein, G. (eds), *Les Ordres mystiques dans l'Islam* (Paris: Éditions de l'École des Hautes Études en Sciences Sociales, 1986).

Zarrinkub, A. H., 'Persian Sufism in historical perspective', *Iranian Studies* 3/3–4 (Summer–Autumn 1970), pp. 139–220.

1 SUFISM'S BEGINNINGS

Background and origins

Vööbus, A., *History of Asceticism in the Syrian Orient* (Louvain: Secrétariat du Corpus Scriptorum Christianorum Orientalium, 1958–60).

Brown, P., *The Cult of the Saints* (Chicago, Ill.: Chicago University Press, 1981).

Viller, M., et al. (eds), *Dictionnaire de Spiritualité* (Paris: Beauchesne, 1932–), articles 'Ébionites', 'Jésus (prière à)', 'Messaliens', 'Mnèmè Theou', 'Mort mystique', etc. One will note in particular the contributions of Antoine Guillaumont on eastern Christianity of Syriac expression.

Corbin, H., 'Manichéisme et religion de la beauté', *Cahiers du Sud* 55/1 (April–May 1963) 102–7.

Halm, H., *Die islamische Gnosis* (Zürich: Artemis, 1982).

Graham, W. A., *Divine Word and Prophetic Word in Early Islam* (Paris: Mouton, 1977).

Smith, M., *Rābiʿa the Mystic and her fellow-saints in Islām* (Cambridge: Cambridge University Press, 1928).

Smith, M., *Studies in Early Mysticism in the Near and Middle East* (London: Sheldon Press, 1931).

Nwyia, P., *Exégèse coranique et langage mystique* (Beirut: Dar el-Machreq, 1970).

Ogén, G., 'Did the term "*ṣūfī*" exist before the Sufis?', *Acta Orientalia* 43 (1982) 33–48.

Merx, E. O. A., *Idee und Grundlinien einer allgemeinen Geschichte der Mystik* (Heidelberg: J. Horning, 1893).

Andrae, T., *In the Garden of Myrtles* (Albany, NY: State University of New York Press, 1987).

The writers and thinkers of the ninth and early tenth century

Ess, J. van, *Die Gedankenwelt von Ḥāriṯ al-Muḥāsibī* (Bonn: Bonn University, 1961).

Zaehner, R. C., *Hindu and Muslim Mysticism* (London: Athlone Press, 1960).

Böwering, G., *The Mystical Vision of Existence in Classical Islam* (Berlin: Walter de Gruyter, 1980).

al-Kharrāz, Aḥmad, *The Book of Truthfulness*, ed. and tr. A. J. Arberry (London: Oxford University Press, 1937).

Madelung, W., article 'al-Kharrāz', in H. A. R. Gibb et al. (eds), *The Encyclopaedia of Islam*, second edition (Leiden: E. J. Brill, 1960–).

Nwyia, *Exégèse coranique*, pp. 231–310.

Radtke, B., *Al-Ḥakīm at-Tirmiḏī* (Freiburg: Klaus Schwarz, 1980).

Chodkiewicz, M., *Le Sceau des saints* (Paris: Gallimard, 1986).

Abdel-Kader, A. H., *The Life, Personality and Writings of al-Junayd* (London: Luzac, 1962).

Massignon, L., *The Passion of al-Ḥallāj* (Princeton, NJ: Princeton University Press, 1982).

Nwyia, P. (ed. and tr.), 'Ḥallāğ: *Kitāb al-ṭawāsīn*', *Mélanges de l'Université Saint-Joseph* 47 (1972) 183–238.

Bibliography 187

2 FROM CONSTRUCTION TO SYSTEMATIZATION (c. 922–c. 1240)

Construction and speculation (c. 922–c. 1020)

Böwering, *The Mystical Vision*, pp. 7–34 and 75–99.
Daylamī, Abu 'l-Ḥasan, *Sīrat-i Abū 'Abd Allāh Ibn Khafīf al-Shīrāzī*, ed. A. Schimmel (Ankara: Türk Tarih Kurumu Basımevi, 1955).
al-Niffarī, Muḥammad, *The Mawáqif and Mukhátabát*, ed. and tr. A. J. Arberry (London: Luzac, 1935).
Nwyia, *Exégèse coranique*, pp. 352–407.
Sarrāj, 'Abd Allāh, *Kitāb al-luma'*, ed. with English summary by R. A. Nicholson (Leiden: E. J. Brill, 1914).
Kalābādhī, Abū Bakr, *The Doctrine of the Sufis*, tr. A. J. Arberry (Cambridge: Cambridge University Press, 1935).
al-Makkī, Abū Ṭālib Muḥammad, *Qūt al-qulūb* (Cairo: A. al-Bābī, 1310/1893).
Daylamī, Abu 'l-Ḥasan, *Le Traité d'amour mystique*, tr. J.-C. Vadet (Geneva: Droz, 1980).
Sulamī, Muḥammad, *The Book of Sufi Chivalry*, tr. T. B. al-Jerrahi (London: East–West Publications 1983).

Reaction and poetic expression (c. 1020–c. 1130)

Maḥmūd ibn 'Uthmān, *Die Vita des Abū Isḥāq al-Kāzarūnī*, ed. F. Meier (Leipzig: F. A. Brockhaus, 1948).
Meier, F., *Abū Sa'īd-i Abu l-Ḥayr* (Leiden: E. J. Brill, 1976).
Hartmann, R., *Das Ṣūfītum nach al-Ḳuschairî* (Glückstadt: J. J. Augustin, 1914).
Hujwīrī, 'Alī, *The Kashf al-maḥjúb*, tr. R. A. Nicholson (Leiden: E. J. Brill, 1911).
Anṣārī, 'Abd Allāh, *Kitāb-i ṣad maydān*, ed. S. de Beaurecueil, *Mélanges Islamologiques* 2 (1954) 1–90.
Anṣārī, 'Abd Allāh, *Manāzil al-sā'irīn*, ed. and tr. S. de Beaurecueil (Cairo: Institut Français d'Archéologie Orientale, 1962).
On Muhammad Ghazālī: Zaehner, *Hindu and Muslim Mysticism*, pp. 153–80.
Ghazālī, Aḥmad, *Gedanken über die Liebe*, tr. R. Gramlich (Wiesbaden: Franz Steiner, 1976).
Arberry, A. J. (tr.), *A Sufi Martyr: the Apologia of 'Ain al-Quḍāt al-Hamadhānī* (London: Allen & Unwin, 1969).
Bruijn, J. T. P. de, *Of Piety and Poetry: the interaction of religion and literature in the life and works of Ḥakīm Sanā'ī of Ghazna* (Leiden: E. J. Brill, 1983).

Brotherhood and theory (c. 1130–c. 1240)

On Ibn Qasī: Dreher, J., *Das Imamat des islamischen Mystikers Abūlqāsim Aḥmad b. al-Ḥusain b. Qasī* (Bonn: thesis, 1985).

Ibn al-'Arīf, Aḥmad, *Maḥāsin al-majālis*, tr. W. Elliott and A. K. Abdulla (Avebury: Avebury Publishing Company, 1980).

Ibn 'Arabī, Muḥyī al-Dīn, *Sufis of Andalusia*, tr. R. J. Austin (London: Allen & Unwin, 1971).

Chabbi, J., ''Abd al-Ḳādir al-Djīlānī, personnage historique', *Studia Islamica* 38 (1973) 75–106.

Gīlānī, 'Abd al-Qādir, *Futūḥ al-ghayb*, tr. A. Ahmad (New Delhi: Kitab Bhavan, 1979).

Suhrawardī, Abu 'l-Najīb, *A Sufi Rule for Novices*, tr. M. Milson (Cambridge, Mass.: Harvard University Press, 1975).

Hartmann, A., *an-Nāṣir li-Dīn Allāh* (Berlin: Walter de Gruyter, 1975).

Suhrawardī, 'Umar, *Die Gaben der Erkenntnisse*, tr. R. Gramlich (Wiesbaden: Franz Steiner, 1978).

For 'Aṭṭār: Ritter, H., *Das Meer der Seele* (Leiden, E. J. Brill, 1955), and Baldick, J., 'Persian Ṣūfī poetry up to the fifteenth century', in G. Morrison (ed.), *History of Persian Literature from the Beginning of the Islamic Period to the Present Day* (Leiden: E. J. Brill, 1981), pp. 120–5.

For the important Iranian mystic Rūzbihān Baqlī of Shiraz (d. 1209), whom it has not been possible to consider here: Corbin, H., *En Islam iranien; aspects spirituels et philosophiques* (Paris: Gallimard, 1971–2), vol. 3, pp. 9–146.

For Kubrā and Dāya: Corbin, H., *The Man of Light in Iranian Sufism* (Boulder: Colo.: Shambala, 1978).

Kubrā, Najm al-Dīn, *Die Fawā'iḥ al-ğamāl wa fawātiḥ al-ğalāl*, ed. (with a long introduction) F. Meier (Wiesbaden: Franz Steiner, 1957).

Rāzī, Najm al-Dīn, known as Dāya, *The Path of God's Bondsmen from Origin to Return*, tr. H. Algar (Delmar: Caravan books, 1982).

Ibn al-Fāriḍ, 'Umar, *The Poem of the Way*, tr. A. J. Arberry (London: Emery Walker, 1952).

Ibn al-Fāriḍ, 'Umar, *The Mystical Poems*, tr. A. J. Arberry (London: Emery Walker, 1956).

On Ibn 'Arabī: Affifi, A. E., *The Mystical Philosophy of Muhyid Dín-Ibnul 'Arabí* (Cambridge: Cambridge University Press, 1939), and Chodkiewicz, *Le Sceau des saints*.

3   ELDERS AND EMPIRES (*c.* 1240–*c.* 1700)

Rulers, collaborators and revolutionaries (c. 1240–c. 1500)

Mongols, Jews, Christians and Iranians (c. 1240–c. 1320)

On Rūmī: Baldick, 'Persian Sufi poetry', pp. 125–8.

Arberry, A. J. (tr.), *Discourses of Rumi* (London: John Murray, 1961).

Rūmī, Jālāl al-Dīn, *The Mathnawī*, ed. and tr. (with commentary) R. A. Nicholson (London: Luzac, 1925–40).

Arberry, A. J. (tr.), *Mystical Poems of Rumi*, first selection (Chicago, Ill.: Chicago University Press, 1968) and second selection (Boulder, Colo.: Westview Press, 1979).

For Najm al-Dīn of Tabriz and other authors of the 'youngmanliness' tradition: Ṣarrāf, M. (ed.), *Traités des compagnons-chevaliers* (Paris: Adrien-Maisonneuve, 1973), and Taeschner, F., *Zünfte und Brüderschaften im Islam* (Zürich: Artemis, 1979).

Collaboration with princes (c. 1320–c. 1405)

For Simnānī: Corbin, *En Islam iranien*, vol. 3, pp. 275–355, and Cordt, H., *Die sitzungen des 'Alā ad-daula as-Simnānī* (Zürich: Juris, 1977).

Digby, S., 'Qalandars and related groups', in Y. Friedmann (ed.), *Islam in India*, vol. 1 (Jerusalem: Magnes Press, 1984), pp. 60–108.

Gaborieau, M., 'Les Ordres mystiques dans le sous-continent indien', in Popovic and Veinstein, *Les Ordres mystiques*, pp. 105–34.

Nizami, K. A., *Some Aspects of Religion and Politics in India during the Thirteenth Century* (Delhi: Idarah-i Adabiyat-i Delli, 1974).

Habib, M., 'Chishti mystics' records of the sultanate period', *Medieval India Quarterly* 1/2 (1950) 1–43.

Lazard, G., 'Le Langage symbolique du *ghazal*', in A. Bausani et al., *Convegno internazionale sulla poesia di Ḥāfeẓ* (Rome: Accademia Nazionale dei Lincei, 1978), pp. 59–71.

For Ḥaydar Āmulī and Ḥurūfism: Corbin, *En Islam iranien*, vol. 3, pp. 149–213 and 251–8.

al-Rundī, Ibn 'Abbād, *Letters on the Sufi Path*, tr. J. Renard (New York: Paulist Press, 1986).

Ibn Khaldūn, 'Abd al-Raḥmān, *Le Voyage d'Occident et d'Orient*, tr. A. Cheddadi (Paris: Sindbad, 1980).

Ibn Khaldūn, 'Abd al-Raḥmān, *The Muqaddimah*, tr. F. Rosenthal (London: Routledge & Kegan Paul, 1958).

For the short treatise on Sufism attributed to Ibn Khaldūn: Nwyia, P., *Ibn 'Abbād de Ronda* (Beirut: Imprimerie Catholique, 1961), pp. l–liv.

Subversion and erudition (c. 1405–c. 1500)

For 'Alī Turka: Corbin, *En Islam iranien*, vol. 3, pp. 233–74.

For Jīlī: Nicholson, R. A., *Studies in Islamic Mysticism* (Cambridge: Cambridge University Press, 1921), pp. 77–148.

Gölpınarlı, A., *Simavna Kadısıoğlu Şeyh Bedreddin* (Istanbul: Eti Yayınevi, 1966).

Aubin, J., *Deux sayyids de Bam au XVᵉ siècle* (Wiesbaden: Franz Steiner, 1956).

Molé, M., 'Les Kubrawiya entre sunnisme et shiisme au huitième et neuvième siècles de l'hégire', *Revue des Études Islamiques* 29/1 (1961) 61–142.

On the early Safavids: Röemer, H., 'The Safavid period', in P. Jackson (ed.), *The Cambridge History of Iran*, vol. 6 (Cambridge: Cambridge University Press, 1986), pp. 189–350.

For Ibn Abi Jumhūr: Corbin, *En Islam iranien*, vol. 1, pp. 48 and 61–4, and Madelung, W., 'Ibn Abî Ǧumhûr al-Aḥsâ'î's synthesis of *kalâm*, philosophy and Sufism', *Actes du 8ᵉ Congrès de l'Union Européenne des Arabisants et Islamisants, Aix-en-Provence 1976*, pp. 147–56.

Jāmī, 'Abd al-Raḥmān, *The Precious Pearl*, tr. N. Heer (Albany, NY: State University of New York Press, 1979).

Trimingham, J. S., *The Sufi Orders in Islam* (Oxford: Oxford University Press, 1971). Has been severely criticized.

The age of the three great empires (c. 1500–c. 1700)

The Ottoman Empire

Kissling, H. J., 'The sociological and educational role of the dervish orders in the Ottoman empire', *Memoirs of the American Anthropological Association* 76 (1954) 23–35.

Kissling, H. J., 'Aus der Geschichte des Chalvetijje-Ordens', *Zeitschrift der Deutschen morgenländischen Gesellschaft* 103 (1953) 233–89.

Faroqhi, S., *Der Bektaschi-Orden in Anatolien* (Vienna: Institut für Orientalistik der Universität, 1981).

Faroqhi, S., *Peasants, Dervishes and Traders in the Ottoman Empire* (London: Variorum Reprints, 1986).

For the important Egyptian mystic 'Abd al-Wahhāb al-Sha'rānī (d. 1565), whom it has not been possible to consider here: Winter, M., *Society and Religion in Early Ottoman Egypt* (New Brunswick, NJ: Transaction Books, 1982), an admirable study, and Vacca, V. (tr.), *Il Libro dei Doni* (Naples: Istituto Orientale, 1972).

The Timurid Empire in India

'Allāmī, Abu 'l-Faḍl, *Akbar-nāma*, tr. H. Beveridge (Calcutta: Asiatic Society of Bengal, 1907–39).

'Allāmī, Abu l'-Faḍl, *Ā'īn-i Akbarī*, tr. H. Blochmann and H. Jarrett (Calcutta: Asiatic Society of Bengal, 1939–49).

Friedmann, Y., *Shaykh Aḥmad Sirhindī* (Montreal: McGill-Queen's University Press, 1971).

Dārā Shukūh, *Majma' al-baḥrayn*, ed. and tr. M. Mahfuz-ul-haq (Calcutta: The Asiatic Society, 1982).

The Safavid Empire in Iran

Roemer, 'The Safavid period'.

Minorsky, V., 'The poetry of Shāh Ismā'īl I', *Bulletin of the School of Oriental and African Studies* 10/4 (1942) 1006a–53a.

Aubin, J., 'La Politique religieuse des Ṣafavides', in R. Brunschvig et al., *Le Shi'isme imamite* (Paris: Presses Universitaires de France, 1970), pp. 235–44.

Rahman, F., *The Philosophy of Mullā Ṣadrā* (Albany, NY: State University of New York Press, 1975).
Hairi, A. H., article 'Madjlisī' in *The Encyclopaedia of Islam*, second edition.

Outside the empires
Eaton, R. M., *Sufis of Bijapur 1300–1700* (Princeton, NJ: Princeton University Press, 1978).
Berque, J., *Ulémas, fondateurs, insurgés du Maghreb* (Paris: Sindbad, 1982).
Ibragimov, S. K., et al. (eds), *Materialy po istorii kazakhskikh khanstv XV–XVIII vekov* (Alma-Ata: Nauka, 1969).

4   INTO THE MODERN WORLD

The eighteenth century

The background
Ohsson, I. Mouragea d', *Tableau général de l'empire ottoman*, vol. 4 (Paris: Imprimerie de Monsieur, 1791), pp. 616–86.

'Abd al-Ghanī al-Nābulusī
Ibn al-Fāriḍ, 'Umar, *L'Éloge du vin*, tr. (with Nābulusī's commentary) E. Dermenghem (Paris: Véga, 1931).
Molé, *Les Mystiques musulmans*, pp. 120–2.

Shāh Walī Allāh of Delhi
Baljon, J. M. S., *Religion and Thought of Shāh Walī Allāh Dihlawī* (Leiden: E. J. Brill, 1986).

Nūr 'Alī-Shāh of Isfahan
Miras, M. de, *La Méthode spirituelle d'un maitre du Soufisme iranien* (Paris: Editions du Sirac, 1973).

The nineteenth century

North Africa
Michon, J.-L. 'L'autobiographie (*Fahrasa*) du soufi marocain Ibn 'Aǧība', *Arabica* 15 (1968) 225–69, and 16 (1969) 25–64, 113–54 and 225–68.
Michon, J.-L., *Le Soufi marocain Aḥmad Ibn 'Ajība et son Mi'rāj* (Paris: Vrin, 1973).
Abun-Nasr, J., *The Tijaniyya* (London: Oxford University Press, 1965).
Evans-Pritchard, E. E., *The Sanusi of Cyrenaica* (Oxford: Oxford University Press, 1949).
Ziadeh, N. A., *Sanūsīyah* (Leiden: Brill, 1958).

Egypt
Jong, F. de, *Ṭuruq and Ṭuruq-linked Institutions in Nineteenth Century Egypt* (Leiden: E. J. Brill, 1978).

Turkey
Faroqhi, *Der Bektaschi-Orden*, pp. 99–127.
Barnes, J. R., *An Introduction to Religious Foundations in the Ottoman Empire* (Leiden: E. J. Brill, 1987).
Kreiser, K., 'Notes sur le présent et le passé des ordres mystiques en Turquie', in Popovic and Veinstein, *Les Ordres mystiques*, pp. 49–61.
Bremer, M. L., *Die Memoiren des türkischen Derwischs Aşçi Dede Ibrāhīm* (Walldorf-Hessen: H. Vorndran, 1959).

The rest of the Muslim world
Algar, H., *Religion and State in Iran 1785–1906* (Berkeley, Calif.: University of California Press, 1969).
Vámbéry, A., *Sketches of Central Asia* (London: Wm H. Allen, 1868).
Ḥājjī, Ismāʿīl, *Taqwiyat al-īmān*, tr. Ali, M. S., *Journal of the Royal Asiatic Society* 13 (1852) 310–72.
Metcalf, B. D., *Islamic revival in British India* (Princeton, NJ: Princeton University Press, 1982).
Gaborieau, 'Les ordres mystiques'.
Triaud, J.-L., 'Le thème confrérique en Afrique de l'ouest', in Popovic and Veinstein, *Les Ordres mystiques*, pp. 271–82.

The twentieth century

Morocco
Brunel, R., *Le Monachisme errant dans l'Islam* (Paris: Institut des Hautes Études Marocaines, 1955).
Crapanzano, V., *The Ḥamadsha* (Berkeley, Calif.: University of California Press, 1973).

Egypt
Gilsenan, M., *Saint and Sufi in Modern Egypt: an Essay in the Sociology of Religion* (Oxford: Oxford University Press, 1973).
Jong, F. de, review of the above, in *Journal of Semitic Studies* 19/2 (Autumn 1974) 322–8.
Jong, F. de, 'Les Confréries mystiques musulmanes au Machreq arabe', in Popovic and Veinstein, *Les Ordres mystiques*, pp. 205–43.

Turkey
Birge, J. K., *The Bektashi Order of Dervishes* (London: Luzac, 1937).

Köprülü, M. F., *L'Influence du chamanisme turco-mongol sur les ordres mystiques musulmans* (Istanbul: Istanbul University, 1929).

The Soviet Union
Bennigsen, A., and Wimbush, S. E., *Mystics and Commissars* (London: C. Hurst, 1985).

South-east Asia
Al-Attas, S. M. N., *Some aspects of Ṣūfism as understood and practised among the Malays* (Singapore: Malaysian Sociological Research Institute, 1963).
Geertz, C., *The Religion of Java* (Glencoe: Free Press, 1960). Has been severely criticized.
Lombard, D., 'Les *Tarékat* en Insulinde', in Popovic and Veinstein, *Les Ordres mystiques*, pp. 139–63.
Vredenbregt, J., 'Dabus in West Java', *Bijdragen Koninklijk Instituut* 129 (1973) 302–20.

Senegal
O'Brien, D. B. Cruise, *The Mourides of Senegal* (Oxford: Oxford University Press, 1971).
Copans, J., *Les Marabouts de l'Arachide* (Paris: Le Sycomore, 1980).
Coulon, C., *Le Marabout et le prince* (Paris: Pédone, 1981).
Schmitz, J., 'Un politologue chez les marabouts', *Cahiers d'études africaines* 23/3 (1983) 329–51.

INDEX I

Brotherhoods, sub-brotherhoods, branches and offshoots

Bakris Named after an aristocratic family which transforms itself into the nucleus of a Sufi organization in Egypt **145**; their head receives 260,000 *paras* a year in the eighteenth century **133**; in the nineteenth century their leaders are given extraordinary powers of supervision over other brotherhoods and religious institutions **145–6**

Bay Fall A branch of the Mourides of Senegal, founded by Ibra Fall (*c.* 1858–1930); their members do not worship or fast, but are famous for self-flagellation and drunkenness **166**

Bektashis Allegedly founded in Turkey around 1300 by a man called Bektash from north-eastern Iran; characterized in the twentieth century by practices shocking to mainline Muslim opinion, such as the consumption of alcohol and dancing with unveiled women; given an official responsibility, at the end of the sixteenth century, for the Janissary soldiers **114**; by the seventeenth century the most disreputable of the recognized brotherhoods in the Ottoman Empire **115**; they take over a well-endowed lodge **117**; in the eighteenth century they perform their exercises behind closed doors, but retain good relations with the government **134**; are dissolved in 1826, and have their property confiscated; the inventories of their possessions show that they produce wine, are orientated towards classical poetry and live comfortably but not luxuriously **147**; the government accuses them of unbelief **147–8**; in 1967 banned in Albania **159**; found in the twentieth century to hold a wide variety of beliefs, notably Shiite and Hurufi; famous for having a great secret, an impressive initiation ceremony and practices which resemble Central Asian Turkic shamanism **160–1**; their modern lodges for celibates in the Balkans hardly distinguishable from Christian monasteries; represent an extremist Christianizing wing of Sufism **169–70**

Chishtis Named after a village called Chisht, in eastern Iran, where their earliest masters are said to have lived; not academic; flourishing in north-western India **97**; the recorded conversations of their leaders give much information about the relationship between elder and disciple, interaction with libertine dervishes and listening to poetry **97–100**; in the sixteenth century one of their members in south-western India manifests a violent hostility to Hindu ascetics **128**; another member is the thinker Wali Allah of Delhi **136**

Darqawis Named after their founder in North Africa, Ahmad al-Darqawi (1760–1823); sometimes linked with the label *neo-sufism,* but highly traditional; they attract 'blame' by colourful behaviour, such as carrying buckets of excrement around in public **141**; one member's autobiography shows him abandoning his wealth to become a beggar and water carrier **141–2**; the Darqawis of Tetouan in Morocco are imprisoned and charged with 'innovation' in wearing the patched frock **142**

Haddawa   Founded by Sidi Haddi (d. 1805) in Morocco; a brotherhood of wandering dervishes, who emphasize celibacy; their associate members are fishermen or artisans **154**; their numbers in the towns have declined; previously close to the soldiery; they show a tendency to pederasty and the consumption of cannabis, preserve a pre-Islamic cult of the cat in an adapted form, possess a slang of their own, and have acted as spies **155**

Hamadsha   Named after their supposed founder in Morocco, 'Ali ibn Hamdush (d. *c.* 1720?); come from the lower classes; associate members alleviate psychological disturbance by entering into trance and head slashing **156**; members are also found in the shanty towns; relate mental illness to the *jinn* (genies); their practices seem to represent influences from the ancient Near East **157**

Kazarunis   Named after Kazaruni of southern Iran (d. 1035), who started an organization of disciples to serve the poor **59–60**; they engage in extra worship and recitation of the Koran; by the fourteenth century have spread to Turkey and China, and are seen as a 'path' or brotherhood **60**; at the beginning of the sixteenth century are wiped out in Iran, with the massacre of 4000 people; live on outside Iran, offering banking facilities for merchants **123**

Khalidis   Founded by Khalid al-Shahrazuri (1776–1827), as a branch of the Mujaddidi ('Renewerist') sub-brotherhood of the Naqshbandi brotherhood, in the Ottoman Empire, where they are persecuted **148**; the autobiography of one nineteenth-century Khalidi bureaucrat shows that he and his 'elder' have anti-European and highly traditional attitudes, in spite of the 'reformist' label often given to the Khalidis **148–9**; come to South-east Asia in the nineteenth century **163**; by 1976 a village of theirs in North Sumatra shows a decline in Sufi activity **164**

Khalwatis   Apparently founded in the fifteenth century, so called because of their concentration on the solitary retreat (*khalwa*) of forty days; linked to the summit of the Ottoman state in the late fifteenth and early sixteenth century; fervently supported by Bayazid II; have followers in the most important government posts under Sulayman the Magnificent; the founding of their lodges subsidized thanks to royal patronage **114**

Kubrawis   Founded by Kubra (d. 1221) of Khwarazm in what is now Soviet Central Asia; spread to Iran and India; characterized by an emphasis on visions and coloured lights **79**; these coloured lights are arranged in sevenfold patterns which seem to reflect Indian influences **95**; in the fifteenth century their visions are used to confirm the mission of a messianic revolutionary **109**

Mawlawis   So called after the title *mawlana* ('our master'), given to their supposed founder in Turkey, Rumi (d. 1273); apparently founded by his son; known as the Whirling Dervishes because of their distinctive dance **91**; at the end of the seventeenth century one member is grand vizier; are seen as academic and respectable **115–16**; in the Ottoman Empire in the eighteenth century retain the affection of the powerful and pray for administrators and jurists; are defended by the writer Nabulusi **134**; in the nineteenth century often include in their ranks administrators who are also Mujaddidis **148**; one such administrator listens to the flute **149**

Mourides An offshoot of the Qadiris in Senegal, so called from the Arabic *murid* ('disciple'); founded by Amadu Bamba (*c.* 1850–1927); noted for the luxurious life-style of their leaders and the skill of their artisans, and characterized by an insistence on working in the service of one's elder **165**; bad cultivators, but politically influential **166**; do not work exceptionally hard **166–7**; in the 1970s their leadership distances itself from the government after earlier collaboration and working as a tool of French colonialism **167**; *see also* Bay Fall

Mujaddidis 'Renewerists', so called after the title *Mujaddid* ('Renewer') of their founder in India, Ahmad Sirhindi (1564–1624); a sub-brotherhood of the Naqshbandis; one member is the thinker Wali Allah of Delhi **138**; they spread to the Ottoman Empire in the seventeenth and eighteenth centuries; include many nineteenth-century westernizing administrators, of whom a lot are killed in 1807 in a revolt **148**; *see also* Khalidis

Naqshbandis Founded by Baha' al-Din Naqshband (d. 1389) of Bukhara in what is now Soviet Central Asia; characterized by their emphasis on a silent 'remembrance of God', as opposed to the usual practice of repeating a formula aloud **111**; extolled by Sirhindi as superior to other brotherhoods because of their distinctive rejection of dancing and music **120**; in 1570 a family of Naqshbandi leaders take power from their Mongol patrons in Chinese Turkestan **131**; are isolated from other brotherhoods in the eighteenth century, but include members of all classes, who gather for extra prayers; one member is the writer Nabulusi **134**; another member is Wali Allah of Delhi **136**; in contemporary Turkey, closely connected with members of the government and other politicians **159**; *see also* Mujaddidis *and* Khalidis

Ni'matullahis Founded in Iran by Ni'mat Allah (d. 1431); they accept Shiism after the Safavid conquest; constitute the main Iranian brotherhood after the decline of the Safavid Sufis; in the seventeenth century their leaders are living in India; are assigned to specific wards of Iranian cities, where they clash with libertine dervishes **126–7**; start a revival in Iran in the late eighteenth century, but are cruelly persecuted **139**

Qadiris Named after their supposed founder, 'Abd al-Qadir of Gilan (d. 1165), a jurist and preacher of Baghdad; now spread from North Africa to Indonesia **71–2**; include in their ranks the heir apparent to the Timurid throne in India **122**; also the writer Nabulusi **134**; and the thinker Wali Allah of Delhi **136**; are identified with the activities of the hero of Algerian resistance to the French, the Amir 'Abd al-Qadir **143**; in nineteenth-century Turkey they illicitly obtain government-owned wood **149**; in West Africa are not vastly different from the Tijanis **152**; in recent years a few of their members in West Java have engaged in the practice of hurting the body with iron spikes **164**; *see also* Mourides

Renewerists *see* Mujaddidis

Rifa'is Named after their supposed founder, who died in 1182, and known in the West as the Howling Dervishes because of their loud 'remembrance of God'; in the Ottoman Empire in the eighteenth century put heated iron instruments in their mouths **134**

Sa'dis   (So called after Sa'd al-Din al-Jibawi (d. 1335), concentrated in Syria, later spread to Egypt) best known for the spectacular ritual in which their leader rides a horse over a long line of his prostrate followers, without apparent injury to them, in nineteenth-century Egypt **146**

Safavids   Named after their founder, Safi 'l-Din of Ardabil in north-western Iran (d. 1334); led by a family of hereditary masters; in the fifteenth century adopt a radical form of Shiism **109**; obtain the tribal loyalty of nomadic Turks and become militarized **110**; at the start of the sixteenth century conquer Iran, and possess widespread tribal support in eastern Turkey **123**; their leaders, ruling as emperors in Iran, have difficulty with their tribal supporters; those members of the brotherhood who represent its oldest traditions are massacred; in the seventeenth century become prison officers, porters and cleaners **125**; replaced by the Ni'matullahis **126–7**; demonstrate that tribal support is a perpetual source of possible revolt **176**

Sanusis   Founded by Muhammad al-Sanusi (1787–1859) near Mecca, but moved by him to Libya, where it engages in academic activities during the nineteenth century **143**; there then follows armed conflict with the French and the Italians (as opposed to collaboration with the Turks and the British) **143–4**; are based on the Libyan tribes and operate in between their sections, providing commercial and legal services; aim at direct communication with Muhammad; reject music and luxury **144**

Shadhilis   So called after Abu 'l-Hasan Shadhili (d. 1258); particularly strong in Egypt and North Africa, where their emphasis on sobriety earns them the label 'the Protestants of Islam'; in the twentieth century one sub-brotherhood in Egypt is the subject of very different observations **158**; a section of another sub-brotherhood performs its 'remembrance of God' to the accompaniment of very violent physical activity, in spite of a supposedly 'reformist' pedigree **158–9**

Suhrawardis   Wrongly thought to have been founded by Abu 'l-Najib (d. 1167) of Suhraward in north-eastern Iran, an academic lawyer in Baghdad; in fact founded by his nephew, 'Umar Suhrawardi (d. 1234), chief religious adviser to the caliph Nasir (1180–1225); particularly important in what is now Pakistan; known for their severity, although some of their members are conspicuous for self-enrichment, collaboration with temporal rulers and enjoyment of worldly pleasures; noteworthy for 'remembrance', with the formula 'There is no god but God', especially among working women **71–5**; their branch in Multan has an academic character and close relations with the Sultan of Delhi **95–7**; this branch's elders have a firm control over their disciples, and complementary employment of academic tutors **98**; tolerate poetry and the symbolism of wine and handsome boys **100**

Tijanis   Founded by Ahmad al-Tijani (1737–1815) in Algeria; they enjoy the patronage of the Sultan of Morocco and expand elsewhere; abandon membership of other brotherhoods and visiting 'friends of God' **142**; are rich **142–3**; collaborate with French colonialism in North Africa and clash with the resistance to it **143**; but in West Africa come into violent conflict with the French and are not vastly different from the Qadiris **151–2**; in the twentieth century obtain the approval of jurists on arrival in South-east Asia **163**

Uwaysis   Mystics who are presented as being instructed by the spirits of physically absent or dead masters; so called after a contemporary of Muhammad named Uways, who is said to have communicated with him by telepathy **28**; the poet Hafiz is seen as an Uwaysi **100**; a brotherhood embodying the Uwaysi tradition is founded by Muhammad Sharif (d. 1555) in Chinese Turkestan **130**; at this time an imaginary history of the brotherhood is compiled by Ahmad Uzgani, who claims that the spirits of previous leaders have told their life stories to him; the brotherhood founded in Chinese Turkestan disappears as the Naqshbandis take power and rule there from 1570 onwards **131**

Whirling Dervishes *see* Mawlawis

INDEX II

Names of persons mentioned

'Abbas I (Safavid ruler) 125
'Abbas II (Safavid ruler) 126
'Abd al-Hamid (Ottoman sultan) 147
'Abd al-Qadir (Algerian amir) 143
'Abd al-Qadir of Fez 130
'Abd al-Qadir of Gilan **71–2**, 164
Abraham 38
Abu Bakr (caliph) 76
Abu 'l-Fadl 119–20
Abu Hashim of Iraq 30
Abulafia, Abraham 87
Abu Mahalli 129–30
Abu 'l-Najib of Suhraward 71–3
Abu Nu'aym of Isfahan 58
Abu Sa'id of Mayhana 60–1
Abu Yazid **35–7**, 46, 47, 49, 53, 55, 62, 64
Adam 7, 19, 25, 82, 91–2, 119
Ahmad of Bareilly, Sayyid 151
Ahmad ibn Idris 159
Ahmad ibn Muhammad ibn Salim 52
Ahura Mazda 23
Akbar (Timurid emperor) **118–20**, 123
'Alawi, Hashim 128
'Ali (first Leader of the Shiites) 76, 91–2, 94, 102, 105, 114, 120, 128, 139, 160
'Ali ibn Hamdush 156
Amadu Bamba 165
Amuli 101–2
Angelus Silesius 45
Ansari 64–5
Aqasi, Hajji Mirza 150
Astarte 157
'Attar **78–9**, 81–2, 90
Augustine 88
Avicenna **61–2**, 73
Awrangzib (Timurid emperor) 113, **122–3**
'Ayisha Qandisha 157
'Ayn al-Qudat 67

Baal Hammon 157
Badr al-Din of Simavna 107–8
Baha' al-Din Naqshband 111
Bahya ibn Paqudah 87
al-Bakri, 'Abd al-Baqi 146
al-Bakri, 'Ali 145
al-Bakri, Muhammad Tawfiq 146
Barhebraeus 88
Bayazid II (Ottoman sultan) 114
Bektash 114
Bihbihani, Muhammad Baqir 139
Biruni 61–2
Buddha 24
Burhan al-Din Janam 128
Burhan al-Din, Shaykh, of Ulakan 164

Chinggis (Genghis) Khan 78, 86, 113, 130

Dante 68
Dara Shukuh (Timurid prince) **122**, 123, 137
al-Darqawi, Ahmad 141
Daya of Rayy **80–1**, 89, 95, 170–1
Daylami 53, **57**,66, 88, 175
devil 40, 43, 67, 78, 80, 90
Dhu 'l-Nun **35**, 40, 49
Diogenes 21
Dostoevsky, Fyodor Mikhailovich 89
Durkheim, Émile 154

Eckhart, Johannes 45

Fadl Allah of Astarabad 103
Farid al-Din of Pakpattan 97–9
Fehmi, Mustafa 149
Fitzgerald, Edward 60
Frederick II of Hohenstaufen 93

Gabriel (angel) 14, 73, 78, 139

Ghazali, Ahmad **65–7**, 68, 72
Ghazali, Muhammad 10, **65–7**, 70, 105, 141
Gregory VII 74
Guru Nanak 118

Haddi, Sidi 154
Hafiz of Shiraz 100–1
Hallaj **46–9**, 50–1, 53, 54, 64
Hammu Qiya 157
Hamza Fansuri 163
Haydar (Iranian seen as founder of Haydaris) 126
Haydar (Safavid leader) 110, 112
Hegel, Georg Wilhelm Friedrich 45, 85
Hermes Trismegistus 80
Hujwiri 60, **63–4**, 68
Husayn (son of 'Ali) 128
Husayn, Sultan (Safavid ruler) 112, 127

Ibn 'Abbad of Ronda 104
Ibn Abi Jumhur 110–11
Ibn 'Ajiba, Ahmad 141–2
Ibn 'Arabi 10, 69, 71, **82–5**, 86, 88, 89–90, 95, 102, 106, 107, 108, 110, 111, 116, 119, 121–2, 125–6, 135–6, 137–8, 163, 171, 173, 174
Ibn al-'Arif 70
Ibn Barrajan 70
Ibn Battuta 96–7
Ibn al-Farid **81–2**, 135–6, 170
Ibn Hud (Spanish prince) 93
Ibn Khafif **52–3**, 55, 57, 59, 175, 176–7
Ibn Khaldun **104–5**, 170
Ibn Masarra 69
Ibn Qasi 70
Ibn Sab'in 93
Ibn Taymiyya 93
Ibn Tufayl 70–1
Ibra Fall 166
Ibrahim Khalil 148–9
Isaac of Nineveh **17–18**, 40
Isma'il (Safavid ruler) 112, **123–5**

Jacob 78
Ja'far (Shiite Leader) 30
Jahangir (Timurid emperor) 121
Jami **111**, 119, 135
Jesus 2, 9, 17, 18–19, 24–5, 48, 49, 54, 55, 84–5, 89–90, 102, 109, 111, 120, 131, 135–6
Jili 107
John the Baptist, Saint 149
Joseph (son of Jacob) 78

Joseph, Saint 29
Junayd (Safavid leader) 110
Junayd of Baghdad **44–6**, 49, 52, 55, 64

Kabir 118
Kalabadhi 55–6
Kazaruni **58–60**, 123
Khalid al-Shahrazuri 148
al-Khalidi, 'Abd al-Wahhab 164
Kharraz **40–2**, 49
Khayyam, 'Umar 60
Köprülü, Muhammad 115
Kubra **79–80**, 95

Lull, Ramón 88

al-Mahdi, Sayyid (Sanusi leader) 143
Mahdi of the Sudan 140
Mahmud II (Ottoman sultan) 146–8
Maimonides 93
Majawi, Fadl Allah **95–6**, 98
Majlisi 127
Makki, Abu Talib **56**, 57, 65
Mani 22
Marx, Karl 45
Mary (mother of Jesus) 25, 29, 131
Mary of Antioch 29
Mary of Egypt, Saint 29. 131
Mary Magdalen, Saint 29
Ma'sum 'Ali-Shah 139
Moses 38, 90
Muhammad, the Prophet 1, 4, 5, 7, 9, **14–15**, 22, **24–8**, 33, 38–9, 41, 42–3, 45, 57, 60, 75–6, 78, 81, 82, 84–5, 91–2, 94–5, 97, 102, 103, 106, 107, 111, 120, 122, 129, 133, 136, 138, 139, 141–4, 146, 151, 154, 160, 176
Muhammad I (Ottoman sultan) 108
Muhammad II (Ottoman sultan) 111, 114
Muhammad IV (Ottoman sultan) 115
Muhammad ibn 'Abd al-Wahhab 133
Muhammad-'Ali (ruler of Egypt) 144–5
Muhammad ibn Salim 52
Muhammad Shah (ruler of Iran) 150
Muhammad Sharif 130–1
Muhasibi **33–5**, 49, 64
Murad II (Ottoman sultan) 115
Musa (Ottoman prince) 107–8

al-Nabulusi, 'Abd al-Ghani 134–6
Nadir Shah (ruler of Iran) 132
Najm al-Din of Tabriz 91–2
Napoleon 140
Nasir (caliph) **72–4**, 76–8

Nasir al-Din of Delhi 98–100
Nesimi 103–4
Niffari 53–4
Ni'mat Allah 127
Nizam al-Din of Bada'un 97–100
Nur 'Ali-Shah 139–40
Nurbakhsh, Muhammad 109
Nusrat al-Din Shah Yahya 101

d'Ohsson, Ignatius Mouragea 134, 170

Paul, Saint 19
Pelagia of Jerusalem, Saint 29
Pharaoh 90
Philo Judaeus 19
Plato 20, 68, 92, 107
Plotinus 20

Qalandar, Hamid 98–9
Qushayri 62–3

Rabi'a of Basra 29–30
Rabi'a of Syria 29–30
Rilke, Rainer Maria 4
Rukn al-Din of Multan **96–7**, 98
Rumi **89–91**, 101, 124, 171, 174, 176

Sadra of Shiraz 125–6
Sadr al-Din of Konya 89–90, 116
Safi 'l-Din of Ardabil 109
Saladin (ruler of Egypt and Syria) 72
Salama Hasan al-Radi 158–9
Salman the Persian 28
Sana'i **68–9**, 79, 92, 172
al-Sanusi, Muhammad **143–4**, 151
Sarraj 55
Selim I (Ottoman sultan) 115
Shadhili, Abu 'l-Hasan 158
Shams al-Din of Bam 108–9
Shams al-Din of Tabriz 90–1, 174

Sibghat Allah, Shah 128
Simnani, 'Ala' al-Dawla 94–5
Sindi 35–7
Sirhindi, Ahmad **120–1**, 122–3, 137–8, 148
Spinoza, Baruch 85
Suhrawardi, 'Umar **73–5**, 77, 80, 98, 100, 174
Suhrawardi, Yahya **73**, 106
Sulami **57–8**, 62
Sulayman the Magnificent (Ottoman sultan) 112, 114

Tahir al-Din of Bam 108–9
Tawfiq (ruler of Egypt) 146
Theophilus of Antioch 29
al-Tijani, Ahmad **142–3**, 144, 151
Timur the Lame 93–4, 103, 106–7
Tirmidhi **42–4**, 49, 50, 84
Traherne, Thomas 173
Turka, 'Ali **106–7**, 110
Tustari **37–40**, 46–7, 49, 52, 56–7, 64

'Umar (caliph) 14, 76
'Umar Tal 151–2
'Uthman (caliph) 24
'Uthman (first leader of the 'Ottoman' Turks) 93
Uways 28
Uzgani, Ahmad 131
Uzun Hasan (Turkoman ruler) 110

Venus 6

Wali Allah, Shah, of Delhi 133, **136–8**, 148

Zarathushtra 23, 68
Zosima 89

INDEX III
Technical terms

A Terms in foreign languages
(Arabic except where stated)

abdal (substitutes)   39, 72
agurram (Berber for 'noble')   156
ahadiyya (Oneness)   83
ahl al-hadith (People of the Tradition)   32
ahl tayhuhiyya wa hayruriyya ('people of wanderinghood and perplexitude')   41
ahwal (states)   3, 35, 65
'alam al-mithal (world of the image)   137
amr ('affair' or 'command')   25
'aql (reason, intelligence, intellect)   43–4
'arif (gnostic, knower)   61
'asabiyya (group solidarity)   105, 176
awliya' Allah (friends of God)   25
awtad ('pegs')   39
'ayn ('quintessence' or 'eye')   38, 124; (Quintessence [of God])   41
'ayyar ('rogue', 'brigand', or an adherent of the 'youngmanliness' tradition)   66

baqa' (survival)   3, 38, 40–2
baraka (blessing)   144, 154
barzakh (interface)   **84**, 102
bay'a (oath of allegiance)   128
bid'a (innovation)   142

dara (a form of the Arabic *dar* (house), used in Senegal to mean a group of young men working to serve an elder)   166
darwish (Persian for 'poor man')   19
dayr (Christian monastery)   59
dhikr (remembrance)   3, 146; *dhikr Allah* (remembrance of God)   **17**, 25

fana' (passing away)   3, 37, 40–2, **45–6**, 87

faqir (poor man)   19
futuwwa ('youngmanliness')   9, 23, **91–2**
fuyud (spiritual overflowings)   142

giruh (Persian for 'group')   64

hadarat ('presences')   88
hadith (Tradition or 'report', literally 'news')   26–8; *hadith qudsi* ('sacrosanct Tradition')   27
halal (lawful)   8
haqa'iq (realities)   36
haqiqa (in Persian *haqiqat*, reality)   84, 100; *al-haqiqa al-Muhammadiyya* (in Persian *haqiqat-i Muhammadi*, Muhammadan Reality)   107, 120; *haqiqat-i Ahmadi* (Persian for 'Ahmadan Reality')   120
haqiqi (real)   68
al-haqq (the Truth)   48, 83, 124
haqq al-yaqin (truth of certainty)   38
haraka jawhariyya (substantive movement)   126
hazirat al-quds (enclosure of sacrosanctity)   137
hikmat al-ishraq (wisdom of Oriental Illumination)   4
hubb (restrained love, affection)   57
hujja (proof)   39
hulul (incarnation)   55
huruf (letters of the alphabet)   **102–3**, 106–7

ijaza (certificate)   76
'ilm al-yaqin (knowledge of certainty)   38
imam (in the sense of 'leader of the

Muslim community') 70
Imam ('Leader', in the Shiite sense of an
  infallible cosmic figure) 30, 67, 109
insan ilahi (divine man) 137
al-insan al-kamil ('Perfect Man') 84
'ishq (passionate love) 57
ishraq (Oriental Illumination) 61, 73
islam (submission) 1
ittihad (unitive fusion) 57, 79, 82, 84, 93,
  95

jabarut (world of divine compulsion) 99

karama (the miraculous grace of God's
  friends) 135
khafi ('concealed') 138
khalifa (caliph, deputy) 60
khalq (creation, created things) 83
khalwa (solitary retreat) 114
khanaqah (Persian for 'lodge' or
  'hospice') 59
khatm al-awliya' (Seal of the Friends) 43
khirqa (patched frock) 76, 105, 136
khulafa' (caliphs, deputies) 14, 75, 123

lata'if (subtle organs) 95

mahadir (locations, levels) 80
Mahdi (ideal or messianic ruler, the
  'divinely guided one') 105, 109, 125,
  140
mahw (effacement) 87
majaz (metaphor) 100
majazi (metaphorical) 68
malakut (world of divine sovereignty) 99
malama (blame) **17**, 57–8
malamatiyya (people of blame) 57–8
manzil (stage) 65
maqam ('station') 65
maqamat ('stations') 3, 34, 35
marabout (French, from the Arabic
  murabit: a word used by French colonial
  writers in North Africa to designate a
  leading Muslim mystic; used in Senegal
  to designate a wide range of people with
  religious functions or knowledge)
  129–30, 144, 155, **165**, 168
ma 'rifa (direct knowledge, gnosis) 35,
  38
mu 'ayana (visual beholding) 38
mujaddid (Renewer) 120
mukashafa (unveiling) 38
murabit (man of religion, man of the holy
  war) **129–30**, 144, 156, 165

muradun ('masters who are desired by
  God') 56
murid (disciple) 165
muridun ('disciples who desire God') 56
mushahada (contemplative witnessing)
  38
muwahhidan-i Hind (Persian for 'the
  unitarians of India') 122

nafs (lower soul, self) 17, 25, 34, 38, 54
nafs al-ruh (lower soul of the spirit) 39
nafs al-tab' (lower soul of nature) 39
nazar ila 'l-murd (gazing at beardless
  boys) 20
nur al-yaqin (light of certainty) 38
nussak (devotees) 29

qadam ('priority') 145
qalandar (a type of libertine dervish) 66,
  68, 98–9, 149
qalb (heart) 25
qiddis (Christian saint) 16
qutb (pole) **105**, 111

rahbaniyya (monasticism) **25**, 34
ribat (lodge, hospice, fortified outpost in
  the holy war) **59**, 129
rida' (acceptance, satisfaction) 62
rijal al-ghayb (men of the unseen) 107
riya' (the sycophantic and hypocritical show
  of religiosity) 34
rububiyya (Lordship) 52
ruh (spirit, higher soul) 17; (Spirit [of
  God]) 25
rukhas (dispensations, relaxations of strict
  rules) 72

salih (pious man) 154
sama' (listening to poetry or music) 35,
  52–3, **99–100**
sayyid (lord) 154
shahid (witness [to the reality of love or to
  universal Beauty]) 80
shath (ecstatic utterance) 35
shaykh (elder) 63, 165
siddiqun (truthful ones) 39
sidq (truthfulness) 40–1
silsila (chain) 75–6
sirr (secret) 38; *sirr Allah* (secret of
  God) 139
sufi 3, 15, 19, 28, **30–2**, 61, 110

tahmil ('relating') 99
ta'ifa (brotherhood) 112

tajalli (theophany, [God's] appearing or self-displaying) 44, 84, 177

tamkin (fixity) 63

tariq (method or 'path') 64, 80

tariqa (in Persian *tariqat*, brotherhood, method, 'path') **59–60**, 64, **73–7**, 112; (in the sense of 'the Sufi Path itself') 17, **59**, 77

tasawwuf (Sufism, wearing wool, belonging to the faith and doctrine of the people called the Sufis, trying to become a Sufi) 3

tashayyu (Shiism, belonging to the Shiite Party) 4

tashkik (ambiguity) 126

tawakkul (trust in God) 40

tawba (repentance) 40

tawhid (the attestation, affirmation, realization or experiencing of God's Uniqueness) 173; *tawhid-i ilahi* (Persian for 'divine affirmation of God's Uniqueness') 119

'ubudiyya (enslavement) 95

ustadh (academic tutor) 98

wahdat al-shuhud (unity of contemplation) 121

wahdat al-wujud (unity of existence) 83, 121

wahidiyya (Uniqueness) 84

wahy (prophetic revelation) 139

wali Allah (friend of God) **16**, 154

waqfa ('staying') 53–4

waqt (moment) 63

al-wujud al-munbasit ('the self-unfolding existence') 125

wusul (arrival) 61

yaki (Persian for 'Oneness') 121

yaqin (certainty) 38

zuhd (renunciation of the world) 40, **170–1**

zuhhad (world renouncers) 29

B English equivalents

acceptance (*rida'*, satisfaction) 40, 55, 56, **62**, 63

ambiguity (*tashkik*) 126

arriving (*wusul*) 2, 61

beholding, visual (*mu'ayana*) 38

blame (*malama*) **17**, 21, 29, 57–8, 66, 141–2, 171; people of blame (*malamatiyya*) 57–8

blessing (*baraka*) 8, 76, 144, 154, 156

brotherhood (*tariqa*) 59–60, 64, 67, 69, **71–7**, 91, 93, 95–7, 100, 112, 113–17, 119, 122, 123, 125, 128, 133–9, 141–51, 154, 156, 158–61, 163–5, 167, 169–70, 174

caliph (*khalifa*, deputy) 72–3, 77, 78, 89–90

caliphs (*khulafa'*, 'deputies') 14, 31, 76, 169

'causes' (*asbab*, visible means of support) 40

certainty (*yaqin*) **38**, 55, 56; light of certainty (*nur al-yaqin*) 38; knowledge of certainty (*'ilm al-yaqin*) 38; quintessence of certainty (*'ayn al-yaqin*) 38; truth of certainty (*haqq al-yaqin*) 38

certificate (*ijaza*) 76

chain (*silsila*) 59, **75–6**

'concealed' (*khafi*) 138; 'most concealed' (*akhfa'*) 138

conjunction (*ittisal*) 2

creation (*khalq*, created things) 83

dancing (*raqs*) 64, 91, 96, 114, 120, 134, 144, 157, 163, 173

deceit (*khud'a*) 36–7

deputies (*khulafa'*) 75, 123, 128, 160, 169

deputy (*khalifa*) 60, 78, 90

dervish (Persian *darwish*) **19**, 170

devotees (*nussak*) 29

disciple (*murid*) 28, 35, 52, 59–60, 65, 70, 73, 75–6, 79–80, 89, 96, **97–8**, 108, 120, 123, 128, 135, 139, 141–2, 151, 165–8, 174

'disciples who desire God' (*muridun*) 56

dispensations (*rukhas*, relaxations of strict rules) 72

divinity (*lahut*) 53

'drinking, of the' (*shurbi*) **91–2**, 117

effacement (*mahw*) 87

elder (*shaykh*) 8, 63, 64, 67, 73–7, 89, 90, 96, **97–8**, 99, 105, 107, 112, 114, 115, 116, 119, 122, 125, 128, 135, 139–40, 148, 149, 151–2, 160, 164–8, 170, 173–4, 176

elder of elders (*shaykh al-shuyukh*) 74

'elder of the elders of the Sufi brotherhoods' (*shaykh mashayikh al-turuq al-sufiyya*) 146

elder of the invisible world (*shaykh al-ghayb*) 80

enclosure of sacrosanctity (*hazirat al-quds*) 137

endings (*nihayat*) 65

enraptured (*majdhub*) 43

enslavement ('*ubudiyya*) 95

Essence (*dhat* [of God]) 80, 81, 83–4, 136

'existence, the self-unfolding' (*al-wujud al-munbasit*) 125

fakir (*faqir*) 19

finding (*wajd*) 41

fixity (*tamkin*) 63

forgetfulness (*nisyan*) 42

friend (*wali*, in Persian *dust*) 44, 48, 95, 176; friend of God (*wali Allah*) 8, **16**, 43, 89, 121, 149, 176; friend of the right of God (*wali haqq Allah*) 43

friends (*awliya'*) 39, 41, 43, 135, 154; friends of God (*awliya' Allah*) 2, 6, 25, 33, 34, 39, 41, 42–3, 44, 49, 57, 72, 84–5, 105, 135–6, 137, 139, 142, 158, 171–2, 177

friendship (*walaya* [with God]) **16**, 39, 41, 42–3, 84–5, 102, 121

frock, patched (*khirqa*) 15, 34, 76, 98, 105, 136, 142

fusion, unitive (*ittihad*) 2, 57, 79, 82, 84, 93, 95

gazing at beardless boys (*nazar ila 'l-murd*) **20**, 134, 173

gem of bewilderment (*hajar al-baht*) 137–8

gnostic ('*arif*, knower) 61

group (in Persian *giruh*) 64

group solidarity ('*asabiyya*) 105, 176

guide (*murshid*) 8

guided, rightly (*muhtadi*) 43

heart (*qalb*, in Persian *dil*) 25, 39, 41, 44, 69, 78–9, 80, 90, 99, 138, 139

hospice *see* lodge

humanity (*nasut*) 53

Illumination, Oriental (*ishraq*) 61, 73, 106, 110, 119; wisdom of Oriental Illumination (*hikmat al-ishraq*) 4, 73, 125

incarnation (*hulul*) 55, 79, 84, 103, 105, 124

I-ness, greatest (*al-ananiyya al-kubra*) 138

innovation (*bid'a*) 42, 142

intellect ('*aql*) 39, **43–4**, 78, 138

Intelligence, Active (*al-'aql al-fa''al*) 69, 73

Intelligence (or Reason), Universal (*al-'aql al-kulli*) 43, 69, 84, 89–91

intelligences ('*uqul*) 43, 61, 91

intention (*niyya*) 34

interface (*barzakh*) **84**, 102, 137

joining (*wasl*) 2

knowledge, direct (*ma'rifa*, gnosis) 35, 38–42, 44, 52, 53, 63, 65

lawful (*halal*) 8; 'the lawful and the pure' (*al-halal al-safi*) 40

leader (*imam*, in the sense of 'leader of the Muslim community') 70, 109

Leader (*Imam*, in the Shiite sense of an infallible cosmic figure) 30, 67, 76, 94, 102, 105, 111, 124, 137, 139

Leaders (*Imams*) 4–5, 26, 33, 76, 94, 102, 110–11, 120, 127

letters of the alphabet (*huruf*) 87, **102–3**, 106–7

light (*nur* [God's]) 38–9, 79, 80, 82

light of Muhammad (*nur Muhammad*) 38, 47, 78

light of sacrosanctity (*nur al-quds*) 138

listening (*sama'*, to poetry or music) · 35, 52–3, 55, 64, 74, 88, 96, **99–100**, 120, 151, 173

locations (*mahadir*, levels) 80

lodge (*ribat, zawiya*, in Persian *khanaqah*) 59, 63, 66, 74, 81, **96**, 104, 113–14, **116–17**, 121, 129, 130, 134, 143–4, 145, 147–9, 154–6, 159–60, 169–71, 174

'looking, permitted' (*nazar mubah*) 57

lord (*sayyid*) 154

Lordship (*rububiyya*) 52, 80

love, metaphorical (in Persian '*ishq-i majazi*) 68, 149

love, passionate ('*ishq*) 57

love, real (in Persian 'ishq-i haqiqi) 68, 149

love, restrained (hubb, affection) 57

man, divine (insan ilahi) 137

Man, Perfect (al-insan al-kamil) **84–5**, 102, 107, 111, 119, 126, 135

'masters who are desired by God' (muradun) 56

men of the unseen (rijal al-ghayb) 107

metaphor (majaz, earthly image) 100

metaphorical (majazi) 8, 68

method (tariq, in Persian also tariqat, 'path') 64, 75, 80

miraculous grace (karama) 135

moment (waqt) 61, 63

moments (awqat) 61

monastery, Christian (dayr) 59, 136, 170

monasticism (rahbaniyya) **25**, 28, 34, 74, 170

monasticism, true (al-rahbaniyya al-haqiqiyya) 54, 170

nearness (qurb) 41, 53, 56

noble (sharif, in Berber agurram) 8, 156

oath of allegiance (bay'a) 128, 135

'one who stands upright at the highest' (al-mustawi al-a'la) 70

Oneness (ahadiyya, in Persian yaki) 83, 121

overflowings, spiritual (fuyud) 142

'passing away' (fana') 3, 10, 37, 39, 40–2, 44–6, 49, 52, 55, 56, 57, 60, 63, 65, 67, 70, 87, 90, 139, 151

'path' (tariqa, method or brotherhood) 60, 75, 77, 136, 138, 148, 151, 160; the Sufi Path itself 3, 17–18, 21, 35, 40, 42, 43, 44, 46, 49, 52, 54, 56, **59**, 61, 62, 63, 65, 67, 70, 77, 101, 110, 150, 162, 170, 174

'pegs' (awtad) 39

pious man (salih) 154

pole (qutb) **105**, 111, 137

presences (hadarat) 88

priority (qadam) 145–6

Proof (hujja) 39

quintessence ('ayn) 38, 124; Quintessence [of God] 41

real (haqiqi) 8, 68

realities (haqa'iq) 36

reality (haqiqa, in Persian haqiqat) 100; the one ultimate Reality 83, 138; reality of Muhammad, Muhammadan Reality (al-haqiqa al-Muhammadiyya) **84**, 107, 120, 137; Koranic reality (haqiqat-i Qur'ani) 120; reality of the Ka'ba (haqiqat-i Ka'ba) 120; Ahmadan reality (haqiqat-i Ahmadi) 120

reason ('aql) 21, **43–4**, 66, 69, 78–9. 90–1, 92

'relating' (tahmil) **99**, 173

remembrance (dhikr) 3, 75, 81, 146, 155; remembrance of God (dhikr Allah) 3, **16–17**, 25, 34–5, 38, 63, 76, 89, 96, 111, 134, 146, 159, 172; remembrance of the tongue (dhikr al-lisan) 74; remembrance of the heart (dhikr al-qalb) 74

renewer (mujaddid) 120, 137

repentance (tawba) 3, 17, 40, 44, 55, 56, 160

retreat, solitary (khalwa) 74, 114, 164

revelation, prophetic (wahy) 139

rogue (or 'brigand', 'ayyar) 66, 77

sacrosanctity (quds or taqaddus) 8

saint, Christian (qiddis) 16

'saying, of the' (qawli) **91–2**, 117

Seal of the Friends (khatm al-awliya') 43, 82, 84–5, 102, 142

Seal of the Prophets (khatam al-nabiyyin) 25, 43

secret (sirr) 38–9, 52, 90, 138, 160; secret of God (sirr Allah) 52, 139

self (nafs) 17, 36, 67; see also soul, lower

show of religiosity (riya') 34

sobriety (sahw) 46, 64, 158

soul, higher see spirit

soul, lower or carnal (nafs) 17, 25, 34, 38–9, 40–1, 42–4, 49, 52, 54, 55, 57, 64, 78, 82, 90, 138; see also self; lower soul of the spirit (nafs al-ruh) 39; lower soul of nature (nafs al-tab') 39

Soul, Universal (al-nafs al-kulliyya) 21, 69, 78, 92, 137

spirit (ruh, in Persian jan) 17, 25, 39, 41, 55, 66, 68, 81–2, 90–1, 99, 135, 137–8, 139–40; the Spirit [of God] **25**, 44, 48, 66, 78–9, 84, 90, 107, 122, 139

stability (thabat) 44

stage (manzil) 65, 70

'state' (hal) 40, 52, 62, 63

'states' (ahwal) 3, 35, 39, 40, 46, 52, 55, 56, 60, 63, 65, 72, 74, 99, 101, 144, 174

'station' (*maqam*)   40–1, 56, 57, 62, 65, 67
'stations' (*maqamat*)   3, 34, 35, 39, 40–2, 46, 49, 52, 55, 56, 60, 62, 63, 72, 74, 101, 170
'staying' (*waqfa*)   53
stupefaction (*dahsh*)   42
substantive movement (*haraka jawhariyya*)   126
substitutes (*abdal*)   39, 42, 72
subtle organs (*lata'if*)   95, 138
Sufism (*tasawwuf*)   **3**, 53
survival (*baqa'*)   3, 38, 40–2, **44–6**, 49, 56, 63, 65
'sword, of the' (*sayfi*)   **91–2**, 117

theophany (*tajalli*, God's appearing or self-displaying)   38, 44, 84, 90, 103, 177; God's most supreme theophany (*al-tajalli al-a'zam*) 137
togetherness (*jam'*)   2
Tradition (or 'report', *hadith*, literally 'news')   5, **26–8**, 39, 42, 48, **75–6**; sacrosanct Tradition (*hadith qudsi*) 27; People of the Tradition (*ahl al-hadith*) 32
trust in God (*tawakkul*)   3, 17, 40, 55, 56
Truth, the (*al-Haqq*, the Real)   48, 83, 103, 124
truthful ones (*siddiqun*)   39
truthfulness (*sidq*)   40–1
tutor, academic (*ustadh*)   96, 98

Uniqueness (*wahidiyya*)   38–9, 44, 49, 53, 69, 79, 83; the affirmation, attesting, realization or experiencing of God's Uniqueness (*tawhid*) 2, 36, 38–9, 48, 57, 58, 65, 78, 158, 173; 'divine affirmation of God's Uniqueness' (in Persian *tawhid-i ilahi*) 119
'Unitarians of India, the' (in Persian *muwahhidan-i Hind*)   122
unity of contemplation (*wahdat al-shuhud*)   **121**, 137–8
unity of existence (*wahdat al-wujud*)   83, 108, 121–2, 136–8
unveiling (*mukashafa*)   38
utterance, ecstatic (*shath*)   35

'wanderinghood and perplexitude, people of' (*ahl tayhuhiyya wa hayruriyya*)   41
witness (*shahid*, to the reality of love or to universal Beauty)   **57**, 80
witnessing, contemplative (*mushahada*)   38
wool, wearer of (*sufi*)   31
wool, wearers of (*mutasawwifa*)   34, 49
world of divine compulsion (*jabarut*)   99
world of divine sovereignty (*malakut*)   99
world of the image ('*alam al-mithal*)   137
world renouncers (*zuhhad*)   29, 71, 170
world, renunciation of the (*zuhd*)   40, 55, 56, 68, 154, **170–1**

'youngmanliness' (*futuwwa*)   9, 23, 58, 66, **77**, **91–2**, 117, 161, 172